Solidarity or Survival?

SOLIDARITY OR SURVIVAL?

AMERICAN LABOR AND EUROPEAN IMMIGRANTS, 1830–1924

A. T. LANE

CONTRIBUTIONS IN LABOR STUDIES, NUMBER 21

Greenwood Press
New York • Westport, Connecticut • London

Library of Congress Cataloging-in-Publication Data

Lane, A. T.
   Solidarity or survival?

(Contributions in labor studies, ISSN 0886-8239 ;
no. 21)
   Bibliography: p.
   Includes index.
   1. Alien labor—United States—History.   2. United
States—Emigration and immigration—History.
3. Trade-unions—United States—Political activity.
I. Title.   II. Series.
HD8081.A5L36   1987   331.6′2′0973   86-25735
ISBN 0-313-25544-X (lib. bdg. : alk. paper)

Library of Congress Catalog Card Number: 86-25735
ISBN: 0-313-25544-X
ISSN: 0886-8239

First published in 1987

Greenwood Press, Inc.
88 Post Road West, Westport, Connecticut 06881

Printed in the United States of America

Copyright Acknowledgment

"American Labour and European Immigrants in the Late Nineteenth Century,"
by A. T. Lane, *Journal of American Studies* 11 (August 1977): 241–60, is reprinted
here by permission of the publisher, Cambridge University Press.

"American Trade Unions, Mass Immigration and the Literacy Test: 1900–1917,"
by A. T. Lane, *Labor History* 25 (Winter 1984): 5–25, is reprinted here by
permission of the publisher.

To my Mother and Father

Contents

Tables

Acknowledgments

I have accumulated many debts in the preparation of this study, and it is a pleasure to record my gratitude to those individuals who have encouraged, stimulated, and otherwise aided me to complete it. I received invaluable advice and practical assistance from Milton Cantor at an important stage in the preparation of the work; without his generous contribution of time and his formidable editorial skills, such merits as the book possesses would have been fewer in number. I am indebted to Philip Taylor for seeing possibilities in my research at an early date. His belief in its value and his readiness to offer assistance were heartening. Daniel Leab showed confidence in a part of the work at a critical time which gave me the encouragement to complete it. Charlotte Erickson made constructive comments on one of the chapters, for which I am grateful. Conversations with my friend and colleague Jack Morrell were invariably supportive and often hortatory; his example and his advice were stimulating and beneficial, even though I did not always measure up to them.

I am grateful to the American Council of Learned Societies for the award of a fellowship which permitted me to undertake research in the United States. The Departments of History of the University of Michigan and the University of Wisconsin-Madison offered me hospitality and assistance which facilitated my work. The receipt of an award from the Twenty-Seven Foundation was valuable in the preparation of the manuscript for publication.

I received indispensable support from the J. B. Priestley Library at the University of Bradford, and I am particularly grateful to the Social Sciences

Librarian, Peter Ketley, for his co-operative and willing help. I drew heavily
on the resources of the Brotherton Library, University of Leeds, the Reading
Room of the British Museum, and the British Library at Boston Spa. Li-
brarians at the University of Michigan, particularly E. Weber of the Joseph
Labadie Collection, the University of Wisconsin, and the State Historical
Society of Wisconsin at Madison were invariably helpful and co-operative.
For the typing and retyping of the manuscript in a succession of versions
I depended on the skill and efficiency of Sue Norman.

My greatest debt is to Jean, Nicholas, and Max for their generosity,
humor, tolerance, and unfailing support.

Solidarity or Survival?

1

Introduction

In the nineteenth and early twentieth centuries vast numbers of Europeans travelled westwards across the Atlantic in search of opportunity or refuge. Most already knew, and the rest would soon discover, how easy it was to gain entry into the most important of western destinations, the United States. After 1880, to be sure, certain categories of immigrants were refused admission by law, but those affected—paupers and criminals, contract laborers and anarchists, the physically diseased and mentally ill—never constituted more than a tiny fraction of new arrivals. For all intents and purposes, European immigrants could anticipate free entry into the United States. It was not until 1917, when Congress approved the administration of a literacy test, which was quickly followed by the tough quota legislation of 1921 and 1924, that serious obstacles were placed in the way of the admission of Europeans.

The freedom of entry characterizing the century before 1917 generally received popular approval. It was widely accepted that European immigration was consistent with America's economic advantage and system of values. Moreover, there was an understandable reluctance on the part of Americans who were immigrants or children of immigrants to deny to others the opportunities from which they themselves had benefitted. However, by the last decades of the nineteenth century, there emerged a growing body of opinion which was concerned about the consequences of mass immigration and urged the enactment of laws to limit entry. The rapid development of restrictionist sentiments coincided with, and was in part caused by, the changing ethnic composition of European immigration in the 30 years after 1880. Instead of a small minority, the arrivals from the southern and eastern regions of Europe—Italians, Slavs, and Jews—made up the overwhelming majority of immigrants to the United States before the First World War. The quota laws of the 1920s made explicit what the literacy test had partially disguised, namely that Americans were not primarily concerned with the numbers but with the quality and type of the newcomers. The restrictive laws which brought to an end a long period of virtually free entry were discriminatory in intent and effect.

The causes of this transformation in popular attitudes have been thoroughly and persuasively discussed by a number of historians, notably by John Higham in his classic work *Strangers in the Land: Patterns of American Nativism, 1860–1925*, published in 1955. However, another intriguing question, but one which has received much less scholarly attention, is the parallel evolution in the attitudes of, in Eric Hobsbawm's term, laboring men. Urban workers employed in manufacturing industry were arguably the section of the American population most directly affected by immigration, especially and increasingly after the American Civil War. The immigrants were generally poor people with few resources, who were compelled by need to take the first available jobs in the locality of their port of disembarkation. This created strong competition for manual work, even though the economy was expanding rapidly and creating numerous additional jobs. Yet, despite the many unfavorable material consequences of immigration for American labor, notably strikebreaking, depression of wages, technological displacement, and worsening of working conditions, labor opinion seems to have been no more restrictionist than public opinion in general. Indeed, insofar as organized labor was slower than the U.S. Congress to endorse the literacy test in the 1890s, it seems to have dragged its feet somewhat on the immigration issue. After 1900, however, labor became a front runner in the immigration stakes, firmly committed to restriction and among the leading pressure groups in American politics on this issue.

Despite the impact of European immigration on the employment and conditions of American industrial workers, labor historians have tended to ignore the response of American labor to foreign-born competitors in the job market. Consequently, the first task of this book is expository: to establish as fully and accurately as possible how labor reacted to the challenge of European immigration in the century before 1924. Initially, most of the research for this study was centered in the post–Civil War period, but it soon became evident that labor's attitudes at this time could not be adequately understood unless there was an explicit comparison with its earlier responses to immigration. Hence, the first chapter of this book tries to identify the opinions of urban craft workers on immigration in the decades before the Civil War, and to relate these opinions to the broader public response to immigration.

In this early period it appeared that attitudes among laboring men were somewhat ambivalent; in general, their response to immigration was tolerant, humane, and generously sympathetic, but from time to time elements of doubt, anxiety, and even antagonism rose to the surface. The doubters and the critics denied that the consequences of immigration were invariably benign and proposed a variety of measures to counter these adverse effects, although they did not advocate governmental restriction on the right of entry. Generally speaking, however, feelings of fraternity held the upper hand, and there were no serious attempts to modify the traditional open door policy regarding immigration before the Civil War.

It was a different matter after the war. There was heightened tension between sentiments of solidarity towards the immigrants and increasing awareness of the dangers of immigration in economic, political, and social life. Gradually labor inched towards adopting a protectionist policy at the expense of fraternal ideals. Nevertheless, the pull of internationalism remained strong and was augmented on occasion by the emergence of organizations in the labor interest which were self-proclaimedly solidaristic, like the Knights of Labor and the Socialist Party. Ultimately restrictionism proved too powerful, and solidarity was discarded as labor's guiding principle in immigration policy. The second major purpose of this book, therefore, is to account for the victory of protectionist forces and to show how each step in a restrictionist direction whetted rather than satisfied the appetite of the restrictionist lobby in the labor movement.

In this study of American labor and *European* immigration, it is particularly important to keep in mind labor's response to Asiatic immigration in the same period. Why did labor lobby for Chinese exclusion as early as the 1860s? What distinctions were drawn between Chinese and European immigrant workers? To what extent was Chinese exclusion a precedent for limiting entry for Europeans? How important was racism in kindling restrictionist sentiments in the labor movement? These are some of the questions posed and discussed in this study, notably but not exclusively in Chapters Three and Nine. A study of labor's discussion of the Chinese issue strongly suggests that the term "Chinese" is a codeword for Southern and Eastern Europeans and that implicit, and sometimes explicit, comparisons are made between the influxes from Asia and Europe and their respective consequences for the American economy and American society. It is helpful for an understanding of labor's attitudes to European immigrants to become aware of why labor rejected the Chinese case as exactly analogous to the European, even though there were many points of comparison.

In discussing American labor we must not forget that the members of labor organizations are also part of the general public and, to a greater or lesser degree, share popular attitudes. In studying the late nineteenth century it is defensible to treat labor as a kind of separate estate possessing a common consciousness as skilled or semi-skilled workers and expressing that consciousness through institutions such as trade unions. But even then, industrial workers were not insulated from general public ideas and values, and in examining labor opinion we become aware of how far that opinion was shaped by familiarity with the widespread popular discussions of the effects of immigration on politics and social behavior. Earlier in the century, when a distinct "labor" consciousness was still embryonic and labor institutions were few and ill-developed, it is more difficult to establish a labor point of view. Far more than in the post–Civil War decades, opinions of urban craftsmen have to be elicited mainly from a study of institutions which were not exclusively working class in membership, notably the various nativist parties and associations which flourished in the antebellum decades. It is surely anachronistic to use the term labor movement in connection with this period, although after the Civil War it becomes increasingly apposite.

The term "labor movement" in the last sentence clarifies the meaning of the term "labor" in the title of this book. This is essentially, though not entirely, a study of labor opinion as expressed through labor organizations like trade unions, labor reform bodies, union federations, and political parties claiming to represent the labor interest. No apology is made for this, although some labor historians might regard it as a return to the dated approach of John R. Commons and his disciples, the so-called Wisconsin School. Recent trends in the writing of American labor history have stressed that the proper subject for labor historians should be the history of American workers, that is, the history of the generally inarticulate, and not the history of their perhaps unrepresentative institutions. The American Federation of Labor (AFL), the federation representing largely craft unions, which is a major subject of study in this book, is often placed in this category.

A number of responses can be made to this criticism. The first is that studies of the American worker at grass-roots level in local communities rarely touch on the subject of immigration specifically, even though they may be mines of information on interethnic relations or on the adjustment of newcomers to the community. Even if successful attempts are made to elucidate local working-class attitudes to immigration, it would be difficult to interpret those findings unless one could place them in the broader context of labor opinion nationwide. How, for example, did the local responses compare with the response of national labor bodies claiming to present the opinion of American laboring men to the legislators in Washington and to opinion formers across the country? One of the purposes of this book, as already noted, is precisely to portray this collective response, to establish the broad contours of labor opinion over a lengthy period, and to provide the national context with which local experiences and attitudes may be compared. Inevitably this national picture will be to some degree provisional, raising questions of fact and interpretation which local studies may help to resolve, and as a result perhaps modifying our understanding of labor history at the federal level. For example, the author's attempts to interpret American labor's shifting opinions on the question of immigration were much assisted by the research of John T. Cumbler into two local working-class communities, as Chapter Seven makes clear.[1]

We should, of course, always keep an open mind about the representativeness of the opinions expressed on behalf of working people by national labor organizations. We have tried to be alert to any signs of dissent from "official" opinion and any evidence which indicates that officially expressed views did not command majority support in the labor bodies themselves. A more systematic attempt to assess the strength of support in the labor movement for one such official decision, the endorsement of the literacy test at the AFL convention in 1897, is made in Chapter Six. The results reinforce the need for caution in evaluating official opinion. But if we cannot be sure, without confirmatory evidence, that national trade unions and their federations represent even their members' opinions accurately, how much less can we rely on their views as representative of opinion in the ranks of the unorganized workers, who constituted the great majority of the urban working class in the United States in the decades before the First World War? A further complication is that most of the unorganized were first-generation immigrants. It is tempting to assume that their attitudes to immigration would have diverged fundamentally from those of official opinion. But even in this respect there are indications from bodies that claimed to provide a voice for these inarticulate newcomers, like the Socialist Party of America, the Industrial Workers of the World, or the few unions which organized low-skilled newcomers, like the International Ladies Garment Workers' Union, that there was a degree of ambivalence about immigration which makes the gap between them and the more conservative labor bodies narrower than might have been predicted.

Still, there are sound reasons for giving priority to establishing opinion in the labor movement over attempts to identify the opinion of a somewhat amorphous working class. These arise from reservations about the possibility of writing American working-class history on the model of recent studies of the English or other European working classes. Whilst the work of E. P. Thompson has provided a model for American labor historians, his categories are not necessarily adaptable to the American environment. David Brody has raised the important question as to whether it is possible to write a "Thompsonian" history of the American working class, owing to the absence of a unified working-class culture in the United States.[2] The formation of class consciousness requires some men, as a result of common experiences, to "feel and articulate the identity of their interests as between themselves, and as against other men whose interests are different from (and usually opposed to) theirs."[3] It was assumed that this polarization of attitudes on the basis of widely differing experiences applied to the emergence of a self-conscious working class differentiating itself from the middle classes. But, in the United States, American working men themselves were as often divided as united by their experiences, since their backgrounds, traditions, ethnicity, values, and languages were so diverse and originated in so many different cultures. Immigration was at the heart of these divisions. Opposition to it by workers whose family roots struck deeper into the American past was partly motivated by the sense that the newcomers were different, that their values and perspectives sharply diverged from those of older stock, and that, albeit unconsciously, they served the interests of the employers. Consequently they were rivals rather than allies, and would remain so until they assimilated American norms. It was perhaps inevitable that the existing labor force would sense a threat from the newcomers and try to protect itself by the enactment of legislation. Alternatively, it might try to follow a solidaristic approach, recruiting immigrant workers into its labor organizations and forming a united front against the employers. So long as the majority of new immigrants originated in those areas of Europe, the North and West, whose culture and ethnicity were not too distant from those of America, the solidaristic option was realistic and was pursued by American labor bodies for much of the nineteenth century. However, when the geographical sources of immigrant recruitment began to change, labor admitted the impracticality of seeking protection through solidarity and moved somewhat erratically before 1900, and more steadily afterwards, towards the restrictionist solution.

If, then, workers were divided and did not share a common class consciousness, what are the implications for writing a history of labor's attitudes to immigration? We should frankly recognize these divisions, accept that they will be reflected in working men's responses to important public issues, and assume that the first generation of immigrants in the work force will tend to be the section most favorably disposed towards immigration. Confirmation of this assumption will await future investigation of this largely unorganized but very numerous element. However, for the purposes of this study, labor is assumed to mean mainly those groups of workers of the second or older generations, usually Northern and Western European in origin, sharing a common consciousness of being American and believing themselves to have acculturated to American norms in industrial and civic life. Moreover, these groups had expressed their commonality of interest in the establishment of defensive institutions motivated by a common strategy. These institutional defenses were provided by the various labor and trade union organizations of the nineteenth and early twentieth centuries, in particular the craft unions that multiplied and prospered after 1880 and associated for joint action in the AFL, which survived when other labor federations based on the principle of all-inclusiveness and solidarity had failed. Brody's aspiration to secure "the common economic ground on which workers of the most diverse loyalties and persuasions might unite" may be realizable in the writing of shop floor history, but it seems unlikely that such a common ground can be identified in the writing of the history of labor and immigration. Attempts to establish it founder on the cultural heterogeneity of the European labor recruits and an understandable incapacity of existing trade unions to organize these newcomers. Solidarity was tried and very reluctantly abandoned; survival only seemed possible if conflicts of interest were recognized and the appropriate defensive measures adopted.

NOTES

1. John T. Cumbler, *Working-Class Community in Industrial America: Work, Leisure, and Struggle in Two Industrial Cities, 1880–1930* (Westport, Conn.: Greenwood Press, 1979).

2. David Brody, "The Old Labor History and the New: In Search of an American Working Class," *Labor History* 20, No. 1 (Winter 1979): 123.

3. E. P. Thompson, quoted in Brody, "The Old Labor History and the New," p. 123.

2

Artisans, Ideology, and Nativism in Pre–Civil War America

Many eighteenth-century Americans would have had occasion to purchase goods manufactured by urban artisans and mechanics. These tradesmen, together with small retailers, suppliers of services, and unskilled day laborers, constituted a substantial proportion of the urban population. Among these artisans the self-employed small masters were almost as numerous as wage earners. The latter, so-called journeymen who had served an apprenticeship, generally aspired to work on their own account. The mentality of urban craft workers was characterized by ambition, pride in economic function, and confidence in the possibilities for social advancement. To be sure, there were complaints that opportunities were narrowing and that craft skills were not being accorded the social respect to which they were entitled, but even so, the values and beliefs of eighteenth-century artisans were quite distinct from those of semi-skilled factory workers a century later. Their possession of indispensable handicraft skills gave them a secure place in society and the shadow of displacement had hardly begun to cross their thresholds.

As small masters and artisans they would, of course, share common interests and ambitions, but workers' organizations in the late eighteenth century were few and far between, and it is impossible to identify anything as coherent and institutionalized as a labor movement. Society was so fluid and the opportunities for social mobility so extensive that rigid and impermeable class barriers could not appear. Consequently, artisans tended to identify with the broader society, and to think of themselves primarily as Americans rather than as members of a particular social class or category.

Following the onset of modern industrialism in the nineteenth century, class and occupational divisions assumed greater importance, and labor came to develop a more distinctive set of beliefs and attitudes reflecting its relation to the means of production.

If we are to understand the evolution of labor attitudes towards immigration in the nineteenth and early twentieth centuries, it is indispensable for us to grasp how Americans viewed immigration in the late colonial and early national periods. In this way we will be able to appreciate the ideological legacy which labor inherited and with which it had ultimately to contend. Moreover, in seeking to persuade the Congress of the United States of the correctness of its views on immigration and of the necessity for incorporating those views in legislation, labor had to take account of public opinion, which in turn was partly the product of traditional values and partly a reflection of the American people's perception of national advantage. Hence the starting point for this study lies in the late eighteenth century, even though labor as a distinct entity scarcely existed and labor institutions were embryonic. Labor's subsequent struggle to convince itself of the necessity to change public policy towards immigration would have been less difficult and anguished if traditional policy had not been so deeply rooted in American values.

Most Americans in the late eighteenth century welcomed immigration and encouraged foreign-born settlers to become American citizens. To be sure, there were currents of opposition and scepticism about the desirability of welcoming all who sought to enter; the very poor, the potentially disloyal, and the politically immature all had their critics, and the colonial period provides examples of attempts to exclude or to discourage such immigrants. Yet suspicion of immigrants was not widely shared, except possibly in time of war. American values and ideology combined to create a strong disposition in favor of those seeking new homes on American shores. Humane feelings, perceived economic and demographic advantages, ideas of natural rights, and the particular quality of American nationalism were among the more important factors behind the American welcome to the foreign-born.

That America should be a refuge or asylum for the victims of European tyranny and oppression, few could doubt. The most eloquent of expatriate Europeans, Thomas Paine, made a powerful plea on behalf of the downtrodden who fled from the cruelty of the European "monster." Paine's words could not fail to inspire Americans, who were keenly conscious of their own European origins and of their families' search for religious and political freedom and economic opportunity.[1]

Thomas Jefferson expressed reservations about immigration in the course of his political career, but he, like Paine, was a champion of America's role of asylum "for those whom the misrule of Europe may compell [sic] to seek happiness in other climes." In the American Canaan, European subjects would be received as brothers and secured against tyranny by the practice of self-government.[2] This appeal to fellow feeling and common humanity was persuasive. Could Americans deny to newcomers the fraternal reception they themselves had been fortunate enough to receive? Even fugitives from the law were welcome, since "seasonable kindness [might] awaken the dormant seed of virtue," especially in the United States, where, it was said, there were "few temptations to vice."[3] Humanity and sympathy were supplemented by the recognition that European despots often expelled from their domains their most freedom-loving subjects, who readily identified with the United States and strengthened the defenses of freedom. It was, therefore, incumbent on Americans to reject the narrow-minded selfishness of the nativists who appeared willing to leave liberty-loving foreigners to the tyrannical embrace of their governments. The appeal of asylum was therefore profound: Americans could relieve suffering by offering freedom, knowledge, and opportunity in place of oppression, superstition, and servitude.

The generous humanity of Americans was reinforced by a wide acceptance of America's providential mission to create a bulwark of liberty in a world of autocracies. The seventeenth-century Puritan settlers thought of themselves as God's Chosen People with a divine mission to sustain and extend true religion. By the second half of the eighteenth century the idea of a Providential Design had become partially secularized. The vast empty spaces of the New World, it was agreed, had been set aside for an experiment in liberty, and humanity's hopes for freedom and justice hung on the success of this experiment. America was a symbol of mankind's hope for a better world; it was not simply the possession of its present inhabitants but a "patrimony" reserved by God for the oppressed of all nations. Moreover America needed constant accessions of new strength if it was to succeed in defending the cause of freedom in a hostile world.[4]

Immigration offered advantages to Americans as well as responsibilities. In her infancy America desperately needed an increase in population to guarantee her external security. Accordingly she "received and caressed strangers from all nations with the utmost warmth and sincerity," and was gratified that most of the newcomers came from the ranks of the enlightened artisans and independent yeoman farmers. Numerous influential Americans paid tribute to the role of the foreign-born in reducing labor scarcity and creating a market for commodities. The immigrants' importance to the development of the national economy was readily appreciated by commercial and manufacturing capitalists in the ante-bellum period, and employers were generally the firmest supporters of unrestricted immigration in the nineteenth century. In the early decades of the Republic, however, most sections of society joined together to welcome immigration on economic grounds.[5]

There was also a current of opinion which believed that the considerable mixing of nationalities which existed in America in the eighteenth century facilitated the creation of a new and superior people or, in J. Hector de Crèvecoeur's terms, a new race of men, "whose labors and posterity will one day cause great changes in the world."[6] Furthermore, immigration was flattering to many Americans in the early nineteenth century, a tribute to American society and institutions which had been chosen in preference to those of other lands. Immigration of such people was an unmixed political and economic blessing.

Perhaps the sturdiest foundations of the traditional American acceptance of immigration were provided by the idea of natural rights and by the particular quality of American nationalism. The rights of man were at the heart of the American Revolution. Each man possessed these rights by virtue of his humanity, his rationality, and his existence as "a precious child of God."[7] Implicit in the rights of life, liberty, property, and the pursuit of happiness was the right to change one's abode. "At all times," wrote Francis Lieber, "men have looked for a better country, when the country of their birth becomes too crowded or too barren. . . . The right to emigrate belongs to the earliest rights of the individual." The right to live, in short, implied a right to migrate.[8] Similarly, the denial of the rights of liberty and protection for property in one society encouraged migration in search of a new homeland where liberty and property could be enjoyed.

The events of the Revolution demonstrated that individuals had a right to choose their allegiance. In the late seventeenth and early eighteenth centuries Americans were beginning to reject the idea of natural allegiance, under which a subject of a monarch remained a subject for ever, in favor of contractual or volitional allegiance which was owed only in return for protection of the natural rights of the citizen. In the context of the 1770s the failure of the British government to defend the inalienable rights of Englishmen, or, as they were termed by 1776, the rights of man, fractured this obligation of allegiance and permitted the colonists to choose a new allegiance in the spirit of liberty The right of contractual allegiance applied equally to the foreign-born, who rejected their natural allegiance to a European prince on account of his failure to protect their rights. Refusal to allow them to choose a new loyalty in the United States could only be construed as a denial of the spirit of the American Revolution and a repudiation of their natural rights.[9]

Finally, the basis of national unity in the United States implied an invitation to emigrate to any Europeans who identified with American ideas and values. The cohesion of American society was not the product of ancient traditions, ethnic and religious unity, a common language, and permanent residence. It was a society possessing "no roots, no memories, no routine, no common ideas, no national character." What, Alexis de Tocqueville asked, was the connecting link between the different elements?[10] The answer lay in ideology; the cohesion of American society resulted from shared values, beliefs, and ideas. The Declaration of Independence and the U.S. Constitution embodied the articulated the ideas which Americans shared—individual liberty, equality, representative government, freedom of expression, and the supremacy of the law. Hence loyalty to principle rather than loyalty to place characterized Americans:

To be an American citizen was justly our pride and our boast. But what was it that rendered it a source of satisfaction and exultation? Was it the soil on which we tread? Was it the natural atmosphere which we breathe? No sir, it was the free and tolerant principles embodied in our institutions, that riveted our attachment to the name of American citizen.[11]

The act of emigration to America, it has been suggested, might in itself be construed as a revolutionary act in that it represented for the individual migrant as strong a commitment to the ideas and values underpinning America as did the Declaration of Independence for a previous generation of Americans. Therefore each immigrant, by the fact of his immigration, was as much an American as the Founding Fathers and as much entitled to residence and citizenship in the Republic.[12]

It is evident from this discussion that strong currents of opinion bore Americans along in the direction of opening their gates to foreigners and treating them on terms of equality after their arrival. Yet the legacy of colonial and early republican history was not entirely free from elements of restrictionism. Doubts had been expressed from time to time about the wisdom of permitting unrestricted immigration or too easy naturalization if the political and religious dominance of existing groups were to be preserved. Some colonies established the precedent of denying political rights to those who seemed to constitute a threat to their security and economic well-being. All the colonies legislated against voting and officeholding by Roman Catholics or Jews. There was equal apprehension over the immigration of paupers, whom all the colonies attempted to exclude. There was anxiety, too, at the wage and price competition emerging from the Scotch-Irish and Palatine German residents of Philadelphia in the mid-eighteenth century.[13]

The views of some of the leading members of Philadelphia society provide an interesting commentary on the immigration question in colonial Pennsylvania and on the current of restrictionism in eighteenth-century America. The major objects of concern were the Scotch-Irish and the Palatine Germans, who entered the colony in large numbers between 1720 and 1750. By the latter date, about 100,000 Germans had settled there. Aside from the economic problems they created in parts of the colony, doubts were expressed about their loyalty, their political maturity, and their willingness to integrate with the host society. Benjamin Franklin questioned their loyalty because of their apparent refusal to participate in the defense of the colony. His suspicions were at their height in 1753 when war in the Ohio Valley was imminent and the French were reported to be establishing a German settlement which would make contact with the Pennsylvania Germans. The latter's political alliance with the Quakers in opposition to conscription and taxation confirmed Pennsylvanians' suspicions about the Germans' loyalty to the British. Moreover, owing to the Germans' unfamiliarity with representative government and democratic institutions, there were accusations that they abused their newly acquired liberty by immature politicking.[14] As the number of Germans grew to about one-third of the population of the colony by mid-century, Philadelphians envisaged the time when Pennsylvania would become a German colony. Hence, for reasons of security, ethnic and cultural homegeneity, and the preservation of English political institutions, Franklin for many years argued against the immigration of non-English settlers "who will never adopt our language or customs any more than they can acquire our complexion."[15]

However, the Seven Years' War ending in 1763 and the subsequent conflict with Great Britain culminating in the Declaration of Independence in 1776 helped to change the attitude of most Pennsylvanians of English origin towards the Germans. The "church," if not the "sect," Germans actively assisted the British against the Indians in western Pennsylvania in the 1750s and later supported the movement for self-determination by the American colonies, in the process finding many opportunities for participation in public affairs. As the English-speaking Americans became more tolerant, the German-Americans in turn became more Americanized, accepting "the dominance of the English element in what is 'American.' "[16]

There were other occasions, notably in the late 1790s and in the 1840s, when opinion was aroused against immigration and there were attempts to make naturalization more difficult. Thomas Jefferson, a libertarian and a firm believer in natural rights, reveals this duality. Whilst his patriotism was "devoid of any narrowness or exclusiveness" and his commitment to the asylum idea total, he was disturbed that the largest proportion of immigrants in the future would originate in the absolute monarchies of Europe, carrying with them to America the principles of despotism. As the newcomers took part in American politics and lawmaking, they would "infuse into it their spirit, warp and bias its directions, and render it a heterogenous, incoherent, distracted mass." Accordingly, Jefferson argued that America should not actively encourage immigration except in the case of "useful artificers," while remaining true to the ideal that all immigrants, whatever their origin or skills, were entitled to the rights of citizenship.[17]

The decade of the 1790s tested the depth of the American commitment to unrestricted immigration and to the easy achievement of citizenship by the foreign-born. Three naturalization acts were passed by the federal government, each more restrictive than its predecessor. The Federalist administration and its supporters in Congress were becoming alarmed at the growing number of politically radical European immigrants, mainly French and Irish, who entered politics on the side of their opponents, the Jeffersonian Republicans The naturalization law of 1798, which increased the period of qualifying residence to fourteen years, was designed to neutralize these newcomers and to deny the opposition a source of additional strength.[18] It was also intended to set at rest fears of a foreign conspiracy aiming to overthrow American institutions. The destructive ambitions of the alleged conspirators were publicized in the United States in 1798 by the Reverend Jedidiah Morse, who accused the Democratic Republicans of being "the dupes and accomplices" of the conspirators and the French and Irish immigrants of being their agents.[19] Most Federalists probably did not take too seriously the idea of an organized conspiracy, but they nevertheless saw dangers in the "promiscuous reception" of aliens, both to their party's standing and to republican institutions. After Jefferson's election to the presidency in 1800, the 1798 measure was repealed, and a new law set the period of qualifying residence for citizenship at five years.[20]

This short interlude of agitated hostility to immigrants in part developed out of colonial precedents and in part prefigured later nativist movements in its use of the conspiracy idea as a political weapon. But with Jefferson's election the appeal of anti-immigrant politics declined, and for the first three decades of the nineteenth century the traditions of asylum, natural rights, and humanity held sway in immigration and naturalization policy. To be sure, some unreconstructed Federalists retained their suspicions of immigrants, nurturing values to which Benjamin Franklin had appealed in the 1750s, above all the equation of national cohesion with cultural homogeneity. It was the responsibility of the immigrants, said John Quincy Adams, to "cast off the European skin, never to resume it" and to encourage their children "[to] cling to the prejudices of this country."[21] Failure to identify with America should disqualify the foreign-born from voting and holding public office. Such sentiments commanded no widespread support until the 1840s and 1850s, when powerful nativist movements developed to highlight the perils of cultural diversity.

Up to this point discussion has centered on the broad trends in public opinion in the young Republic. It remains to try to identify opinion among the artisan and mechanic classes of the Eastern towns. It is important to do this in order to appreciate the starting point from which subsequent "labor" opinion was to evolve. According to one historian, the artisans were proud of their contribution to the achievement of American independence and sought an honored place in American society as testimony to their efforts. Their self-image was that of independent, honorable, and respectable producers whose role and influence in politics should be commensurate with their social position and economic importance. Their contributions to the nation's life demanded that they be treated with dignity and respect. Yet there were forces in society which sought their own economic advantage at the expense of the artisans' vaunted independence. A "mechanic" wrote that the so-called monopolists would reduce wages to the point where the independent spirit "so distinguished at present in our mechanics, and so useful in republics, will be entirely annihilated. The workmen will be servants and slaves, and their votes must always be at the command of their masters."[22] The slavery or "vassalage" against which artisans fought was a continuation, in a different guise, of the subordination to the British which the Americans had to endure before independence, and included in that subordination was the submission to an "aristocratic" way of life that consigned the mechanic to an inferior social position.

It is therefore not surprising that in the period 1795–1810 the artisans of New York City voted heavily for the Jeffersonian Republicans, perhaps by as much as 60 percent. The latter's fight against the "monocratic" dispositions of the Federalist leaders, most notably Alexander Hamilton, earned the approval of the egalitarian mechanics, who were further conciliated by the respect paid to them by Jeffersonians seeking approval and political support. The most tangible mark of that respect was the readiness of the Republicans to place representatives of the artisan class on the ballot. By contrast the Federalists were openly scornful of mechanics' pretensions to political influence and spoke disparagingly of their qualities and achievements. They were evidently unwilling to concede the mechanics' claim to equality and independence, further alienating artisans by their unpopular pro-British foreign policy.[23] By the end of the 1790s the Republicans were an altogether more attractive party to the bulk of the artisans, and they made a particular appeal, it has been suggested, to workers in the less prosperous crafts, to those whose crafts were most in need of protection from British imports, to the newer immigrants, especially the Irish and the French but to a lesser extent the English and the Scots, and finally to those who had played an active part in the Revolution and who "responded to the revival of the 'Spirit of '76.' "[24]

General support for the Republican party by artisans probaby ensured their opposition to the Naturalization Act of 1798. While some members of the artisan community advocated extremely liberal terms for naturalization, there is no evidence that they commanded wide support among their fellows. The inference to be drawn from the party loyalty of most artisans is that they approved repeal of the 1798 act and a restoration of the conditions for naturalization set out in the act of 1795. However, there is some evidence that the welcome for immigrants was not unconditional. In particular, mechanics were unsympathetic to measures designed to help immigrants and others at the expense of the craft workers. A notable example was the proposal of the mayor of New York in 1803 to assist new immigrants, the sick, the handicapped, and exconvicts to learn mechanical trades through the agency of municipally operated workshops. Opposition to the plan was partly directed at its monopolistic elements, and partly at the apparent identification of high-status mechanics with "the rabble" of the city.[25] It would appear, then, that hospitality and welcome to the foreign-born on the part of the artisans depended on the preservation and enhancement of their own economic and social position. If that was not under threat, then the Jeffersonian Republicans could command support both from the artisan community and from recent immigrants resident in towns, many of whom were artisans themselves.

The corpus of ideas and values in regard to immigration which American society inherited from the eighteenth century pointed in two different directions, although these ideological strands were of unequal influence. On the one hand there was the dominant theme of welcome and hospitality based on economic advantage, humanity, and natural rights; on the other, the recognition that immigration could create serious problems of adjustment to the foreign- and native-born alike, that it represented a threat to external security and to the integrity of American political institutions, and that it created enclaves of the foreign-born which remained undigested by American society. For most of the colonial period and the first decades of the independent Republic the majority of Americans were not disposed to place obstacles in the way of immigration, nor seriously to impede the achievement of political rights by the foreign-born. Artisans were apparently no exception; in the first three decades of the nineteenth century they accepted immigrants from Europe without significant protest and in a spirit of fraternity. But in the two decades before the Civil War, when the flames of nativism were rekindled, the urban artisans' solidarity with newcomers from abroad was put to a severe test, and many craft workers yielded to the claims of personal and group survival.

It is true that a welcome was still given to substantial numbers of European immigrants who admittedly made a valuable contribution to the economic development of the United States. However, a large and growing proportion of newcomers, mainly Irish in nationality and Roman Catholic in religion, were regarded with suspicion and hostility by American artisans, despite evident claims to sympathy arising out of their harrowing experiences in Europe. It appears that the decade of the 1830s was crucial in the evolution of urban workers' attitudes. An energetic attempt to maintain working-class solidarity in the face of ethnic and religious diversity petered out during the period of economic depression and falling living standards at the end of this decade.

However, the attitudes of American artisans to immigration should not be studied in isolation. The urban craftsmen were influenced by middle-class opinion, and the policies they advocated partly reflected their perception of what was popular among the wider electorate. Nativist parties and other organizations received considerable, though fluctuating, support in the two decades before the Civil War, exerting most influence in the towns and cities of the Atlantic seaboard, notably New York, Philadelphia, and Boston. We know that there was considerable "working-class" membership in these nativist organizations, and a grasp of their objectives and policies takes us several steps along the path to understandintg the nativism of the artisans.

However, only a portion of the urban skilled workers joined these nativist organizations, many remaining loyal to the major political parties of Democrats and Whigs. Furthermore, trade unions and working men's organizations existed at intervals during this era, and their aims and political programs are relevant to determining the extent of working-class nativism. A division of opinion among artisans on the immigration issue was to be expected since the eighteenth-century legacy of ideas about immigration was not monolithic, and the social and economic forces which were tending to undermine solidaristic sentiments were uneven in their impact, varying from craft to craft and region to region. However, one important strand of working men's opinion was represented in the nativist organizations, and they deserve brief discussion.

The most prominent nativist association in the 1830s was the so-called Native-American Party, whose formation resulted from a desire to mobilize emerging anti-Catholic forces to lobby hard for Protestant rights.[26] Protestant apprehensions about the increasing influence of Roman Catholics in American politics had deepened as a result of lurid newspaper articles on the subject. The disruption of Protestant meetings by Catholic mobs, the formation of an Irish-American regiment in New York as part of the state militia, and Democratic electoral victories in New York achieved with the help of the Irish provided evidence, for impressionable minds, of a Catholic plot.[27]

The severe economic depression beginning in 1837 temporarily diminished the force of nativist sentiments, but by the early 1840s anti–Roman Catholic and anti–Irish forces were gathering for a second attack on the enemy. By 1843 they had coalesced into a new political organization called the American Republican Party, which made important gains in elections in 1844 and 1845 in New York, Philadelphia, Boston, and Baltimore, the most striking achievement being in New York City, where the party obtained 23 percent of the vote. However, many supporters of the new party were appalled by the rioting and public disorder of nativist mobs in 1844, particularly in Philadelphia, and began to return to their old political allegiances. Public hostility towards the Irish community was weakened further as a result of the Mexican War, in which many Irish volunteers fought for their adopted country and earned the respect of the native-born. However, by the late 1840s this modest *rapprochement* between the Roman Catholic and Protestant communities was overturned as a result of the intense political controversy over the future of the territories annexed from Mexico.[28]

The subsequent nativist revival was not immediately embodied in a new political party to succeed the American Republicans. Instead, a number of secret nativist organizations were formed to provide fraternal benefits for their native-born members. The growth of secret orders like the United Americans, the United American Mechanics, the United Sons of America, the Junior Sons of America, and the Order of the Star Spangled Banner implied that the eighteenth-century tradition of internationalism was weakening somewhat in the face of rival religious and ethnic allegiances, and that occupational solidarity was similarly failing to command the primary loyalty of the artisans in particular crafts.[29]

By the mid–1850s the time was ripe for the re-emergence of a nativist political party, and in 1854 the American Party evolved out of the Order of the Star Spangled Banner. Its electoral achievements were immediate, dramatic, but short-lived, and after 1856 it was a spent force. This last upsurge of nativism before the Civil War was the product of several political and demographic developments. The Irish famine, for example, had caused an enormous outflow of population from Ireland to the United States in the late 1840s and early 1850s and had greatly increased the numbers of Irish crowding into the Eastern cities. The attendant social and economic problems were compounded by the increased political participation of Irish Catholics. Scare stories about a papal plot began to circulate again, and were given greater substance by the reopening of the school question and the emergence of the trusteeship issue. The momentum to create a nativist political party was increased by the palpable failure of the existing parties, particularly the Whigs, to grapple with the problems posed by the Irish Catholics. New and honest political representatives of a new and honest party were urgently sought.[30]

This brief outline of nativist movements in the decades before the Civil War raises two important questions about their membership. Firstly, how much support did they receive from the artisans and mechanics of the Eastern towns and cities? Second, since rioting and street demonstrations were a feature of nativist protests, what was the social composition of the mobs who burned Roman Catholic churches and brawled with the Irish? Fortunately some detailed studies exist of the social and occupational membership of nativist organizations, and there is some indication of the composition of nativist street gangs which engaged in riot and arson.

There is wide agreement that urban artisans and craftsmen were very prominent in nativist organizations, both among the leadership and the rank and file. In 1843, out of the 48 leaders of the American Republican party in New York City whose occupations could be identified, about half were craftsmen and shopkeepers and the remainder were in white-collar and professional categories.[31] Analysis of a large sample of the most active members of the party in Philadelphia shows that artisans were in a majority, and in the working-class Kensington ward party candidates for the 1845 election included a blacksmith, a tailor, a carter, and a cabinetmaker. Leaders of the American Party in Pittsburgh, less than a decade later, were both younger and poorer than most political leaders; more than one-half were under 35 and almost 50 percent were artisans or clerks. In the Massachusetts legislature in the 1850s, nativist representatives were predominantly artisans from the building trades and manufacturing shops, allied with clerks and clergymen.[32] The rank and file and the less active supporters of the various nativist bodies showed an even more pronounced working-class or craft character. A self-appointed spokesman of the laboring community affirmed that the bulk of the nativist party in 1844 was composed of the "suffering working classes smarting under the effects of competition" and "incensed on seeing foreigners promoted to office." In Boston and New York City most of the party's support derived from "small shopkeepers, laborers and mechanics" with a sprinkling of professional men. A decade later the Know-Nothings attracted a great deal of working-class support, and it is a striking fact that the artisans' share of the membership in nativist parties exceeded their proportion in the population.[33]

The evidence about the status and occupations of those participating in nativist riots is less conclusive. Street violence was more common in the 1830s and 1840s than in the pre–Civil War decade. Some indication of the character of the nativist crowds is available from the lists of those injured or arrested and from police reports and newspaper accounts. It appears that young men drawn from the ranks of apprentices and journeymen in the traditional crafts were the most prominent group. The convent at Charles-town was burned by Boston workingmen; those killed or wounded on the nativist side in the Kensington Riots were all employed as apprentices and craft workers. None was known to be a member of the American Repub-lican Party, although they were obviously susceptible to the anti-Catholic rhetoric of the time.[34]

Substantial numbers of artisans were evidently attracted by the nativist parties and fraternal organizations in the ante-bellum years. Many sup-porters of the Democratic Party, which traditionally claimed the allegiance of most urban artisans, transferred their support to the rival nativist parties in the 1840s and 1850s.[35] But it is one thing to demonstrate significant artisan involvement in nativist organizations, quite another to determine what proportion of artisans in the community cast their lots, however temporarily, with the nativists. Although we know that some members of trade unions supported nativist organizations in this period, it is impossible to estimate what proportion of the membership was sympathetic to the nativist cause. Consequently it is difficult to assess the extent to which the traditional ideal of fraternity had become devitalized among the skilled workers.

Nevertheless, it is indisputable that inroads were made into solidaristic and internationalist traditions in the pre–Civil War period among the Amer-ican urban workers. Why was this? What factors impelled artisans and master craftsmen in the direction of nativism against the weight of their previous traditions, and what precisely did they hope to gain by supporting the various nativist organizations? We can best approach this question by way of a brief discussion of the mentality of nativists in general.

Nativism arose out of anxiety and even fear at the presence of large numbers of the foreign-born in American society. These apprehensions stemmed from a belief that the foreigners could not, or would not, absorb American values and modes of behavior, and that their failure to assimilate would undermine the coherence and homogeneity of American society. These fears recall the forebodings of Benjamin Franklin almost a century earlier, and, like him, nativists set out to defend core values and to preserve the integrity of American institutions. Underlying nativist fears was the suspicion that failure to assimilate was, in itself, evidence of disloyalty to America. It is difficult to improve on John Higham's definition of nativism as "intense opposition to an internal minority on the ground of its foreign (i.e. 'un-American') connections" and a "zeal to destroy the enemies of a distinctively American way of life."[36] The severity of the nativists' countermeasures will suggest the degree to which the dominant eighteenth-century legacy of fraternity towards new immigrants was being diluted in these decades.

We can now try to identify the factors which impelled some American artisans and mechanics to embrace the politics of nativism. First we must remember that American artisans were an integral part of American society, susceptible to the same prejudices and bearers of substantially the same values and beliefs as other Americans. This does not mean that artisans were indistinguishable in their norms and patterns of behavior from the rest of society, but rather that their group consciousness was insufficiently powerful to erect solid barriers between them and other social groups. Consequently the popularity of nativism among urban skilled workers was partly attributable to general changes in ideas and social values taking place at the time, and partly to the particular circumstances that confronted mechanics and craftsmen, which were not shared in that precise form by any other social group.

Historians have produced a variety of explanations for the emergence of, and the cyclical fluctuations in, nativist movements. Nativism was derived, so it is said, from simple dislike of particular ethnic groups of foreign origin, a dislike founded on prejudice and drawing on widely diffused ethnic stereotypes. Prejudice was by definition irrational, arising from the social and psychological insecurities of the nativists themselves, which in turn were often the product of social strains, individual and class anxieties, and failure to achieve cherished positions in the social structure. Immigrants were therefore selected as scapegoats for the frustrations and disappointments experienced by individuals and social groups.[37]

Some historians have expressed dissatisfaction with this interpretation, while admitting that many individuals were tempted into nativist movements by the force of prejudice. Higham for example, contends that the power of status rivalries underlay much nativist behavior. The desire of groups to improve their economic and social position generated conflicts of interest between these new pretenders and the existing holders of power and influence. Put under pressure by newcomers from abroad, the native-born often succumbed to the temptation to draw upon ethnic stereotypes and to engage in nativist politics as a means of waging the battle for social prestige. For example, Higham argued that the movement to restrict immigration at the end of the nineteenth century may be seen as an attempt to reduce conflict between those already part way up the social ladder and the foreign-born newcomers who were pressing upwards and challenging the position of those above them.[38]

A very direct form of this competition seems to have occurred between native-born and immigrant skilled workers over jobs in the manufacturing sector. But this seemed less threatening than the conflict arising from technological innovation, which led to the displacement of skilled workers by semiskilled machine operators, many of them of foreign origin.[39] This interpretation of the dynamics of nativism emphasizes genuine conflicts of interest between the native- and foreign-born. It does not categorically deny that the irrationalist use of myths and stereotypes stimulates hostility but de-emphasizes it as a motivator of nativist behavior. Accordingly, fluctuations in the power and influence of nativist movements are most fully explained by reference to the precise historical circumstances from which they emerge and into which they recede. Economic depression, technological innovation, and intense competition for jobs, power, or status will spawn defensive organizations among the victims of change, who may or may not attempt to discriminate against the recently arrived foreigners. Whether they remain fraternal and solidaristic or draw upon ethnic stereotypes to inflame feelings depends on a delicately balanced relationship between a number of factors: the ethnicity, religion, and culture of the newcomers; their absolute numbers and proportion in the total population; their degree of geographical concentration; their range of skills and occupations; their willingness to adjust to American customs; and the influence of traditional ideas of fraternity, natural rights, and asylum. In short, it is the interaction among inherited values, economic and technical change, and the characteristics of the immigrant community which determine whether a social group under threat selects the foreign-born as a target of attack.

Do these general explanations of the emergence of nativism help us to understand why many artisans and skilled workers abandoned or modified the tradition of solidarity inherited from an earlier period in the nation's history? An appraisal of the trends in American economic life in the decades after 1815 shows why artisans felt it was necessary to join organizations which were not initially nativistic for their own defense. That many of them ultimately turned to nativism is attributable both to the intensification of economic crises in the 1830s and 1850s and to the changing ethnic composition of European immigrants. Most important of all, native-born artisans could detect a connection between the destabilizing effects of commercial and technical change and the arrival of unskilled immigrants. These are the factors which peculiarly affected artisans and helped to shape their attitudes, but we must also remember that artisans shared with other sections of society an anxiety about foreign-born participation in politics and the consequences of that for American republican institutions. However let us begin by locating the germs of artisanal nativism in the interaction between their self-perception and the changes being forced upon them by economic developments.

The dynamism and fluidity of the United States in the several decades before the Civil War was disturbing and perplexing even for those who gained material advantage. For those, like the urban artisans, who were often the victims rather than the beneficiaries of change, the psychological consequences were more serious, provoking bitterness and resentment and promoting the formation of defensive organizations. The traditional values, beliefs, and attitudes which shaped their behavior seemed to conflict with the demands of a technologically innovative and increasingly commercialized society. Finding their expectations frustrated, they tried to identify the sources of their difficulties and to devise effective countermeasures for restoring their former economic and social status.[40]

The artisans' capacity to adjust to the changing world was impeded by their very flattering self-image. This in turn was derived from their economic function, their political role, and their indispensable contribution towards the achievement of American independence and the defeat of "aristocracy." Their long period of apprenticeship endowed them with the high levels of skill required for self-employed or master status. It was the possession of a skill, and the capacity to produce goods, which differentiated them, they believed, from the unskilled workers and, indeed, from the merchants. They felt they possessed the most highly prized quality of all, independence, which formed the basis of their self-esteem and dignity, preserving them from the subservience of wage slavery and fitting them for responsible participation in politics. It was the wisdom of the mechanics that prevented the corruption of the republican ideal at the hands of the wealthy. "However Snobdom may scorn and smear," one tribute began, "the mechanic is the very blood and muscle of society. Remove him and you strike out of existence the pivot element upon which all the machinery of society depends."[41]

An important and highly prized constituent of the independence of the artisans was their autonomy in the work process. This enabled them to determine the pace, duration, and timing of work and the frequency and length of leisure periods. One does not need to subscribe to the "hedonistic" interpretation of pre-industrial life, in which work is seemingly fitted into the interstices of alcohol consumption, cockfights, sporting contests, and country rambles, to appreciate the value of determining when and how long one works. Even though the freedom of journeymen was restricted in this respect, their expectation of achieving master status for themselves sweetened the pill.[42]

But by the 1820s the traditional world of the artisan and mechanic was under threat from the widening of the market and the consequential innovations in the manufacturing process. Industrialization, in Susan Hirsch's vivid phrase, was "the graveyard of the artisan class," and the fervent wish of one citizen of Newark, New Jersey, that "pursuits *so* honorable and useful [should] result in individual prosperity and happiness" found no response among the dynamic entrepreneurs of the new order. Inevitably the artisans compared the present with the past and judged the emerging order in the light of traditional values.[43] It was apparent to them that the division of labor, the rationalization of tasks, and the increasing use of machinery undermined their dignity, their pride, and, above all, their independence. The deterioration in their economic and social position can be measured in a number of ways.

One of the most obvious was the diminished opportunity for self-employment among skilled workers. In Philadelphia County the proportion of master craftsmen to the total workforce fell by more than half between 1820 and 1860, and the proportion of journeymen to masters approximately tripled. As the proportion of self-employed declined, the size of the workplace increased, with the result that in Philadelphia in 1850 the average size of a shop was about ten workers.[44]

Accompanying the reduction in selfemployment, indeed partly caused by it, was the decline in skill. This was devastating for traditional artisanal independence, and hence for the self-esteem and social status of the urban craftsman. Moreover, the inexorable decline into permanent wage-earning status of many actual or prospective master craftsmen, coupled with closer supervision of the production process by the employers, reduced the artisans' control over income and hours and pace of work. Even more important, artisans gradually ceased to own the means of production and were compelled to sell their labor rather than their products, a notable decline into dependence. The increased use of the term "factory hands" brutally summarizes the loss of human dignity involved in the transition from artisanal to capitalist production.[45]

The reduction of artisanal autonomy in the work process was an inevitable result of craft decline. In a situation where competing employers were frustrated in their drive for higher profits by the sporadic work habits and traditional easygoing approach of their employees or subcontractors, it was inevitable that they would exercise closer supervision of the work process to improve efficiency and to inculcate desirable qualities of industry, discipline, and regularity in the work force. The transition from "traditional" to "modern" values was inevitably painful for most workers, representing the forcible loss of autonomy, the decline in skill, and the associated fall in status and self-respect that "took a great deal of joy out of life."[46]

Furthermore, the decline into dependence and the rise of the new employing class drew threatening clouds over the future of republican institutions and placed a question mark over the political role of the urban workers. Having taken pride in their independence as the most important qualification for voting, they were dismayed by their descent into economic dependence, since it left them open to the criticism that, as mere wage earners, they were the helpless agents of their employers and unfit for the suffrage.[47]

Inevitably the artisans reflected on the causes of their decline and what, if anything, could be done about it. They concluded that it was inherent in the process of economic modernization in a free-market economy. Capitalist development inevitably produced an unjust society in which worthy producers were denied their proper rewards. They derived this conclusion from the labor theory of value, which was the subject of some discussion in the early 1830s.

The employment of this theory is important to our understanding of the artisans' response to economic and social change: it shows that they were prepared to adopt a solidaristic approach to their problems. Their initial target was the capitalists and financiers, not fellow workers from abroad. The theory taught them that the labor of the "producing classes" was the source of all wealth, and therefore capital was simply accumulated labor. However, under capitalism, labor and capital had been divided and capital had been appropriated by nonproducers, or capitalists. Society was therefore split into two conflicting interests, the useful producers and the parasitical nonproducers. Justice demanded that the producers receive a full or fair share of the wealth produced. The pioneering trade unions of the 1830s, the cooperative associations and ten-hours movements of the late 1840s and the reconstituted trade unions of the early 1850s were all, in their different ways, constructive attempts to improve the material conditions of the producing classes, among which the urban mechanic had an honored place.[48]

Self-defense by artisans involved all producers working together to thwart the ambitions of the "capitalist" element. If foreign workers undercut existing wages, as they sometimes did, the solution, many believed, was to recruit them into trade unions. Hence, numerous unions were formed in Philadelphia in the 1830s, composed mainly but not exclusively of skilled mechanics of many nationalities, grouped loosely together under the umbrella of the General Trades Union of the city. In this instance the unity of the producers appears to have overcome their ethnic and religious differences, and their solidarity encompassed both unskilled and skilled workers. Unity was fostered by the willingness of many foreign-born skilled workers to ally with their native-born counterparts in seeking to maintain wages and conditions. The trade unions, too, played their part in setting up labor exchanges to disseminate information about job opportunities and wage rates among newly arrived immigrants. Union recruitment of newcomers in the early 1850s was facilitated by conducting union meetings and publishing journals in more than one language. In these instances the awareness of common "class" objectives overcame ethnic and religious antagonisms.[49]

This "co-operative" approach to their problems by urban workers is evidence of a conviction that solidarity was the most effective means of ensuring survival. However, when this faith weakened during the nativist hysteria of the 1840s and 1850s, solidarity and survival were widely thought of as opposites, and competition increasingly displaced co-operation in the relations between native- and foreign-born workers. The main vehicles of the conflict strategy were the various nativist parties and associations already referred to, whose membership was disproportionately drawn from the ranks of urban artisans and craftsmen. But members of trade unions also expressed sharp opposition to immigration, asserting that it was the major cause of strife between capital and labor.[50] Notwithstanding this evident hostility, some nativist union officials continued to recruit foreign-born workers in their trades. Given the changing composition of immigration in ethnic, religious, and occupational terms and the fact that the Irish Catholics were the nativists' major target, there was probably little change in attitude to traditional kinds of immigrants, Protestant in religion and yeoman farmer or skilled craftsman in occupation, although they too would be adversely affected by nativist political proposals.

The question remains as to why the initial solidaristic approach to the problems of dependence and declining status on the part of urban artisans was pushed aside by the politics of nativism in the early 1840s. There appear to be two broad reasons for this. The first is that the economic depression which began in 1837 and lasted into the 1840s had a damaging effect on working-class organizations. A substantial reduction in wage rates coupled with a rise in unemployment produced a heavy fall in trade union membership, and many unions did not survive. Strikes became rare and despairing, and the embryonic sense of working-class unity was undermined. From looking to collective security through solidarity, artisans now turned to ethnically based organizations and to the politics of temperance, education and religion.[51]

The second reason was that the urban artisans, as serious casualties of change and economic depression, were able to identify a particular group in society, the Irish, as being largely responsible for their decline in occupational, political, and social status. Their antagonism towards this group arose from their recognition, in part as a result of the depression, that self-defense was better achieved by ethnic competition than class collaboration. The latter depends on sentiments of solidarity which were ill-developed towards the Irish, whose values, behavior, physical concentration, and population growth were alarming to native-born Americans, and seemed to constitute a genuine threat to the dominance of traditional American values and to the integrity of American political institutions.

The native-born artisans became aware of the dramatic increases in immigration in the three decades before 1860. In the 1830s there were approximately half a million immigrants, in the 1840s about one and three-quarter million, and in the immediate prewar decade about two and one-half million. The bulk of these newcomers were Irish or German Roman-Catholic peasants. The impact of these new arrivals on the host society was very considerable. In 1789 the Roman Catholic population of the United States was around 30,000, but by 1860 it had increased to about 3 million out of approximately 30 million, and its rate of growth exceeded that of the population as a whole, which itself was increasing very rapidly.[52]

Another characteristic of the post–1840 immigrants was their high concentration in urban industrial locations; consequently the ethnic and religious character of the population of many American cities was transformed, to the dismay of the native-born inhabitants.[53] The problems of concentration were exacerbated by the tendency of the Irish to congregate in a relatively few sections of the cities and to create recognizably Irish districts. The development worried the native-born, who saw in it an impediment to assimilation. Furthermore, the Irish communities seemed to be a major source of the increasing number of social problems which bedevilled the cities. This criticism had some objective basis, and it would be mistaken to view it as simply the fruit of prejudice and bigotry.[54] For example, the poverty of the Irish newcomers provided cause for complaint. The low wages in unskilled work, the frequent periods of unemployment, and the high rates of mortality among the male wage earners tended to increase dependency and to throw many Irish onto poor relief or into almshouses, increasing the burden of public support. The rapid increase in Irish immigration also placed enormous strain on the housing market in the Eastern cities, producing appalling overcrowding and very unhealthy living conditions.

Similarly, the Irish were held responsible for the increasing corruption of politics and for the decline of republican values. The source of these problems was the extraordinary increase in the size of foreign-born vote, rising from 1 in 40 of the total electorate in 1830 to 1 in 7 in 1845 and continuing to grow. Many of these voters had been able to evade the naturalization law and to cast their votes soon after arrival. The party politicians quickly recognized that elections could be decided by the vote of the Irish-Americans, and both parties made overtures to the community's leaders.[55] Critics of Irish political participation compared their behavior with that of Jefferson's "independent" voter who, through his ownership of property, exercised individual judgment in placing his vote. By contrast the Irish appeared to vote *en bloc* for venal politicians, ruthessly pursuing sectional self-interest without regard to the wider issues of public welfare.[56]

Moreover, anti-Irish hostility was intensified by the widely held suspicion that the Irish Catholics were the advance guard of European reaction, intent on destroying republicanism in America.

Finally, and from the native artisans' viewpoint most importantly, the Irish were identified as agents in the process of economic modernization. The adoption of task differentiation and mechanization was facilitated by this increasing supply of cheap, unskilled labor, notably in industries like sewing, shoemaking, cabinetmaking, and carpentry. The essentially class opposition to innovative capitalists was transformed into ethnic antagonism when these "accumulators" employed workers of a different ethnicity or religion. When one ethnic group is markedly cheaper than another, the higher-paid workers face not only the loss of their jobs but the equally disturbing likelihood of a long-term worsening of working conditions. It is not surprising, therefore, that there was a widespread dismissal of Irish claims on American solidarity; the Irish were perceived less as fellow laborers than as the minions of capital.[57]

This narrowing of sympathy among native-born artisans for recently arrived Irish immigrants may therefore be attributed to a potent combination of rapid social and economic changes and the ethnic, religious, occupational, and other characteristics of the newcomers. The weakening of solidarity prepared the way for artisans to support the emergent nativist organizations. But what did they hope to gain by this and what specific objectives did they have in mind?

As a way of approaching this question, let us briefly consider the policies of the nativist parties and try to deduce from them the nature of their appeal to artisans. These parties believed that their major task was to reduce the pernicious political influence of the foreign-born population. They did not propose to abolish the traditional right of asylum; indeed, the American Republicans reaffirmed their conviction that "without any distinction as to political creed or religious faith . . . we invite the stranger, worn down by oppression at home, to come here and share with us the blessings of our native land.[58] But one of these blessings was the right to participate in American politics. Nativists believed that this right was too cheaply obtained and that naturalization should be conditional on immigrants abandoning old loyalties. Nativists contended that only a prolonged period of residence in the United States could weaken former ties and guarantee sufficient assimilation to permit naturalization.[59]

Omitted from the political programs of nativist political and fraternal organizations is any reference to legislative restrictions on immigration.[60] Instead, nativists advocated ways of reducing the impact of the foreign-born in politics. Two main methods were suggested: to restrict the holding of public office to the native-born, and to extend the period of residence for naturalization from 5 to 21 years. At a state level nativists sometimes tried to limit or to remove the voting rights of naturalized citizens or, at the very least, to insist that voting rights should be restricted to citizens, something which was not always done.[61] Nativists also fought a vigorous propaganda battle against the insidious influence of the Roman Catholic church in American politics. This fight was especially keen over the use of the Protestant Bible in the public schools, considered by many as an essential means of protecting American institutions against the forces of Catholic reaction and of preserving opportunity for Protestants against their Catholic rivals.[62]

Little was heard from the various nativist organizations about actually restricting the number of foreign-born entering the country. True, the Know-Nothing party in one state, in attempting to present itself as the friend of working men, argued that improvements in artisans' standards of living were partly dependent on immigration restriction. Some of the nativist secret societies also required their members to oppose the immigration of foreign paupers and criminals, and individual nativists occasionally advocated the "arresting" of immigration. But immigration restriction generally received low priority from nativists.

This conclusion poses a problem of interpretation, since there is an apparent conflict between the increasing opposition of artisans to immigrants on economic grounds and the objectives of the nativist defense organizations which they joined in growing number after 1840. After all, the policies of the nativist parties were not obviously designed to offer protection against economic vicissitudes or changing methods of production. Therefore it is tempting to infer from the policies of the nativist organizations that nativists, including working-class ones, primarily objected to the political power of the Irish Catholics, which permitted them to defend and to promote their objectionable cultural and religious values. Michael Feldberg is one historian sympathetic to this view, warning against reducing working-class nativism to economic causes or "to a class consciousness turned sour in a long depression." The bitter clashes between the Protestant and Irish Catholic communities over temperance, Sabbatarianism, public education, and immigrant participation in politics, he reminds us, had a life of their own and were not surrogates for latent economic conflict, being part of a struggle in which each community attempted to assert its superiority over the other. Hence, either simple dislike founded on prejudice, or the self-conscious evocation of stereotypes to wage the battle for supremacy, explain the participation of many artisans in the nativist movements of the time.[63]

Feldberg's cautionary words about the dangers of economic reductionism are not misplaced. Yet it may be equally misleading to take the nativist parties' political programs at face value, at least as far as their working-class supporters were concerned. After all, artisanal support for the nativists was not based simply on opposition to the foreign-born on cultural and religious grounds but reflected a determination to protect artisan wages and working practices from intense competition on the part of cheap foreign-born labor.

It must, of course, be conceded that the most effective means of achieving this objective was by immigration restriction, and this, as we know, was not seriously proposed by the nativist parties. But there were considerable obstacles in the way of adopting such a policy in the 1840s and 1850s. The practical and philosophical difficulties of the artisans should not blind us to the possibility that they saw in the nativist parties a potential for economic self-defense. The collapse of their class-based organizations of the 1830s left artisans with few alternatives for selfprotection in the commercial and manufacturing revolution than taking place, the effects of which were exacerbated by the acute depression after 1837. The nativist bodies were the best available means of erecting a defense against economic disaster, not least because of their potential for attracting wide political support. Moreover, their attacks on the Irish centered on a group which appeared to collaborate with the economic modernizers in undermining the traditional methods of production, and hence in subverting the social status of the "independent" artisans.

Evidence in support of this "economic" interpretation of nativism is of two kinds. Some working-class nativists, it has been suggested, hoped that the postponement of naturalization, the exclusion of the foreign-born from political office, and the maintenance of the Protestant Bible in the public schools would deter some potential immigrants from leaving their European homelands.[64] In retrospect it is easy to see that this was a vain hope, but, given contemporary assumptions about the motives for immigration, it was a not unreasonable expectation at the time.

A more practical and effective means of economic self-defense lay in the nativists' attempts to establish religious and cultural homogeneity, and by so doing to confer on Protestant workmen an economic advantage over their Irish Catholic rivals. The roots of the artisans' support for the politics of cultural superiority lay in the Protestant revivalism of the late 1830s. The temperance movement, an integral part of the revival, gained numerous working-class converts. Many valued it for its practical utility in ensuring economic and personal survival in an insecure world. For example, temperance secured an advantage for the sober worker in the labor market over his inebriated, ill-disciplined, and unreliable competitor. In particular, it promised success against the hard-drinking, unskilled Irish workers, who, in their turn, resented the attack on their culture from self-righteous Protestants claiming moral superiority.[65]

Survival by self-help could also be advanced through the widening of opportunity provided by an improved public education system. The Protestant coloration of the public schools offered competitive advantages to Protestant children, as well as helping to ensure the dominance of traditional Protestant culture in America. Hence nativists urged that no concessions should be made to Roman Catholic demands for the allocation of tax revenue for the construction of Catholic schools or for the replacement of the Protestant Bible in the public schools.[66]

Whilst the nativist parties, it may be conceded, offered the possibility of economic and status advantages to their supporters, immigration restriction would undoubtedly have had a more favorable and direct impact on the wages and conditions of the native-born. However, there were insurmountable political and philosophical obstacles to the adoption of such a policy. There would, for example, have been widespread popular opposition to any scheme to limit the supply of already scarce labor. The nativists' political proposals were a different matter, since their impact on immigration would probably have been marginal. Moreover, while employers were opposed to immigration restriction, they would exercise no restraining hand on ethnic hostility, since it served their interest to divide the working class along ethnic and religious lines. Working-class nativists, we may conclude, could expect little political success for a party advocating immigration restriction, but could expect widespread sympathy for proposals to limit the political rights of the foreign-born.

Internal doubts were probably as effective as external restraints in ensuring that distrust of and apprehension about the foreign-born did not culminate in proposals to limit immigration. The tradition of hospitality, asylum, and natural rights deriving from the eighteenth century was still influential, not least among artisans. That careful regard was paid to these values is evident from the nativists' defense of their proposals to restrict office-holding and to extend the period of residence for naturalization. This sensitivity to the criticism that they were abandoning traditional values helped to inhibit artisans from making the direct attack on immigration which their economic interest conceivably demanded.[67]

It is easy to see why the support Americans gave to nativist organizations has been widely attributed to simple religious bigotry, nativism being just one more episode in the bitter hostility between Protestantism and Roman Catholicism. However, that conclusion is not totally persuasive, even though it is undeniable that some artisans were deeply prejudiced. The decision to work through nativist organizations was a perfectly rational method of artisan self-defense, given the political and ideological constraints of the 1840s.

In the three decades before the Civil War, then, the well-established tradition of artisan fraternity towards newcomers to the United States began to be modified. Many of the old craft skills became obsolete under the impact of commercial and technological transformation, and the casualties of this process, the artisans and mechanics, looked for the means of defending their economic and social position. The attempt to form a class alliance against the innovators in the 1830s perished with the post–1837 economic depression, and was only tentatively revived in the following two decades. The emergence of nativist parties and organizations appeared to offer a partial solution to the artisans' difficulties, and their considerable support for these bodies testified not only to the misgivings they shared with other sections of society about the presence of growing numbers of Irish Catholics in the United States, but also to their rational identification of the Irish with the forces of economic modernization.

The politics of solidarity may, in certain circumstances, transcend ethnic and religious barriers; but in the 1840s Protestant revivalism heightened anti-Catholic sentiments, and the Catholic Irish in turn became obdurate in their determination to preserve their ethnic and religious identity under Protestant attacks. The achievement of solidarity implies both an invitation and a sympathetic response. When neither was forthcoming, the politics of survival took over. This ethnic competition was kept within fairly narrow bounds, however. The practicalities of politics and the economic and philosophical arguments against legislative restriction on immigration created a climate in which full-blooded economic protectionism on behalf of the urban artisans was never on the political agenda. The Civil War was a watershed in this respect. In the postwar world, for the first time in the history of the Republic, organized urban workers began to agitate against the immigration of foreign labor. Yet we should be in no doubt that the origins of working-class xenophobia are to be found in the ante-bellum period, and the forces which produced and molded it can be seen in embryo at this time.

NOTES

1. Thomas Paine, *Common Sense*, in Moncure Daniel Conway, ed., *The Writings of Thomas Paine*, 4 vols. (New York: Putnam's, 1894–96), Vol. 1, pp. 100–101.

2. Thomas Jefferson to George Flower, 1817, quoted in Hans Kohn, *The Idea of Nationalism: A Study in Its Origins and Background* (New York: Macmillan, 1961), p. 310.

3. Joseph Priestley, "A Charity Sermon for Poor Emigrants" (1797), in Edith Abbott, ed., *Historical Aspects of the Immigration Problem: Select Documents* (1926; rpt. New York: Arno Press, 1969), pp. 707–11.

4. Merle Curti, *The Roots of American Loyalty* (New York: Columbia University Press, 1946), pp. 4–5; Kohn, *Idea of Nationalism*, 269–73; Yehoshua Arieli, *Individualism and Nationalism in American Ideology* (Cambridge, Mass.: Harvard University Press, 1964), pp. 42–43; Thomas L. Nichols, *Lecture on Immigration and the Right of Naturalization* (New York, 1845), in Abbott, *Historical Aspects*, pp. 750–53; Rush Welter, *The Mind of America, 1820–60* (New York: Columbia University Press, 1975), p. 63.

5. Samuel F. B. Morse, *Imminent Dangers to the Free Institutions of the United States through Foreign Immigration* (1835), in Abbott, *Historical Aspects*, p. 450; Samuel Whelpley, *A Compend of History from the Earliest Times*, 8th ed. (1825), ibid., p. 728; Curti, *Roots of American Loyalty*, pp. 80–81; Welter, *Mind of America*, 324.

6. Curti, *Roots of American Loyalty*, pp. 70–71; J. Hector St. John de Crèvecoeur,

Letters from an American Farmer, in Abbott, *Historical Aspects*, p. 419; Thomas L. Nichols, *Lecture on Immigration*, p. 751.

7. Conway, *The Writings of Thomas Paine*, Vol. 3, p. 271; W. H. Hadow, *Citizenship* (Oxford: Clarendon Press, 1923), pp. 168–70.

8. Quoted in John A. Hawgood, *The Tragedy of German-America* (London: Putnam's Sons, 1940), p. 285; Nichols, *Lecture on Immigration*, p. 750.

9. James H. Kettner, "The Development of American Citizenship in the Revolutionary Era: The Idea of Volitional Allegiance," *The American Journal of Legal History* 18 (July 1974); 211, 220, 232.

10. Alexis de Tocqueville, in a letter to a friend, quoted in Arieli, *Individualism and Nationalism*, p. 19.

11. Welter, *Mind of America*, p. 42, quoting John Norvell's speech to Michigan's first constitutional convention. See also Kohn, *Idea of Nationalism*, pp. 290–91; Arieli, *Individualism and Nationalism*, 24, 52, 185–87.

12. Parke Godwin, "Secret Societies—The Know Nothings," *Putnam's Monthly* 5 (January 1855), in Abbott, *Historical Aspects*, p. 800; Kohn, *Idea of Nationalism*, p. 309; Welter, *Mind of America*, p. 401.

13. Ira M. Leonard and Robert D. Parmet, *American Nativism, 1830–1860* (New York: Van Nostrand Reinhold Co., 1971), pp. 11, 14; letter of Benjamin Franklin to James Parker, 20 March 1751, in Leonard W. Labaree, ed., *The Papers of Benjamin Franklin* (New Haven: Yale University Press, 1961), Vol. 4, p 120.

14. Letter of Benjamin Franklin to Peter Collinson, 9 May 1753, in Labaree, *Papers*, Vol. 4, pp. 483–85; Glenn Weaver, "Benjamin Franklin and the Pennsylvania Germans," *William and Mary Quarterly* 14 (October 1957): 540–42; Curti, *Roots of American Loyalty*, p. 74; also Franklin to James Parker, 20 March 1751, in Labaree, *Papers*, Vol. 4, p. 120.

15. Carl and Jessica Bridenbaugh, *Rebels and Gentlemen: Philadelphia in the Age of Franklin* (1942; rpt. New York: Oxford University Press, 1962), p. 53; Arieli, *Individualism and Nationalism*, p. 46.

16. Weaver, "Benjamin Franklin," pp. 546–48, 553, 559.

17. Kohn, *Idea of Nationalism*, pp. 273, 309; Thomas Jefferson, *Notes on the State of Virginia*, in Merrill D. Peterson, ed., *The Portable Thomas Jefferson* (1975; rpt. Harmondsworth, England: Penguin Books, 1977), pp. 124–25; Curti, *Roots of American Loyalty*, p. 69.

18. Curti, *Roots of American Loyalty*, p. 73; James Morton Smith, *Freedom's Fetters: The Alien and Sedition Laws and American Civil Liberties* (Ithaca, N.Y.: Cornell University Press, 1956), pp. 22–23; Leonard and Parmet, *American Nativism*, p. 22.

19. Seymour Martin Lipset and Earl Raab, *The Politics of Unreason: Right-Wing Extremism in America, 1790–1970* (London: Heinemann Educational Books, Ltd., 1971), pp. 35–36.

20. Smith, *Freedom's Fetters*, 27, 30; Curti, *Roots of American Loyalty*, p. 75.

21. Thomas J. Curran, *Xenophobia and Immigration, 1820–1930* (Boston: Twayne Publishers, 1975), p. 20; Leonard and Parmet, *American Nativism*, 24, 49–50.

22. Howard B. Rock, *Artisans of the New Republic: The Tradesmen of New York City in the Age of Jefferson* (New York: New York University Press, 1979), pp. 8–9, 192, 283.

23. Ibid., pp. 27, 69, 71.

24. Alfred Young, "The Mechanics and the Jeffersonians: New York, 1789–1801," *Labor History* 5 (1964): 247, 250–52, 255–57, 269–70.

25. Rock, *Artisans of the New Republic*, pp. 50, 65–66.

26. Curran, *Xenophobia* pp. 29–30.

27. Ibid., pp. 25–29.

28. Ibid., pp. 35, 43; Jean H. Baker, *Ambivalent Americans: The Know-Nothing Party in Maryland* (Baltimore: The Johns Hopkins University Press, 1977), p. 4; Lipset and Raab, *Politics of Unreason*, p. 50; David Montgomery, "The Shuttle and the Cross: Weavers and Artisans in the Kensington Riots of 1844," *Journal of Social History* 5 (Summer 1972): 437–39; Michael Feldberg, *The Philadelphia Riots of 1844: A Study of Ethnic Conflict* (Westport, Conn.: Greenwood Press, 1975), pp. 172–74; Sam Bass Warner, Jr., *The Private City: Philadelphia in Three Periods of Growth* (Philadelphia: University of Pennsylvania Press, 1968), p. 153.

29. Curran, *Xenophobia*, p. 43; Bruce Laurie, " 'Nothing on Compulsion': Life Styles of Philadelphia Artisans, 1820–1850," in Milton Cantor, ed., *American Workingclass Culture: Explorations in American Labor and Social History* (Westport, Conn.: Greenwood Press, 1979), p. 116; Thomas Richard Whitney, "A Defense of American Policy as Opposed to the Encroachments of Foreign Influence" (1856), in Abbott, *Historical Aspects*, p. 324; Baker, *Ambivalent Americans*, p. 6.

30. Curran, *Xenophobia*, pp. 52–54, 60–61; Michael F. Holt, "The Politics of Impatience: The Origins of Know Nothingism," *Journal of American History* 60 (Sept. 1973): 314–18, 323–24; Baker, *Ambivalent Americans*, pp. 8–22.

31. Lipset and Raab, *Politics of Unreason*, p. 51.

32. Montgomery, "The Shuttle and the Cross," p. 429; Feldberg, *Philadelphia Riots*, pp. 51–52, 55; Holt, "Politics of Impatience," p. 319.

33. Feldberg, *Philadelphia Riots*, pp. 46, 55, 164–65; Lipset and Raab, *Politics of Unreason*, pp. 50–51, 55–57; *Working Man's Advocate*, 23 March 1844, quoted in John R. Commons et al, eds., *A Documentary History of American Industrial Society* (1910–11; rpt. New York: Russell and Russell, 1958), vol. 7, p. 90; Laurie, " 'Nothing on Compulsion,' " pp. 116–17.

34. Feldberg, *Philadelphia Riots*, pp. 51, 67, 107; William V. Shannon, *The American Irish* (New York: Collier, 1974), pp. 42–45.

35. Michael Feldberg, "The Crowd in Philadelphia History: A Comparative Perspective," in Cantor, *American Workingclass Culture*, p. 88; *Working Man's Advocate*, 23 March 1844, quoted in Commons et al., *Documentary History*, vol. 7, p. 90; Lipset and Raab, *Politics of Unreason*, pp. 51, 55.

36. John Higham, *Strangers in the Land: Patterns of American Nativism, 1860–1925* (1955: rpt. New York: Atheneum, 1963), p. 4.

37. See, for example, Ray Allen Billington, *Protestant Crusade, 1800–1860* (New York: Macmillan, 1938), and Richard Hofstadter, *The Paranoid Style in American Politics* (London: Jonathan Cape, 1966).

38. John Higham, "Another Look at Nativism" in Higham, *Send These to Me: Jews and Other Immigrants in Urban America* (New York: Atheneum, 1975), pp. 107, 113.

39. Edna Bonacich, "A Theory of Ethnic Antagonism: The Split Labor Market," *American Sociological Review* 37 (1972): 554; Laurie, " 'Nothing on Compulsion,' " p. 114.

40. See quotation from Zygmunt Bauman, in Herbert G. Gutman, *Work, Culture,*

and Society in Industrializing America: Essays in American Working-Class and Social History (New York: Alfred A. Knopf, 1976), pp. 16–18.

41. Howard B. Rock, *Artisans of the New Republic*, pp. 8–14, 71, 135–36, 191–92, 225; Herbert Gutman, "Labor's Response to Modern Industrialism," in Howard H. Quint, Milton Cantor, and Dean Albertson, eds., *Main Problems in American History*, 2 vols. (Homewood, Ill.: Dorsey Press, 1972), Vol. 2, p. 74; Feldberg, *Philadelphia Riots*, p. 68; Susan E. Hirsch, *The Roots of the American Working Class: The Industrialization of Crafts in Newark, 1800–1860* (Philadelphia: University of Pennsylvania Press, 1978), p. 123; Alan Dawley, *Class and Community: The Industrial Revolution in Lynn* (Cambridge, Mass.: Harvard University Press, 1976), pp. 59–61.

42. Laurie, " 'Nothing on Compulsion,' "pp. 97, 100–101.

43. Hirsch, *Roots of the American Working Class*, p. 15; Gutman, "Labor's Response," p. 74.

44. Stuart Blumin, "Mobility and Change in Ante-Bellum Philadelphia," in Stephan Thernstrom and Richard Sennett, eds., *Nineteenth-Century Cities: Essays in the New Urban History* (New Haven: Yale University Press, 1969), p. 199; Rock, *Artisans of the New Republic*, pp. 257, 268; Hirsch, *Roots of the American Working Class*, pp. 78–79; Laurie, " 'Nothing on Compulsion,' " p. 93; David Montgomery, "The Working Classes of the Pre-Industrial American City, 1780–1830," *Labor History* 9 No. 1 (Winter 1968): 10–11. Goldin and Sokoloff suggest that "as the size of a firm or its scale of production increased, so did the proportion of the firm's work force made up of women and children," dramatically illustrating declining opportunity for skilled males; see Claudia Goldin and Kenneth Sokoloff, "Women, Children, and Industrialization in the Early Republic: Evidence from the Manufacturing Censuses," *Journal of Economic History* 42, No. 4 (December 1982): 752.

45. Hirsch, *Roots of the American Working Class*, pp. xv, xvii–xviii, 7–8, 90; Warner, *Private City*, pp. 65, 72; Norman J. Ware, *The Industrial Worker, 1840–60* (1924: rpt. Quadrangle Paperbooks, New York, 1964), pp. xiv, 106–7; Dawley, *Class and Community*, pp. 61–64.

46. Laurie, " 'Nothing on Compulsion,' " 104; Paul Faler, "Cultural Aspects of the Industrial Revolution: Lynn, Massachusetts, Shoemakers and Industrial Morality 1826–1860," in Cantor, *American Workingclass Culture*, pp. 121–22, 128–29, 133–39; Alan Dawley and Paul Faler, "Working Class Culture and Politics in the Industrial Revolution: Sources of Loyalism and Rebellion," ibid., pp. 62–63; Gutman, *Work, Culture, and Society*, p. 37.

47. Gutman, *Work, Culture, and Society*, p. 50; Rock, *Artisans of the New Republic*, p. 280; Gutman, "Labor's Response," pp. 74–75.

48. Commons et al., *Documentary History*, Vol. 5, pp. vi–vii, 24, 27–33; Dawley and Faler, "Working Class Culture," p. 55; Laurie, " 'Nothing on Compulsion,' " pp. 111–13; Dawley, *Class and Community*, pp. 64–65.

49. Robert Ernst, *Immigrant Life in New York City, 1825–1863* (New York: Columbia University Press, 1949), pp. 101, 107–8: Montgomery, "The Shuttle and the Cross," pp. 417, 419; Feldberg, *Philadelphia Riots*, p. 47.

50. *Voice of Industry*, 9 October 1845, quoted in J. R. Commons et al. *History of Labor in the United States*, 4 vols. (1918: rpt. New York: Augustus M. Kelley, 1966), Vol. 1, p. 488; Ernst, *Immigrant Life*, pp. 102–3.

51. Curran, *Xenophobia*, p. 32; Ware, *Industrial Worker*, pp. 27–28; Warner, *Private*

City, pp. 74, 76; Montgomery, "The Shuttle and the Cross," pp. 420–21; Laurie, " 'Nothing on Compulsion,' " pp. 94–95.

52. Curran, *Xenophobia*, pp. 23–24; Ware, *Industrial Worker*, p. 11; Lawrence J. McCaffrey, *The Irish Diaspora in America* (Bloomington: Indiana University Press, 1976), p. 89.

53. Leonard and Parmet, *American Nativism*, p. 33; Peter R. Knights, *The Plain People of Boston, 1830–1860: A Study in City Growth* (New York: Oxford University Press, 1971), pp. 33–34, 47.

54. Shannon, *American Irish*, p. 40; Holt, "Politics of Impatience," p. 323; Laurie, " 'Nothing on Compulsion,' " p. 114; Feldberg, *Philadelphia Riots*, pp. 33–34.

55. Oliver MacDonagh, "Emigration During the Famine," in R. D. Edwards and T. D. Williams, eds., *The Great Famine: Studies in Irish History, 1845–52* (Dublin: Browne and Nolan, 1956), p. 383; Feldberg, *Philadelphia Riots*, pp. 30–31; Lipset and Raab, *Politics of Unreason*, p. 50; Baker, *Ambivalent Americans*, pp. 19–21.

56. MacDonagh, "Emigration," p. 383; Curran, *Xenophobia*, p. 25.

57. Bonacich, "Theory of Ethnic Antagonism", pp. 553–54. Occasionally the Irish were denied "producer" status on the implausible grounds that they all kept liquor and grocery stores. See Laurie, " 'Nothing on Compulsion,' " p. 115.

58. Feldberg, *Philadelphia Riots*, p. 60.

59. Ibid., p. 61; Samuel C. Busey, *Immigration, Its Evils and Consequences* (New York: De Witt and Davenport, 1856), pp. 5–7; *Address of the Delegates of the Native American National Convention, Assembled at Philadelphia, July 4, 1845, to the Citizens of the United States*, in Abbott, *Historical Aspects*, pp. 745–46.

60. Immigration restriction did not become a lively political issue until after the Civil War, and in that respect internationalism remained strong in the prewar period.

61. Curran, *Xenophobia*, pp. 36, 51, 59; Baker, *Ambivalent Americans*, p. 4; Feldberg, *Philadelphia Riots*, p. 64; An American, *The Sons of the Sires: A History of the Rise, Progress, and Destiny of the American Party* (Philadelphia, 1855), in Abbott, *Historical Aspects*, pp. 790–91.

62. Curran, *Xenophobia*, p. 59; Warner, *Private City*, p. 144.

63. Feldberg, *Philadelphia Riots*, p. 65.

64. Busey, *Immigration*, p. 137; Feldberg, *Philadelphia Riots*, p. 49.

65. Laurie, " 'Nothing on Compulsion,' " pp. 108–11; Faler, "Cultural Aspects of the Industrial Revolution," pp. 146–47; Montgomery, "The Shuttle and the Cross," p. 421.

66. Montgomery, "The Shuttle and the Cross," p. 421; Feldberg, *Philadelphia Riots* p. 49; Laurie, " 'Nothing on Compulsion,' " p. 111.

67. Feldberg, *Philadelphia Riots*, p. 65.

3

The Developing Response of Urban Labor to Immigration, 1860–1873

During the American Civil War from 1861 to 1865, and in the immediate postwar period, urban wage earners in the United States experienced a fall in living standards and a worsening of working conditions. Wartime price rises exceeded wage increases, the gap between the two being widest in the early years of the war. The *New York Tribune* recorded that the cost of living doubled between 1860 and 1864, whilst wages increased by no more than 20 percent. Subsequent calculations show that although real wages did not fall as precipitately as the *Tribune* stated, their decline was nevertheless quite marked. Increases in rents and in clothing and food prices, all of which exceeded general price increases, were particularly burdensome through being such a large proportion of family expenditure. Although wages were beginning to increase more rapidly towards the end of the war, wage earners as a whole were worse off than they had been in 1860.[1]

Peace produced economic problems of a different sort. In early 1865 some employers attempted to reduce wages in expectation of declining demand once the conflict was over. The federal government's postwar policy of contracting the greenback currency intensified the fall in prices and increased unemployment, which was further augmented by the demobilization of Civil War veterans and by the increase in European immigration following the end of hostilities. However, real annual earnings began to rise after 1867 owing to the stabilization of wages and the continued fall in consumer prices. Of course, the price levels and rates of growth of some industries deviated significantly from the general trends; employees in these sectors fared better or worse than the average worker whose fortunes have been briefly outlined.[2]

The general worsening of the living standards of urban workers during the Civil War and the immediate post–Civil War period should be considered in the context of the long-term disruption of traditional craft skills by rationalization and innovation in the productive process, which was briefly discussed in the previous chapter. The impact of change was uneven; industries most severely affected were consumer goods industries like clothing, boots and shoes, textiles, light engineering, woodworking, and cabinetmaking, whereas the capital goods industries, like coal mining and iron and steel, were as yet relatively untouched.[3] The undermining of skill was very disturbing for artisans. William Sylvis, the iron molders' leader, was apprehensive lest his craft cease to exist. The major threat to it in the 1860s came, not from machinery, but from the more systematic division of labor introduced by employers before the Civil War to cut manufacturing costs. The simplified operations encouraged employers to recruit and train "greenhands" for specialist tasks, at lower wages than those of the competent skilled molders. These innovations were anathema to the molders, even though their countermeasure of reducing the proportion of "helpers" and apprentices to skilled workers was relatively successful in the decade after 1858.[4]

The effects of mechanization were most acute in this period in the shoe and coopering industries. As late as 1850 hand labor was still dominant in the shoe industry, although in the preceding decades numerous changes had occurred in the organization of production. But the introduction of the pegging machine in 1857 and the McKay sole-sewing machine in 1862 "usurped not only the highest skill of the workman but also his superior physique."[5] The inevitable resistance of the artisans was directed less at machines than at the process of displacement, by which skilled workers were replaced by unskilled greenhands or forced to take a less skilled task at lower wages. Craft yielded to machine in cabinetmaking, too, when wood turning became automatic and large factories transformed "a once flourishing craft into a small remnant." Earlier the cotton textile industry had established power-driven machine production in spinning and weaving in place of old craft skills.

Rationalization and innovation in the work process had far-reaching practical and psychological effects, which in turn generated protest and opposition from skilled workers.[6] The two major targets of criticism were the capitalist employers, sometimes described as "accumulators," and their manipulable allies, the unskilled machine tenders. The hiring of cheaper native or foreign-born labor to mind the machines drove a deep wedge between skilled and unskilled workers, since it was from the reservoir of unskilled labor that semiskilled machine minders were chiefy drawn. The immigration of large numbers of unskilled workers and their employment by innovating capitalists often gave an ethnic dimension to this hostility.

The decline in real wages and the continuing threat of economic modernization, plus a collection of other grievances, persuaded urban workers of the necessity for organization. Only a handful of the national trade unions formed in the 1850s survived into the 1860s, among them the Typographers, the Stone Cutters, the Hat Finishers, the Iron Molders, and the Machinists. The formation of local unions and city trades assemblies during the war revealed that locally negotiated improvements could not be sustained in the absence of national bargaining units. Consequently the surviving national trade unions were joined by newly formed unions of locomotive engineers, cigar makers, bricklayers, shoemakers, iron workers, and anthracite miners. Altogether 26 new national unions were formed between 1864 and 1874, and probably a larger proportion of the labor force was organized in trade unions in the pre–1873 decade than at any other time before 1900.[7]

Discontent with the performance of local and national unions, particularly their ineffectiveness in preventing state legislatures from passing employer-sponsored laws, persuaded some members to establish a national labor organization. Furthermore, the failure of strike action by the molders and others in 1867–68 created some disillusionment with conventional industrial action and strengthened the resolve among labor leaders to develop a central labor federation to engage in political propaganda and pressure group politics. The resultant National Labor Union (NLU) was attended by delegates not just from trade unions, but from trades assemblies, Eight-Hour Leagues, and other labor organizations throughout the United States.[8]

The outstanding personality and driving force behind the NLU was William Sylvis of the Iron Molders. Believing that trade unions and strikes were incapable on their own of improving the working conditions of the urban labor force, he strongly urged reform of the political and economic structure by means of political action through the agency of a national labor organization. Hence the NLU was, from its inception, a politico–reform organization, which adopted an almost Lassallean position in its emphasis on the primacy of politics.[9]

Although invitations were issued to a variety of labor and labor-reform organizations, the overwhelming majority of delegates to the NLU were wage earners, not the middle-class sympathizers with reform who frequently dominated such bodies. Even so, the NLU did not become a federation of national trade unions or a trades union congress. At its first convention in Baltimore in 1866 only two national trade unions were represented, although officers of three national unions were sponsored by trades assemblies and other national officers were present throughout. The congress was dominated by representatives of local unions and trades assemblies, with a handful of delegates from Eight-Hour Leagues.

The reforms proposed and supported by the NLU evolved from the recognition that economic developments were undermining the producer philosophy and the labor theory of value, which were widely accepted by artisans' organizations in the Jacksonian period.[10] Economic modernization, technical innovation, and the enlargement of the units of production gave rise to fears that the class of small independent master craftsmen would disappear. By the 1860s the protests against the reduction of economic opportunity were supplemented by the complaints of wage earners in modern factories who, in the face of postwar unemployment and the apparent failure of strikes to defend wage levels, advocated the abolition of the wage system itself, which was responsible for the virtual enslavement of the worker and the increasing maldistribution of income. Whether the ultimate aim of the reformers was to strengthen and enlarge the class of self-employed artisans, or to accept the trends towards industrial concentration whilst adopting new methods of rewarding labor, is a subject for debate. However, it is clear that the reforms were designed to restore individual opportunity and social mobility on the basis of a more equitable division of income between capital and labor.[11]

In retrospect it appears that the reforms were overambitious and, while valuable in themselves, unlikely to achieve the social reconstruction desired. The eight-hour bill, proposals for monetary reform, a program of co-operative production and distribution, and land reform were the major policies of the NLU, supplemented by conventional trade union activity and laws to improve working conditions and to reduce the number of competitors in the labor market. In this last respect the rather incongruous alliance of women and children, convicts, and immigrant workers under contract was identified as the major problem, and appropriate legislation was proposed to deal with it. If the NLU can rightly be thought of as aiming at social reconstruction, it also sought modest practical action to safeguard the position of wage earners in a competitive labor market. This dual character of the NLU, both reform body and labor organization, produced some ambivalence as regards the immigration of European workers and created tension, as yet rather muted, between solidarity and survival.[12]

According to the producer philosophy, to which many members of the NLU subscribed, there was only one division among men, that between the labor class and the class that was parasitic upon it. Consequently there should be no distinctions between workers on the grounds of race or nationality. But such distinctions had been and were being made, and not all who toiled and spun were permitted to claim membership of the producer class. Blacks, American Indians, and, by 1860, the Chinese in California were excluded from this fraternity. The Democratic Party, which was the main bearer of the producer philosophy, was traditionally hostile to the claims of black equality, and, on a practical level, Northern workingmen were conscious of the economic competition of black workers. Rivalry for jobs, combined with a belief in the racial inferiority of blacks, was a potent legacy to the urban workers of the 1860s.[13]

The emancipation of the slaves and the end of the Civil War created the possibility of black labor migration from the South to the Northern cities in the search for work. A substantial section of the white urban work force rejected calls for solidarity with black workers. They believed that the most effective method of protecting their jobs, and one which matched their feelings of social superiority, was to exclude the black worker from membership of trade unions.

By contrast, some urban "producers" adopted a different approach. One Boston source contended that black persons must be "elevated to the intelligence and rights which white workingmen enjoy, so that they can cooperate with them, or they will operate against them by underworking. . . . Capital knows no difference between white and black laborers; and labor cannot make any, without . . . tearing down the walls of its defense."[14]

These feelings were shared by prominent figures in the NLU and were eloquently expressed in the "Address to Workingmen" issued before the NLU convention in Chicago in 1867. This address is a striking example of the producer philosophy coming to terms with the necessity to include all workers, irrespective of race or color. The rhetoric was stirring: it was a "grand ennobling idea that the interests of labor are one; that there should be no distinction of race or nationality . . . that there is one dividing line, that which separates mankind into two great classes, the class that labors and the class that lives by others' labor."[15]

Expediency seemed to be a stronger element in the attitude of William Sylvis, who feared that antagonism between blacks and whites would "kill off" trade unions and induce blacks to vote against the party of labor for which he was working. For organizational and political reasons, therefore, an alliance between blacks and whites was necessary, even though Sylvis could not wholeheartedly accept black people, expressing distaste for both interracial marriages and mixed juries.[16]

Faced with a division of opinion in its ranks, the NLU was paralyzed, unable to implement some of the noble sentiments of brotherhood expressed at its conventions. By 1869, however, the central organization was willing to grasp the nettle, though few unions were prepared to accept black artisans as members, relegating them instead to "Jim Crow" locals. In this they were acquiescing in the prejudices of their members for the sake of survival. These prejudices were so strong in many local unions that "any attempt to disregard or override them will almost inevitably lead to anarchy and disintegration." The NLU was unable to persuade unions of the wisdom of recruiting black workers, and a dual structure of white and black trade unions resulted.[17]

The inclusiveness of the producer category was limited further when the question of Chinese membership arose. Most Chinese workers resided in

California, where, as Saxton has shown, they "fitted readily into that mental compartment which in the East had been reserved for blacks"; that is to say, they were both economic competitors and racial inferiors. Why the analogy of black workers was used in the Chinese case helped to explain the reasons for American workers adopting attitudes towards Chinese immigrants which differed from those they were to hold towards incoming Europeans.[18]

In the first place, the Chinese population of California had increased rapidly in the 1850s and 1860s, though no faster than the total population of the state. In the 1870s the Chinese comprised about 9 percent of the population, though probably as much as 25 percent of the wage-earning class. Secondly, although the economic prosperity of the Civil War years continued until 1869, the completion of the first transcontinental railroad in that year permitted cheap goods and cheap labor to enter from the East, followed shortly afterwards by a depression and its accompanying unemployment. The high expectations of the California labor force ensured that unemployment produced a higher than normal degree of resentment and indignation. California was a dream which had been partly realized, providing jobs and entrepreneurial opportunities for enterprising immigrants from the Eastern and Midwestern states. The maturing of the California economy and its more complete integration into the American economy reduced "the freedom of movement, the newness, the magnificent bounty and opportunity. Illusions though these may have been, their vanishing left a taste of tragedy."[19]

In circumstances like these the victims of change seek reasons for their worsening economic and social position. In this case, Chinese laborers were identified as major labor-market competitors who could be blamed for falling wage rates. But the Chinese were particularly singled out because the clash of economic interest was not softened by any sense of identity or fraternity. The Chinese were commonly thought of as inferior to whites, degraded in their habits of life, and unassimilable to American values and behavior. Henry George was only the most prominent of those who believed that the Chinese could not be raised to the American level of civilization.[20] It was inevitable that many Americans moving west, who believed in the racial inferiority of black people, would transfer their racial attitudes to the Chinese. Furthermore, the Chinese were particularly disliked for their servility to the big capitalist interests, acting as the unthinking agents of monopolistic corporations like the Central Pacific Railway. Migration in pursuit of individual opportunity was one thing; the mass importation of workers by, or on behalf of, large employers was quite unacceptable. In this respect the Chinese were guilty of helping to undermine American economic individualism by strengthening corporate capitalism. In sum, the labor competition of the Chinese in an economic depression, the frustration of white expectations as the California economy matured, and a widespread belief among the white community in the racial inferiority of the Chinese combined to produce a virulently anti-Chinese movement in the state.

The NLU could not avoid the debate on Chinese immigration. There were tolerant voices in its ranks reiterating the economic arguments in favor of unrestricted immigration: labor was in relatively short supply and additions to the work force would generate higher levels of production. American workers were therefore advised to welcome anyone, "Chinaman, African, or native of any country coming voluntarily to this soil" in the interests of increasing national wealth. Moreover, labor opposition to the Chinese simply divided worker from worker and served the interest of the employers.[21]

But this tolerance of the Chinese was not shared by all members of the NLU. One of its most prominent figures, A. C. Cameron, editor of the *Workingman's Advocate*, believed the Chinese were racially inferior, a "base people," who would "water down the old Caucasian race." The *Arbeiter Union* opposed the Chinese on the practical grounds that their absorption of American standards would be an exceedingly lengthy process. It was generally felt that continued immigration would simply nullify the limited degree of assimilation achieved by an earlier generation.[22]

Initially, members of the NLU could unite on a policy towards the Chinese despite these disagreements. In a debate at the 1869 convention on the Burlingame Treaty concluded between the United States and China in the previous year, the delegates agreed to call for the prohibition of coolie importation, but affirmed that "voluntary Chinese immigration ought to enjoy the protection of the laws like other citizens."[23] In opposing the importation of Chinese coolies the NLU could claim that it was not overtly discriminating against the Chinese in comparison with European immigrants because it was at the same time opposing the importation of European labor under contract. However, there was covert discrimination, since the proportion of "voluntary" Chinese immigrants was believed to be so small.

Even this surface equality of treatment had disappeared by the time of the NLU convention in the following year. In the interval, the Chinese problem had become a reality for some workers in the Eastern states. As a result of a wage dispute with the shoemakers' union, an employer, C. T. Sampson, engaged 75 Chinese to work in his shoe factories in North Adams, Massachusetts. The alarm occasioned by this importation of "a servile class of laborers" and by what it portended brought the national labor movement into even closer accord with the attitudes of California artisans. Acting on these fears, the NLU called for the abrogation of the Burlingame Treaty, with the clear implication that "voluntary" Chinese immigration should be treated differently from voluntary immigration in general. This opened the way for excluding all Chinese immigrants, whether imported or voluntary.

Whilst this would have made very little practical difference, it did necessitate a new rationale for exclusion.

The experience of the 1860s, then, had the effect of narrowing the concept of "producer." Attempts to include the black worker had foundered on the rock of racial prejudice, and in California the tradition of "thinking racially" expedited the consignment of the Chinese to the category hitherto reserved for blacks. Despite somewhat timid attempts to resist the California example, the NLU succumbed to racial fears in 1870 and favored the exclusion of the Chinese from the United States, tarnishing the "grand ennobling idea" of the unity of the producers. However, no immediate attempt was made to narrow even further the community of producers, and voluntary immigration from Europe, which accounted for the overwhelming majority of newcomers, was not seriously challenged. Labor's response to European immigrants can best be examined in the context of immigration trends in the 1860s and of efforts to stimulate emigration from Europe by government and industry.

After the 1857 economic depression and through the early years of the Civil War the flow of immigrants declined. This, combined with army recruitment, led to a shortage of labor, particularly of skilled workers. Towards the end of the war, employers recognized that the resumption of large-scale immigration would help to solve the labor shortage. "All agree," one of them reported, "in desiring the influx of the hardy toilers of Europe in greater numbers than they have ever come." In similar vein a congressional committee affirmed: "The nation wants people; working, enterprizing people, people with capital; people with skill in business; people who will go into the vast regions of unoccupied country and till the soil; people who will develop our rich and inexhaustible mines."[24] In addition, a resumption of large-scale immigration would help to strengthen the hands of the employers against the emerging labor organizations.

The Republican Party was not unresponsive to this propaganda; both Abraham Lincoln and W. H. Seward, his secretary of state, favored large-scale immigration and were prepared to use government to encourage it. The 1864 Immigration Act, which placed the force of law behind a contract made between a prospective immigrant and an American employer, was the main result at the federal level of the campaign to induce more Europeans to migrate to the United States. Seward also circularized U.S. consuls in Europe to inform them of the high rate of wages in the United States, but drew the line at subsidies or loans to immigrants, which remained the function of private enterprise. In this congenial environment a number of companies were formed, the best-known being the American Emigrant Company, whose purpose was to supply American manufacturers with skilled foreign labor. For a number of reasons these companies ran into difficulties and transported to the United States only a few hundred workers under the 1864 act. Once immigration began to increase significantly there seemed to be less need for federal government involvement, and the 1867 downturn in the economy temporarily reduced the need for labor and reinforced congressional opinions that the 1864 act served no purpose. In general employers were happy to seek what workers they needed from the stream of immigrants, resorting to a contract only in exceptional circumstances when workers with rare skills were required, and then using informal channels and business contacts rather than an emigration agency.[25]

The stream of post–Civil War immigrants was significantly widened by the activities of a variety of recruitment agencies operating in Europe. Among these were the agents of Midwestern and Southern state governments, railway land companies eager for settlers to take up railway land, and steamship companies anxious to fill all their berths on westward-bound ships. Perhaps the most prominent were the labor agencies which recruited labor in Europe and steered it to jobs in the United States, taking suitable commissions along the way. Most of their recruitment did not involve the drawing up of formal work contracts, although it was undeniable that much of this immigration was, to a greater or lesser degree, subject to inducement and persuasion.[26]

Immigration in the postwar decade, therefore, resulted almost exclusively from the work opportunities made available in a rapidly expanding economy. Immigration figures for the decade of the 1860s compare quite favorably with the preceding and succeeding periods, despite low totals in the early years. By 1870 the number of foreign-born inhabitants of the United States represented about 14 percent of the total population, although their proportion in the workforce was higher, probably about 20 percent, owing to the relatively large proportion of young unmarried men in the immigrant population.[27]

If these figures are broken down by industry and region, one finds that immigrants outnumbered the native-born in the textile mills of Massachusetts and in 35 other occupations, although of these only mining ranked among the large industries. But in some places the foreign-born majority was considerable. At the end of the Civil War there were nearly twice as many immigrants in the manufacturing industries of New York and Chicago as native-born workers. Of the nation's six largest cities only Philadelphia had more native-born workmen than immigrants in the manufacturing industry. David Wells, special commissioner of the revenue, reported in 1866 that the great demand for skilled labor had "occasioned a change in the character of workmen employed in various mechanical establishments of the country. Formerly these operatives were almost exclusively of American birth; now a large proportion are of foreign birth." In fact this proportion of the foreign-born in the entire American population was greater than the share of the Chinese in the California population, and their proportion in the workforce was comparable.[28]

It seems clear that conditions of employment for American workers were being threatened by developments in the economy in the 1860s. Immigration was increasing, inflation ate away at living standards during the Civil War, and after the war, though real wages stabilized and even increased, periodic though short-lived depressions temporarily reduced employment. Long-term developments in methods of production were accompanied by the gradual supersession of the class of small independent producers and their replacement by large employers of labor, thus reducing opportunity for economic and social mobility among the wage-earning population. In California, thwarted aspirations had found a scapegoat in the Chinese immigrants. Was a similar response to European immigrants emerging in the Eastern urban areas in the 1860s, or was the noble ideal of the unity of the producers to be upheld?

On the whole, labor organizations attempted to face the problems presented by European immigration within the framework of solidarity and tolerance. Free and voluntary immigration was regarded as legitimate and analogous to most previous immigration. This did not prevent trade union leaders from trying to dissuade European workers from emigrating during periods of unemployment in the United States. But the question of introducing legal restrictions on such immigration did not arise, since the object of labor's hostility was so-called alien contract labor, which was excluded from the brotherhood of the producers owing to its subservience to the employing class. Acting as the uncritical agents of employers in labor disputes, contract laborers were regarded as traitors by their fellow workers, and their treachery destroyed any obligations owed to them as members of the producer class. The development of labor attitudes towards European immigration in the 1860s arose out of the interaction of traditional values with the actual economic conditions of the period.

After the Civil War employers attempted to adjust to declining demand and falling prices by cutting wages, thus provoking strikes by their workers. In response, employers tried to break the strikes using imported European workers, some of whom were alleged to be under contract. Strikebreaking infuriated those on strike, who tended to equate it with alien contract labor. Contract labor was particularly offensive to trade unionists because the contract effectively removed the new worker from the "organizable" labor force and prevented him from responding to fraternal appeals from his fellow workers. Consequently, the 1864 Immigration Act, and the emigrant companies which recruited workers under contract, became the principal targets of resentful trade unionists. Their brief but energetic campaign against the contract labor provisions of the act came to an end when the act was repealed in 1868. But repeal left a question mark over the matter of contract labor and strikebreaking, since it simply withdrew legal protection from the contracts; importation of contract labor was not itself prohibited. Further strikebreaking by contract laborers might induce trade unions to try to ban contract labor altogether. For the moment labor was happy to assume that, without protection in the courts, the provisions of the contract would be evaded and employers would no longer have an incentive to use the contract system.[29]

The passage of the 1868 Immigration Act did not solve other problems associated with immigration. Labor leaders were aware that even free and voluntary immigration could cause problems for their members. However, they were inhibited from proposing legislative restrictions on this type of immigration by their acceptance of traditional American values, by fellow feeling for people seeking opportunity and escaping oppression, by their understanding of natural rights, and by recognition of the economic advantages of immigration. Consequently, in order to reconcile traditional freedoms with the protection of wages and jobs they pursued a policy of voluntary persuasion towards their European fellow workers. Their general strategy was to increase the flow of information to Europe on the state of the American economy and to try to reach agreement with European, mainly British, trade unions on voluntary limitation of European emigration at times of economic depression in the United States. There are many examples of this type of trade union activity.

William Jessup of the New York Ship Joiners corresponded with Robert Applegarth of the London Society of Carpenters and Joiners, requesting co-operation between the two organizations in an attempt to end the competition of foreign workers fostered by American employers. Applegarth's response was to suggest an amalgamation of the two unions to promote a sense of solidarity and mutual sympathy among the members, possibly taking as his model the British Amalgamated Society of Engineers, which had American members. The engineers' union, in fact, provided a good example of consideration for its members' interests on both sides of the Atlantic when, in 1871, it prohibited its British members from receiving union emigration benefits if more than 7.5 percent of union members in the proposed destination were unemployed.[30]

William Sylvis also attempted to protect the interests of members of his molders' union by establishing transatlantic co-operation with his British counterparts, though with little success. Sylvis was bitter about the English union encouraging its unemployed members to emigrate as a means of maintaining wage rates in Great Britain. He suggested to the English molders' officials that accurate information about employment prospects in their trade in the United States, supplied by him, should be distributed to English molders contemplating emigration as a counter to the propaganda of emigrant agencies. This and other attempts to provide English molders with accurate information were unsuccessful, which so incensed Sylvis that during the depression in the American iron trade in 1867–68, when three-quarters of his members were unempoyed, he wrote to the Scottish molders' union denouncing their emigrant scheme "as a direct and outrageous fraud practised upon your own members and a gross imposition on us."[31]

Having experienced the limitations of bilateral discussions with his molders' union counterparts in the United Kingdom, Sylvis was eager to promote the NLU as a means of exerting pressure on British trade unions and of enlightening British workers about actual conditions in the United States, in the hope that immigration would become self-regulating. At its 1867 convention Sylvis proposed the creation of "an inter-continental agency" to counteract "the intrigues of capitalists." This led *The Times* of London to attack the NLU as a nativist organization, which it plainly was not. Sylvis was neither a xenophobe nor a chauvinist but sought international labor cooperation. He recognized that solidarity implied not simply voluntary restrictions on emigration at times of economic depression in the United States, but also American labor support for union and reform struggles in Europe, which might help to improve wage levels there and diminish the attractiveness of American employment. American self-interest, as well as fraternal feeling for fellow "producers" in Europe, dictated international labor co-operation.[32]

Shortly before his death in 1869, Sylvis wrote to the General Council of the International Workingmen's Association, eloquently urging the necessity for international labor solidarity. Their cause was a common one: it was "war between poverty and wealth: labor occupies the same low condition and capital is the same tyrant in all parts of the world." Sylvis and his fellow union leaders in the 1860s interpreted fellowship as having three related meanings. First, the American door should not be barred to immigrants fleeing from oppression and seeking a better life in the United States. Second, international labor co-operation should guide the flow of immigrants, so that "avaricious capital" could not use it to the detriment of American artisans. Finally, American labor organizations should do all in their power to assist fellow trade unionists in Europe to improve wage levels and effectuate reforms.[33]

Since the American experience of dealing with individual British trade unions was only partly successful, it was probable that sooner or later the NLU would respond to the invitations of the First International to send a delegate to its annual congress. Sylvis favored affiliation to the International as a method of achieving the NLU's objectives regarding European immigration. Closer relations between the two organizations were facilitated by the International's own record on immigration, which Karl Marx himself came to endorse. Marx had denied that impoverished immigrants menaced the standard of living of the existing workforce. The so-called immiseration of labor would occur according to the laws of capitalist development whether or not immigration took place. However, Marx became aware that the insular British trade unionists might be prepared to co-operate with other European labor movements in the forum of the International if the Europeans would accept the need to reduce the number of immigrants from the continent of Europe to Great Britain. Accordingly he was prepared to disregard his own ideas about international solidarity to meet the interests of British artisans. In making the International the agent of restricting the entry of foreign craftsmen into Great Britain, Marx was not so much modifying his theory of inevitable immiseration as ignoring it in the interests of achieving closer international cooperation between labor movements.[34]

When the Americans saw examples of the International's willingness to use co-operative methods to limit harmful immigration, they were more disposed to accept invitations to attend its congresses.[35] J. G. Eccarius, the secretary of the International, was aware of American anxiety over immigration and, in his invitation to the NLU, raised the prospect of effective action on the issue. A. C. Cameron, the American delegate to the Basle Congress of the International in 1869, underlined American priorities in his speech by confining himself almost entirely to the subject of immigration, frankly but insensitively declaring that the only interest of American workers in the International was to establish it as an agent of immigration control. Cameron suggested that the International and the NLU jointly establish an Emigrant Bureau to gather and disseminate accurate information about wages, conditions of labor, and industrial disputes in the United States. Cameron also requested the General Council of the International to try to prevent European workers being hired to break American strikes.[36]

The General Council subsequently agreed to both proposals. Their willingness to do so was presumably increased by Cameron's assurances that the Americans had no desire to restrict "legitimate" immigration. "No rational being," he asserted, "objects or can object to the workman of the old world leaving its over-crowded marts, and seeking to better his condition in our own land." Men of this type "strengthened our hands," in contrast to the class of men "who are brought to thwart the legitimate claims of our mechanics, to pauperize labor and flood the market."[37]

Cameron's statement was a fair and accurate representation of American labor sentiment in the late 1860s. But it was based on a number of questionable assumptions and failed to come to terms with reality. Was it reasonable to make a rigid distinction between voluntary or legitimate immigration and induced or imported immigration? Cameron was surely incorrect to imply that imported immigrants were not seeking to better their condition. Nor was he on firm ground in assuming that once an intending, "legitimate" immigrant was fully apprised of the employment situation in the United States, he would voluntarily abstain from immigration or, to use Cameron's words, "cut off his right arm [rather] than defraud his brother of his dues." The acceptable level of those "dues" might well be a subject of dispute between immigrants and their American cousins. It is conceivable that as far as American labor was concerned there would always be reasons for saying that the time was not right for immigration. It is hard to envisage circumstances when immigration would actually "strengthen the hands" of American labor, as Cameron asserted.[38]

American workers had, then, not thought through the problems arising out of European immigration, problems of lower wages, worsened conditions, accelerated mechanization, strikebreaking, and so on, which were caused by both imported and voluntary immigration. Imported labor was excluded from the solidarity of the producers owing to its dependence on the employers. However, solidarity was still deemed to apply to voluntary immigrants and, in their case, methods of dissuasion were to be used until economic conditions in the United States improved.[39] As long as a plausible case could be made that the overwhelming majority of "harmful" immigrants were the instruments and dupes of American employers and that further, tougher legislative action was still available to deal with them, American labor could duck the issue of what to do about voluntary immigrants who were deaf to American pleas to stay in Europe. Labor chose to ignore Henry Carey's claim that the expansion of the American economy and the resulting increase in jobs would attract sufficient foreign workers to meet the labor needs of the employers without recourse to additional inducements. Hence organized labor retained the comfortable option, should it choose to use it, of proposing restrictions on immigration without necessarily infringing ideals of solidarity. Consequently, the long-established traditions of asylum and hospitality for voluntary immigrants still held sway in the labor movement.[40]

Despite the economic and technological problems facing American workers in the 1860s, there was no resurgence of the working-class nativism that had characterized the two previous decades, nor was the California example followed of proposing the complete exclusion of competing immigrant workers, in this case, the Chinese. In asking why not, we may also identify the circumstances which might provoke a less liberal reaction to European immigrants than had characterized the 1860s. An informed prediction of this sort may then be tested by comparing it with the actual development of working-class attitudes in subsequent decades.

Nativism failed to reappear as a widespread popular movement in the decade after the Civil War, notwithstanding that the number of European immigrants remained high and that the majority still originated in Ireland and the German states, though joined by larger numbers from Scandinavia and Great Britain. The demise of nativism can be attributed to two major factors. Much of the apprehension and anxiety of the 1850s had now been dissipated by the South's defeat in the Civil War and the restoration of the Union. With the benefits of the economic legislation enacted during the war and the promise of the completion of the first transcontinental railroad, a prosperous economic future beckoned. Optimism succeeded pessimism, hope, despair. It was, in Higham's words, a generation of "exuberant materialism and expansive confidence."[41] Talk was now of wages, strikebreaking, employment contracts, and the like, not of temperance, the school question, and foreign conspiracy.

A second factor in the disappearance of nativism was the gratitude owed by the North to the Irish- and German-Americans who had displayed such conspicuous gallantry in the Northern armies in the cause of Union. Their loyalty to the Union, measured by their willingness to die for it, dispelled the fear that they owed a superior allegiance to a foreign power and conspired to subvert American institutions. The contacts which war had fostered between soldiers of different ethnicity and religion helped to overcome stereotypes and increase mutual regard. "There were now," wrote William Shannon, "common memories and common sacrifices that linked Americans across the rifts of differing cultural backgrounds and national ancestry." "The war," in Oscar Handlin's words, "had provided an issue on which the Irish did not menace, indeed supported, the existing social order and its ideals."[42] The fact that Irish-Americans shared a common interest with native Protestant workers in excluding blacks from the labor market was an added commendation. Hence antagonism to immigrants in the postwar world was directed against particular categories which created identifiable economic problems. Ethnic and cultural divisions in the workforce loomed less large than class differences between honorable "producers" on the one hand and parasitical "non-producers" with their imported and subservient lackeys of whatever nationality on the other.

It remains to ask why urban workers in the East did not follow the California example and try to exclude immigrant labor competition. Economic and social conditions in East and West were not dissimilar: a rapid increase in immigration, coinciding with economic hardship for sections of the labor force; fluctuations in the economy causing unemployment and uncertainty; a contraction of economic opportunity and the dashing of expectations. In the East the spread of new technology, the reorganization of production methods, and the rise of a new class of capitalists seemed to presage the decline of the independent producer. Those who fled to California as the last remaining outpost of producerism and individual opportunity found they had merely deferred swallowing the bitter pill of disillusionment. The contrast between the prosperity of the war years and the depression after 1867 was more extreme in California, the disenchantment more profound, and this partly explains the virulence of the opposition to the Chinese. Yet the severity of labor's proposals in their regard was made possible by acute racial antagonism and by the consequential elimination of any feelings of solidarity. In other words, class identity could not be sustained in the face of ethnocultural divisions; furthermore, the Chinese incurred the additional odium of being imported under contract. By contrast, European immigrants in the East were not objects of racial prejudice, and ethnic and cultural identity reinforced producer solidarity. Even the Irish had crossed the line into at least a modest acceptability.

In concluding this chapter we can try to envisage the circumstances under which the solidarity of native-born and immigrant workers would be

eroded, and the ever-present tension between the imperatives of self-preservation and fraternity sufficiently heightened to tip the balance in favor of
self-protection. Tolerance for foreign workers might diminish if the following conditions were met: an economic depression in which wages and
conditions of urban workers were adversely affected and foreign workers
identified as job competitors; a significant increase in the proportion of
foreign-born workers in the labor force; an intensification of technological
change and work reorganization leading to skill displacement and the sub-
stitution of native-born skilled workers by semi-skilled machine operators,
many of them foreign-born; a higher proportion of immigrants from the
rural areas of Europe having no familiarity with trade unions and labor
organizations, and hence less amenable to appeals for labor solidarity; the
suspicion that immigrants were not free agents but under contract to employers; the conviction among the indigenous workforce that newcomers
were either culturally or racially inferior and could not assimilate American
standards and values, leaving no alternative to exclusion or restriction if
tolerable working and living conditions were to be retained; and, finally,
the recognition that new arrivals constituted a threat to republican institutions and even to national security. Whether this model provides an adequate explanation of labor's increasingly restrictive approach to European
immigration in subsequent decades should emerge from the discussion of
labor opinion in the following chapters.

NOTES

1. Philip S. Foner, *History of the Labor Movement in the United States*, 4 vols.
(1947; rpt. New York: International Publishers, 1962), Vol. 1, p. 326; Lance E.
Davis, Richard A. Easterlin, and William N. Parker, eds., *American Economic Growth:
An Economists' History of the United States* (New York: Harper and Row, 1972), p.
123; David Montgomery, *Beyond Equality: Labor and the Radical Republicans, 1862–
1872* (1967; rpt. New York: Vintage Books, 1972), pp. 96–97, quoting from Wesley
Mitchell's cost of living index; Clarence D. Long, *Wages and Earnings in the United
States, 1860–1890* (Princeton, N.J.: Princeton University Press, 1960), p. 111.

2. Long, *Wages and Earnings*, p. 111; Stanley L. Engerman, "The Economic
Impact of the Civil War," *Explorations in Enterpreneurial History*, Second Series, 3,
No. 3 (1966), pp. 178–83.

3. Davis, Easterlin and Parker, *American Economic Growth*, p. 123; Montgomery,
Beyond Equality, p. 264; John R. Commons et al., *History of Labor in the United
States*, 4 vols. (1918; rpt. New York: Augustus M. Kelley, 1966), Vol. 2, pp. 68–
76, 123; see also Chapter Two.

4. Jonathan P. Grossman, *William Sylvis, Pioneer of American Labor* (New York:
Columbia University Press, 1945), pp. 135–42.

5. Commons et al., *History of Labor*, Vol. 2, p. 76; Clyde Griffen, "Workers
Divided: The Effect of Craft and Ethnic Differences in Poughkeepsie, New York,
1850–1880," in Stephan Thernstrom and Richard Sennett, eds., *Nineteenth-Century
Cities: Essays in the New Urban History* (New Haven: Yale University Press, 1969),

pp. 84–86; John R. Commons, *American Shoemakers, 1648–1895; A Sketch of Industrial Evolution* (Cambridge, Mass.: Harvard University Press, 1909), pp. 72–74, reprinted from the *Quarterly Journal of Economics* 24 (November 1909); Charlotte Erickson, *American Industry and the European Immigrant, 1860–1885* (Cambridge, Mass.: Harvard University Press, 1957), p. 126.

6. Griffen, "Workers Divided," pp. 83–92; Clifton K. Yearley, Jr., *Britons in American Labor: A History of the Influence of the United Kingdom Immigrants on American Labor, 1820–1914* (1957; rpt. Westport, Conn.: Greenwood Press, 1974), pp. 16–17; Massachusetts Bureau of Labor Statistics, *Annual Report*, 1872, pp. 341–42; for a different opinion on the effect of mechanization on creativity and self-satisfaction, see Howard M. Gitelman, *Workingmen of Waltham: Mobility in American Industrial Development 1850–1890* (Baltimore: The Johns Hopkins University Press, 1974), p. 73.

7. Foner, *History of the Labor Movement*, Vol. 1, pp. 235–46, 326–27, 355–62; Henry Pelling, *American Labor* (Chicago: University of Chicago Press, 1960), p. 38; Commons et al., *History of Labor in the United States*, 4 vols. (1947): rpt. New York: International Publishers, 1962), Vol. 2, pp. 45–48; Montgomery, *Beyond Equality*, pp. 139–41; Lloyd Ulman, *The Rise of the National Trade Union* (Cambridge, Mass.: Harvard University Press, 1955), p. 19.

8. Foner, *History of the Labor Movement*, Vol. 1, pp. 352–55, 361–62, 417; Montgomery, *Beyond Equality*, pp. 175–76.

9. Norman J. Ware, *Labor in Modern Industrial Society* (New York: Heath and Co., 1935), p. 178; Gerald N. Grob, *Workers and Utopia: A Study of Ideological Conflict in the American Labor Movement, 1865–1900* (Evanston, Ill.: Northwestern University Press, 1961), p. 27; William M. Dick, *Labor and Socialism in America: The Gompers Era* (London: Kennikat Press, 1972), pp. 10–11.

10. See Chapter Two.

11. Montgomery, *Beyond Equality*, pp. 177, 444–45; Grob, *Workers and Utopia*, pp. 11–15.

12. Montgomery, *Beyond Equality*, p. 177.

13. Alexander Saxton, *The Indispensable Enemy: Labor and the Anti-Chinese Movement in California* (Berkeley: University of California Press, 1971), pp. 23–27.

14. *Boston Daily Evening Voice*, official organ of the Workingmen's Assembly of Boston and Vicinity, quoted in Foner, *History of the Labor Movement*, Vol. 1, pp. 392–93.

15. Foner, *History of the Labor Movement*, Vol. 1, p. 396.

16. Montgomery, *Beyond Equality*, p. 228; see also Grob, *Workers and Utopia*, pp. 22–23.

17. Foner, *History of the Labor Movement*, Vol. 1, pp. 375, 398–99, 401 (quoting from the *Printers' Circular*, organ of the Typographical Union).

18. In developing the argument which follows I am much indebted to Saxton.

19. Saxton, *Indispensable Enemy*, pp. 3, 7, 15–16.

20. Ibid., p. 103.

21. Foner, *History of the Labor Movement*, Vol. 1, pp. 488–89.

22. Ibid., p. 489.

23. *Boston Commonwealth*, 25 June 1870, quoted in John R. Commons et al., eds., *A Documentary History of American Industrial Society* (1910–11; rpt. New York: Russell and Russell, 1958), Vol. 9, pp. 85–86; Saxton, *Indispensable Enemy*, p. 101;

Charles R. Leinenweber, "Immigration and the Decline of Internationalism in the American Working Class Movement, 1864–1919" (Ph.D. diss., University of California, Berkeley, 1968), pp. 43–46; Commons et al., *History of Labor*, Vol. 2, p. 150.

24. Morrell Heald, "Business Attitudes toward European Immigration, 1861–1914" (Ph.D. diss., Yale University, 1951), pp. 40, 43; *Report of Hon. D. A. Wells, Special Commissioner of the Revenue, Dec. 1866*, quoted in Edith Abbott, *Historical Aspects of the Immigration Problem: Select Documents* (1926; rpt. New York: Arno Press, 1969), p. 354.

25. Erickson, *American Industry*, pp. 9–10, 20–27, 29, 45; Montgomery, *Beyond Equality*, p. 23.

26. Erickson, *American Industry*, pp. 68–82.

27. Peter Roberts, *The New Immigration* (New York: Macmillan, 1912), p. 162; Simon Kuznets and Ernest Rubin, *Immigration and the Foreign-Born* (New York: National Bureau of Economic Research, 1954), p. 39; Harry Jerome, *Migration and Business Cycles* (New York: National Bureau of Economic Research, 1926), p. 49; Long, *Wages and Earnings*, pp. 113–14.

28. Montgomery, *Beyond Equality*, pp. 35, 37; Abbott, *Historical Aspects*, p. 354.

29. Montgomery, *Beyond Equality*, pp. 23, 149, 390–91; Grossman, *William Sylvis*, pp. 145–46.

30. Foner, *History of the Labor Movement*, Vol. 1, pp. 410–11; Erickson, *American Industry*, p. 56.

31. Grossman, *William Sylvis*, p. 147; Foner, *History of the Labor Movement*, Vol. 1, pp. 410–11; Erickson, *American Industry*, p. 54; Samuel Bernstein, *The First International in America* (New York: Augustus M. Kelley, 1962), p. 30.

32. Grossman, *William Sylvis*, p. 258; Leinenweber, "Immigration and the Decline of Internationalism," p. 38.

33. *Report of the Fourth Annual Congress of the International Workingmen's Association, 1869*, quoted in Commons et al, *Documentary History*, Vol. 9, pp. 340–41; Grossman, *William Sylvis*, p. 149.

34. Commons et al, *Documentary History*, "Introduction to Volumes 9 and 10," by J. R. Commons and Charles B. Andrews, Vol. 9, pp. 28–31; Julius Braunthal, *History of the International, 1865–1914* (1961; rept. London: Nelson, 1966), pp. 99–100, 113–14.

35. For example, the General Council of the International voted to help check the importation of European strikebreakers at the request of the New York Compositors' Union. See Foner, *History of the Labor Movement*, Vol. 1, p. 411.

36. Bernstein, *First International*, pp. 32–33; Leinenweber, "Immigration and the Decline of Internationalism," pp. 40–42; Foner, *History of the Labor Movement*, Vol. 1, p. 412.

37. *Workingman's Advocate*, editorial letters November–December 1869, quoted in Commons et al., *Documentary History*, Vol. 9, pp. 348–49.

38. *Workingman's Advocate*, November–December 1869, in Commons et al. *Documentary History*, Vol. 9, pp. 349–50.

39. Charlotte Erickson, "Encouragement of Immigration by British Trade Unions," *Population Studies* 3(1949): 270–71; Yearley, *Britons in American Labor*, pp. 56–57.

40. Montgomery, *Beyond Equality*, p. 24.

41. John Higham, *Strangers in the Land: Patterns of American Nativism, 1860–1925* (1955; rpt. New York: Atheneum, 1963), p. 17.

42. Oscar Handlin, *Boston's Immigrants* (1941; rpt. New York: Atheneum, 1969), pp. 210–11; William V. Shannon, *The American Irish* (New York: Collier, 1974), p. 59.

4

The Knights of Labor and Solidarity

In the decade after 1877 the Knights of Labor became the dominant labor organization in the United States and the virtually undisputed spokesman for American working people. An attempt to identify labor opinion in the 1880s must mainly focus on the views and attitudes of this so-called order. Founded in 1869 in Philadelphia by Uriah Stephens and other members of a declining garment cutters' benefit society, the Knights remained a secret society until 1879. It grew slowly until the depression of 1873, when it was able to recruit some local branches of collapsed national trade unions which, in the face of an employer antiunion offensive, were glad to shelter under the "umbrella of secrecy" provided by the Knights. However, the Knights offered more than a temporary haven; it seemed to provide a basis for the establishment of the One Big Union which could counteract employer power through the strength and solidarity of the membership.[1]

In 1878 a general convention of the local assemblies of the Knights was held, at which a preamble and platform were adopted and Stephens was elected General Master Workman. In the following year secrecy was largely abandoned as the economy began to recover and industrial tensions diminished. The Knights became much more active in recruiting new members and in popularizing the order's views on economic and social questions. Membership rose briskly from 19,000 in 1881 to 111,000 in 1885. But this substantial increase seemed insignificant compared with the sevenfold rise in the membership in the course of the next year, which brought the total to 700,000. However, the year 1886 marked the peak of its power and influence. Its next strike failed, its leadership was indecisive over the cam-

paign for the eight-hour day, and negotiations with unions of craft workers
to secure a *modus vivendi* broke down, resulting in the establishment of a
rival labor federation, the American Federation of Labor, in 1886. Disillusionment and disappointment accounted for massive desertions from the
Knights, and by the end of the decade membership was down to 100,000
and still declining.

In less than a decade the Knights developed a critique of American society
and a set of policies overtly based on the principle of solidarity which, if
widely adopted, would have restored individualism, equality of opportunity, and social responsibility to American life. What is striking about its
position on European immigration, a growing problem in the 1880s according to many Knights, was its adoption of a restrictionist policy which
was apparently at odds with its commitment to the ideal of solidarity. The
extent of this conflict depends upon an assessment of the meaning or meanings which the Knights attached to the term solidarity, and of the precise
purposes it had in mind in its support of immigration legislation. Which
European immigrants, for example, did it seek to exclude from the United
States? Why was it increasingly critical of immigration in the 1880s? Why
did it choose one method of restriction rather than others? Why was it blind
to the probability that this method would not work? These are the major
questions to be addressed in this chapter.

The theme of solidarity is central in the history of the Knights of Labor.
The organization was rooted in the reform unionism of the 1860s; in terms
of policy it was in direct line of descent from the National Labor Union,
and its prominent figures grew to maturity in the atmosphere of ante-bellum
reform movements. Stephens and T. V. Powderly, who succeeded him as
head of the order, plus other notable figures like Charles Litchman, John
Hayes, and Thomas B. Barry retained the ideal of a society dominated by
small, independent producers.[2] For them the term "producer" included all
who produced wealth, whether skilled artisans or unskilled machine minders, small manufacturers or farmers, shopkeepers or clerks. The few excluded categories, like stockbrokers and bankers, were involved in financial
speculation and removed from the actual process of production. The
Knights had no quarrel with "legitimate enterprise or necessary capital,"
but they objected to what they termed "the money power" or "wealth,"
by which they meant the financial manipulators and the powerful but remote
controllers of capitalist production, who were steering the economy in the
direction of huge units of enterprise, a permanent wage-earning class, and
diminished opportunities for the small entrepreneur. Their aim was to restore equality of opportunity and to make "every man his own master,
every man his own employer."[3]

The early leaders of the Knights, therefore, saw their mission as being
"to lift up, to dignify, to disenthrall labor." The purpose of the order, for
Stephens, was no less than the elevation of man. This emphasis on moral

regeneration was evident in the preamble to the Knights' constitution of
1878, which proclaimed that the true standard of individual and national
greatness was "moral worth, not wealth."[4] Arguably one of the major
achievements of the ante-bellum artisan workshop, which remained the
ideal of many of the founders of the order, was its preservation of moral
worth through marrying the twin virtues of individualism and fraternity.
Individualism could lead to "success," but only in the limited context of
small-scale economic activity, thus helping to preserve the sense of concern
and responsibility one worker felt for another. In the modern factory, by
contrast, individualism and responsibility had become divorced, impersonality and inhumanity reigned, and wealth alone became the criterion for
measuring individual achievement.

Stephens' commitment to fraternity had a religious origin: sharing in the
Fatherhood of God, men were brothers, with obligations to care for each
other.[5] Yet no one expressed the ideal of brotherhood more eloquently than
an anarchist member of the order, Joseph Labadie, for whom the chief and
crowning glory of the Knights was "the mingling of skilled and unskilled
labor—the fraternization of all who earn their bread by the sweat of their
brow, regardless of their wages, social position, their country, creed or
clothes, their commingling of intelligence and ignorance, conservatism and
radicalism." The all-inclusiveness for which Stephens and Labadie stood
was expressed in the Knights' famous solidaristic motto: "An injury to one
is the concern of all." How infinitely superior this was, thought Labadie,
to the "narrow-minded, tight-chested, small-souled, selfish, exclusive and
aristocratic trades unionism."[6]

However, it is imperative to recognize that by no means all members of
the Knights shared Stephens's and Labadie's idealism, although they might
pay lip service to it. Many, while accepting solidarity, saw it as a means to
an end rather than an end in itself. Still others were distinctly antipathetic
to the ideal or the tactic of solidarity. These differing attitudes can be
illustrated by a brief discussion of the motives of members joining the order.
Many joined the Knights as means of preserving their local or national labor
organizations, others because the order seemed to be successful at conventional trade union functions. Indeed, the original assembly of the Knights
in Philadelphia was composed of skilled garment cutters, and in the 1870s
the order provided a home for a number of disintegrating national and local
trade unions, as well as incorporating so-called mixed assemblies of skilled
workers from a variety of crafts whose numbers were too small to support
separate local unions. This focus on skilled workers was in fact a conscious
policy; in 1876 membership was limited to those who thoroughly understood the trade which they followed. Apparently no provision was made
at that point for the entry of the broad category of unskilled producers.[7]

However, after 1877 a change came about. The industrial disputes of that
year, and the increasing evidence of the power and determination of capital,

had shown the ineffectiveness of small craft unions in defending their members. But even if all the skilled workers had placed their organizations under the protection of the Knights in the cause of unity, this would not have solved the problems created by technological change, which was undermining craft skills and creating new classes of displaced craft workers and semi-skilled machine minders.[8]

Powderly was convinced that the Knights should recruit these unskilled and semi-skilled workers because only the solidarity of all producers could restrain the power of capital and provide hope that a new order could be created. During the period of breakneck expansion of the Knights between 1881 and 1886, its recruiting policy seemed to reflect Powderly's philosophy. Most new members were probably semi-skilled or unskilled laborers, farmers, shopkeepers, and small masters or proprietors, a high proportion of whom lived in the Midwest. Furthermore, in this region and possibly elsewhere the Knights had a much higher proportion of native-born members than the trade unions, a fact which helps to account for the strength of the producer philosophy within the order.[9]

However, it would be wrong to overlook the fact that skilled workers were recruited in substantial numbers in the 1880s. Even in 1886, at least half the membership was composed of skilled craftsmen, and in industrializing states like Illinois the proportion was as high as two-thirds.[10] A number of national trade unions were incorporated in the order as district assemblies; and the Knights fulfilled, albeit without enthusiasm, some trade union functions, particularly in the period of its greatest fame in the mid–1880s. It is probable that a considerable number of the new members of that period were mainly attracted by the successful strikes in which the Knights engaged.

The Knights' elected leaders became conscious of the differing aspirations and needs of their members and tried to take account of them. On the one hand they continued to promote the producer philosophy and to campaign for currency and land reform, the establishment of producer cooperatives, and government action against monopolies. On the other, they adopted a number of trade union measures, among them improvements in safety and health, enforcement of hours legislation, and the abolition of convict labor.[11]

Yet these adjustments highlighted the duality of the organization. The majority of members in the 1880s were probably uninfluenced by, or even impatient with, the philosophy of the original leadership. Skilled, and even unskilled, workers seeking immediate material improvements through collective bargaining and successful strike action would probably find little to attract them in the producer philosophy and the reform proposals of Powderly and his followers. The watchword of solidarity, if it meant anything to the newcomers, meant something very different from what it had meant to Stephens and the founders of the organization. An understanding of the meaning or meanings attributed to solidarity by the membership is indispensable for grasping the Knights' attitude to European immigration in the 1880s.

It may be assumed that the more inclusive and solidaristic a labor organization shows itself to be, the greater is the likelihood of a tolerant and magnanimous attitude towards newcomers to the labor force, including immigrants. Evidently some Knights committed themselves, in a sort of mystical fervor, to a quite literal interpretation of the meaning of solidarity, under which the barriers of race, creed, color, sex, and occupation would be swept aside in the cause of brotherhood.[12] Probably only those who shared the Christian principles of Stephens or the anarchist ideas of Labadie would have embraced this version of solidarity, according to which immigrants, being producers, would be warmly received, and any limitations on immigration, perhaps in times of high unemployment in the United States, would be entirely voluntary on the part of the potential immigrants themselves. This interpretation of solidarity probably gained greater publicity than its limited support justified owing to the prominence of its adherents in the order.

However, perhaps the majority of members meant something different by the term, even before the massive growth of the order in the 1880s. It was widely recognized in the mid–1870s that a major threat to skilled workers originated in the process of technological change as directed by capital, and that the most effective means of preserving labor's dignity and independence in the face of this threat lay in creating a solid front of workers who would recognize the necessity for mutual support. During the economic depression of the mid–1870s, when immigration was relatively insignificant and overwhelmingly from Northern and Western Europe, the term solidarity probably bore little connotation of fraternity with foreign-born workers, at least for a majority of the Knights. Its meaning was more limited: it offered a method of uniting the interests of skilled and unskilled producers in a period of technological change and capitalist aggression.

Advocates of solidarity may therefore be conveniently divided into two groups, "enthusiasts" and "instrumentalists." The former understood the universalistic implications of the term, recognizing that it implied a whole-hearted acceptance of immigration; the latter interpreted it more narrowly, seeing it as a means of building a bulwark against capitalism with no immediate reference to immigration at all. Even in the 1870s the majority of members may have been instrumentalists, and the balance was tipped even further in their direction by the mass recruitment of new members. This difference of opinion about the meaning and implications of the term solidarity had practical consequences when immigration became a live issue again in the 1880s. "Enthusiasts" opposed proposals for immigration restriction whilst "instrumentalists" recognized that a tightening up of the immigration law was necessary, but in such a way as not to conflict with their own definition of solidarity. However, before this subject is examined more closely, some attention should be given to why European immigration became an important political issue for the Knights in the 1880s.

The form of immigration which was particularly unwelcome was inaccurately referred to as alien contract labor. In the 1860s the term meant skilled European workers migrating to the United States under written contract of employment. The National Labor Union had insisted that labor contracts involving foreign workers should not be enforceable in U.S. courts.[13] The Knights adopted a different policy towards contract labor, calling for an end to the importing of workers under contract, and reiterating this demand with increasing force in the early 1880s. The initiative in the Knights' 1880s campaign was taken by the Window Glass Workers, who constituted a skilled assembly in the order. However, these workers and the official leadership of the Knights differed over the meaning of alien contract labor. The former defined it in the manner of the 1860s: skilled workers imported from Europe under written contract to American employers. The leadership broadened the meaning to embrace unskilled workers too, and in particular penurious and so-called "degraded" unskilled workers originating in Southern and Eastern Europe. The reasons for this change of emphasis are worth examining.[14]

Strikebreaking by foreign-born workers was a major grievance of labor organizations in the 1870s and 1880s. In the economic depression of 1873–78 and the less severe downturn after 1882, employers attempted to reduce wages, provoking retaliatory strikes by their employees. Employers struck back by hiring foreign-born workers in order to maintain production and to break the unions. An example of this process was the calling of numerous strikes by the Miners' National Association in the bituminous coal fields of Pennsylvania, Ohio, and Indiana between 1872 and 1875. The employers' response was to bring in Swedish, German, and then Italian immigrants to replace the striking workers. In the great strike in Hocking Valley, Ohio, in 1884, Italian, Polish, and Hungarian strikebreakers recruited by labor contractors in Chicago, New York, and Buffalo were again prominent. Foreign-born strikebreakers were just as conspicuous in the anthracite and coking districts of Pennsylvania, where railroad companies had taken over many of the independent mines and ruthlessly crushed employee opposition to changes in working conditions. The bitter resentment of the workers was directed not just at the companies but at their apparent accomplices and agents, the unskilled foreign-born strikebreakers.[15]

Outside the coal industry, the employment of such workers was most common in the railroad, iron and steel, and textile industries. In railroad construction the employment of strikebreakers was rare though not unknown, but in track maintenance and freight handling, where employment was on a more permanent basis, strikes were met by employers with the same methods as in mining. One labor leader described how the railroads had broken a strike of New Jersey freight handlers in 1882 by bringing in

Italians from the Port of New York, who were kept from contact with the strikers by being forced to eat and sleep in the holds of the vessels on which they were working.[16] In the iron and steel and textile industries, employment of recent immigrants was more closely associated with mechanization than with strikebreaking, though there were occasions when strikes accelerated the introduction of new machinery and the displacement of skilled workers. In cigar making too, strikes were broken by the employment of unskilled Southern and Eastern Europeans to operate the new machinery available to the industry.[17]

In all these industries labor associated the foreign-born workers with mechanization, the growth of corporate power, and strikebreaking. Their connection with such hated developments demonstrated a lack of moral worth and an absence of solidarity with their American comrades. In allowing themselves to be imported under contract and hence to destroy the livelihood of American workers, they forfeited the claims of solidarity. It seemed that labor's natural allies in the production process had united with its enemies. It was not unreasonable, therefore, to deny them a fraternal welcome, indeed to restrict their entry by law.[18]

Strikebreaking and wage cutting were not the only offenses of these newer immigrants, in labor's opinion. Their peculiar dependence, indeed servility, was a product of their poverty on arrival. This in turn resulted from their lowly economic status; they constituted, it was said, the "riff-raff" and "scum" of Europe, illiterate, unskilled, and ignorant. They imported their demoralizing and degraded habits of life, which they showed no signs of abandoning. Labor observers stressed the filth and squalor of their living conditions, their revolting diets, their primitive and disgusting sanitary arrangements, and their bouts of heavy drinking. Their servility contrasted with the occasional outbreaks of uncontrolled violence in which they indulged. It was not always clear from these criticisms whether the deplorable qualities exhibited by the immigrants were the products of poverty and ignorance, or of a conscious decision to live as cheaply as possible in order to maximize savings. Many observers took the latter view, condemning the newcomers' preference for remitting savings to their countries of origin to spending their income on goods produced in the United States.[19]

Their apparent determination to return home when enough had been saved highlighted another immigrant characteristic condemned by labor critics: their ignorance of the United States except as the provider of economic opportunies. Immigrants allegedly refused to take an interest in American institutions, laws, and social customs, and rejected the opportunity to assimilate and become good American citizens. However, there was a suspicion that the failure to assimilate was not a question of will but of incapacity; the newcomers were simply incapable "of enjoying, appreciating, defending and perpetuating the blessings of good government" and therefore had no claim on America, which was "intended for a race of

freemen."[20] By failing to identify with the United States they revealed
themselves as un-American. They therefore forfeited any claim on the hospitality which Americans had generally extended to European immigrants.
In other words, the newcomers had to earn the solidarity of American
workers by willingly accepting American values and conforming to
American standards. If they were incapable of that, they should be denied
entry.

Whilst the Window Glass Workers and the Knights' leadership had different targets among the immigrants, they agreed that the undesirables had
one thing in common: they travelled under inducement, which, in the view
of their critics, guaranteed their complete dependence on their American
employers. They had not chosen to emigrate of their own free will, unlike
earlier generations of immigrants who had in most cases quickly identified
with the United States. This "voluntaryism" flattered Americans and
strengthened their belief in the virtues of their society. By contrast, immigrants under inducement were motivated by a simple determination to
exploit American economic opportunities for all they were worth before
returning to their homelands. The refusal of such immigrants to accept,
still less to admire, American customs and attitudes was regarded as insulting. In a word, induced immigrants were parasitic on the United States,
and should be excluded from the country. By contrast, the door should
still remain open for those who, "of their own free will, seek a home in
the United States, come to be its citizens and help build up the country by
their intelligence and industry."[21]

It will be apparent that opponents of immigration in the labor movement
desperately needed to establish the fact of inducement if they were to loosen
the grip of ideas of solidarity and libertarianism in immigration policy which
had strongly influenced public attitudes before 1880. If it could be shown
that there was a connection between the undesirable qualities of many recent
immigrants and the apparently new phenomenon of widespread inducement, the argument for restriction would be strengthened. Labor's case that
inducements were a major stimulus to immigration did not lack foundation.
To demonstrate this, a brief review of the use of inducements to encourage
immigration may be helpful.

The traditional, most widely known form of induced immigration was
the importation of skilled labor under written contract, a method which
enjoyed a brief heyday immediately after the Civil War. However, by the
late 1860s American employers found that they could obtain most of the
skilled labor they required through the normal processes of immigration.
Furthermore, the use of contracts often had unsatisfactory results, partly
because of the high expenses involved and partly because employees under
contract frequently evaded their contractual obligations, especially after the
passage of the 1868 law. In those rare cases where insufficient skilled labor
was available from normal immigration, employers often avoided formal

written contracts in their recruiting efforts in Europe, preferring to advertise, to employ their European business agents, or to persuade their immigrant employees to send for friends and relatives.[22] Consequently, in the early 1880s the flow of skilled alien workers under contract had slowed to a trickle. However, some small groups of American skilled workers still claimed to be adversely affected by the importation of artisans under contract. One such group was the Window Glass Workers, who spearheaded the movement for an Alien Contract Labor Law to ban the import of skilled workers under written contract. Subsequently the Knights threw itself into the campaign and in doing so broadened the meaning of the term contract labor to include unskilled, impoverished, degraded, and unassimilable European labor. The transformation in meaning was remarkable but not irrational.

The Knights had correctly recognized the role of so-called labor agencies in the immigration of much unskilled labor. Recruitment by this method had occurred in the rural areas of Western and Northern Europe in the 1860s and early 1870s before agencies had begun to operate in the South and East.[23] But in the 1880s labor claimed that recruitment by agencies, *padroni*, and bosses was a new phenomenon exclusively associated with the "new" immigrants. Whilst this was inaccurate, it is nevertheless true that the large majority of unskilled immigrants recruited by these means originated in the Southern and Eastern regions of Europe. Where the Knights of Labor and the craft unions went wrong was in assuming that this imported or recruited labor was under written contract. Considering the complexity of the issue and the Knights' own philosophical standpoint, it is not surprising that the order fell into this error. But though it was wrong in this, it was essentially correct in recognizing that unskilled labor brought in by varying kinds of labor agencies was as effectively under the control and direction of the employers as contract labor was. How this system of recruitment worked is not completely clear, since testimony is contradictory and witnesses before congressional committees often had reason to be evasive. Nevertheless, the main outlines are not in dispute.

A number of agencies induced Europeans to emigrate to the United States. Among them were Southern and Western states seeking settlers, particularly in the early postwar years; railroad companies hoping to dispose of their land grants; steamship lines trying to fill space in ships sailing westwards across the Atlantic; and labor bureaus anxious to supply workers for the ever-expanding American economy. The latter were the main targets of labor critics in the 1880s. Known variously as agencies, bankers, or *padroni*, they fulfilled the role of middlemen between the American employers on the lookout for unskilled labor, especially during strikes, and the populations of Southern and Eastern Europe who were not averse from emigrating, if only temporarily, to the United States. These labor agencies became associated in the public mind with the introduction of Hungarian, Polish, and

Italian immigrants into the construction, railroad, mining, and steel industries.[24]

In Europe they employed a variety of inducements. Agents working on commission toured the hinterland of the ports assuring potential recruits of an abundance of jobs in the United States and offering vague promises of work. Printed information about steamship sailings and the cost of passage was circulated. Prepaid tickets were made available on the understanding that the price would be repaid to the labor agency in New York out of future earnings. Almost certainly no written contract was involved. The immigrant's almost complete dependence on the labor contractor for work on arrival, his ignorance of the language, and a sense of honor regarding the repayment of debt ensured that most immigrants did not leave the agency until they had paid it what they owed. The agents provided labor on demand to American employers, taking a commission from the employer, or the immigrant, or both. A batch of workers sent to an employer were usually accompanied by an interpreter, sometimes called a boss, who would seek the concession from the employer of provisioning or housing the men.[25] Once the work ran out, the employees probably returned to the agency, being accommodated in boarding houses owned by the agent and able to use the banking, money changing, and remitting services provided. The difference between the agency and the *padrone* system, with which it has sometimes been confused, lay in the different method of operation. The *padrone*, having recruited labor in Italy, attached it directly to himself, hiring it out *en bloc* at a fixed rate, and paying less than that in wages. The labor bureaus flourished because they seemed to give some sort of guarantee of work in the New World, because they solved some of the most awkward early problems of adjustment for the new arrivals, and because they provided a convenient means by which American employers could recruit labor.[26]

Many foreign-born witnesses before a select committee of the House of Representatives, known as the Ford Committee, denied that they would have emigrated without the blandishments of the labor agents. Yet some immigrants preferred to sell property or to borrow money from friends or relatives in order to pay for their passage. There is, in fact, considerable evidence that perhaps only about one-third of the immigrants from Southern Europe came on prepaid tickets, and that the greater proportion of these were purchased, not by agencies, but by friends and relatives already resident in the United States. Moreover, it is probable that after a few years of the "new" immigration, the major inducement offered to Europeans lay not in the activities of labor agents but in the so-called "emigrant letters" sent to them by relatives on the other side of the Atlantic.[27] Of course, in times of economic depression such letters probably deterred emigration through their depiction of bleak economic prospects.

Contemporary labor critics probably overstressed the role of inducements and loans offered by labor agencies compared to that played by family and friendship networks. Yet in the early days of immigration from Southern and Eastern Europe, when the Knights of Labor was at the peak of its influence, such familial connections could not have been widely established. Furthermore, whatever the method of financing the passage, new immigrants invariably arrived in the United States in desperate need of work, with few financial resources, and deeply ignorant of working conditions and the role of trade unions.[28]

The Knights of Labor confused the issue when it referred to this labor as being under written contract. Only in the case of a tiny minority of skilled workers were such contracts in force. All that existed for the majority of new immigrants were vague and general assurances of work. Subservience was achieved not by a contractual bond but by the deep ignorance of the United States on the part of induced workers. As their ignorance diminished, their dependence on the employers weakened, but the ever-increasing number of new arrivals offered employers a ready source of dependent labor to replace those whose broader knowledge of American industry encouraged them to support organized labor.

Allegations by the Knights of Labor that inducements to emigrate in the 1880s were a new and rapidly growing phenomenon with damaging consequences for working people in the United States were not without foundation. The establishment, to its own satisfaction at least, of the fact of inducement was crucial in making the case for a tougher immigration law. It insisted that immigrants who had been persuaded by the agents of capital to seek employment in the United States had forfeited claims to solidarity from their American brothers. By contrast, adherents of an "enthusiastic" conception of solidarity still remained loyal to the open door, but they were in a minority. The claims of solidarity had little appeal to many members of skilled trade assemblies in the Knights. It was the supporters of an "instrumental" idea of solidarity who were most affected by the revelations of the widespread practice of inducement. Aiming to strengthen the bonds between producers, both skilled and unskilled, in the interests of forging a grand alliance against finance capital, these Knights believed that the claims of solidarity applied only to those who placed themselves unequivocally in the producer camp. But "induced" immigrants excluded themselves by their identification with the employers and by their evident unwillingness to strike roots in the American community. In short, there was no obigation to offer solidarity to those who did not seek it.

If the "instrumental" form of solidarity offered little resistance to tighter immigration controls on induced immigrants, we now have to ask why the Knights chose to support the Alien Contract Labor Law of 1885 as its favored measure of restriction. It was of course true that contract labor and induced labor shared a common dependence, but it did not follow that the method devised for dealing with the one was appropriate for the other. The

Knights' somewhat puzzling mistake was to believe that it was. Its support for this legislation was unaccompanied by evidence that the immigrants to whom it objected were under written contracts. At hearings before a committee of the House of Representatives, the "only solid evidence" about immigrants under written contract was provided by the Window Glass Workers, who could reasonably expect to benefit from a change in the law. By contrast, the Knights' own testimony that the inducement offered to unskilled immigrants was in the form of a written contract was "remarkably weak." Despite the realistic opinion of one labor leader that the 1885 law would not affect a very large number of immigrants and was likely to be evaded, labor's expectations about the results of the act were generally inflated.[29]

It is important to ask why this was so, since the answer may provide a clue to the Knights' general approach to the problem of European immigration. Was its support of the bill due to confusion, to wishful thinking, to political opportunism, or to inhibitions in proposing more radical measures which would violate traditional ideals of internationalism and solidarity? It is impossible to give a categorical answer, since all these elements, in varying degrees, contributed to the decision. However, it seems probable that misunderstanding of the character of induced immigration played an important part, combined with a deep need to believe that the proposed law would work, given the absence of available alternatives.

Confusion and misunderstanding undoubtedly existed. Some leaders were unable to distinguish the informal agreements between labor agents and potential immigrants from the formal written contracts which were the subject of the bill. There was some excuse for this, since, in the words of one labor spokesman, "the question is quite a new one and will take some time for labor organizations to investigate it alone."[30] Furthermore, business, the one section of the community which was well informed on the supply of foreign labor, had no interest in entering the debate and correcting labor's misconceptions. Business interests could support the bill with impunity, since exclusion of the handful of immigrants under written contract constituted no threat to their supply of labor. Moreover their support could be seen as a *quid pro quo* for a more positive labor attitude to the tariff.[31]

The confusion among the Knights about contract labor ensured that many followed the firm lead given by one of its own assemblies, the Window Glass Workers, which confidently analyzed the threat to itself from foreign contract labor and prescribed an appropriate remedy. Furthermore, it was in the glassworkers' interest to persuade the order that the problem of impoverished degraded immigrants could be alleviated by the passage of the alien contract labor law. Both business and elements among the skilled workers had a stake in obscuring the probable ineffectiveness of the proposed legislation as far as the immigration of unskilled workers was concerned.

Moreover, there was a recent precedent for believing that the proposed legislation would be effective. The prohibition of Chinese coolie immigration in 1882 seemed to offer a way of treating induced and dependent immigrants. To be sure, the Chinese case did not provide an exact analogy, but it gave several pointers to the most appropriate legislation. Supporters of the 1885 bill observed that the new immigration from Europe resembled that from China in its degradation, its poverty, its dependence, and its alien customs. Furthermore, it was widely believed that the Chinese were under contract. John Swinton, the distinguished labor editor, claimed that the situation of the so-called Hungarians in the coke regions of Pennsylvania was essentially the same as that which induced Congress to prohibit the importation of the Chinese. "Italians and Hungarians," he asserted "are now brought to this country in precisely the same manner that [sic] the importation of the Chinese was begun seventeen years ago," claiming that both the Chinese and the Italians had been imported under contract to work for railway and other companies.[32]

Swinton concluded from this comparison that the arguments used in favor of excluding the Chinese applied equally to the Italians and the Slavs. The latter, like the Chinese, refused to become citizens; they crowded out unskilled and, indirectly, skilled American workers; their major aim was to maximize their savings preparatory to returning home; in industrial conflict, their barbarous and violent methods resembled those of guerilla warfare; and, most shocking of all, their manner of life was degraded, and degrading to those Americans who came in contact with them. In the Mulberry Street area of New York City, he concluded, the living conditions of the Italian inhabitants resembled those in San Francisco's Chinatown. The filth, wretchedness, vice, and absence of sanitation were common to both; only the opium was missing from the Italian quarter. It seemed appropriate to workingmen to refer to the Italians as the "Continental Chinese" or "imported slaves."[33]

Since it was generally accepted that the Chinese came under contract, it was an easy step to infer that the Italians were under the same inducement. Some argued that similar problems demanded similar solutions and that the Italians and Slavs, like the Chinese, should be rigorously excluded. But that was only a minority view. Most labor leaders shrank from advocating this solution and instead seized on the Alien Contract Labor Law as the best answer to the problem. Why did they hesitate about total exclusion, and does the reason for their scruples help to illuminate their decision to support the apparently inappropriate 1885 bill?

Henry George distinguished between Chinese immigrants and the new immigrants from Europe by observing that the latter had the capacity to assimilate.[34] Many Knights would not have shared this view, but another barrier stood in the way of treating Chinese and Slavs or Italians in precisely the same manner. Any attempt at total exclusion would fall foul of a still strong American libertarian and egalitarian tradition. Unless it could be demonstrated quite unequivocally that all the Italian and Slavic newcomers were the pawns of the labor agents and the dupes of the employers, and that none had been responding to the age-old dream of individual opportunity, it would be unjust to exclude them all. Consequently, an immigration law was required that would discriminate between immigrants capable of assimilation and of solidarity with American workers, and those totally dependent on the employing class, between, that is, voluntary and induced immigrants.

For the Knights of Labor as for other labor organizations, the whole topic of immigration restriction was a very sensitive one and had to be handled with great care. There was a built-in resistance to limitations on free movement; all who were concerned with immigration, a leading Knight reported, "felt the delicacy of the subject" and shrank "from the public expression of views regarded as widely at variance with the spirit of our institutions." One labor journal attributed the difficulties of dealing with the immigration problem to the "shrinking and irresolution" of American workingmen. The Knights' own emphasis on solidarity no doubt also played a part in sensitizing some of its members to idealistic objections to all forms of immigration restriction.[35]

Two of the most forceful and prominent opponents of restriction in the order were Joseph Labadie and Judson Grenell, both supporters of an "enthusiastic" conception of solidarity. Labadie was sharply critical of the restrictionists on three major counts. First, the policy of restriction weakened labor's challenge to the unjust privileges of capitalists and monopolists by dividing the working class on ethnic or religious grounds. Second, restrictionist laws were contrary to the natural right of every human being to choose freely his place of work and residence. Americans who were themselves "foreigners" or the descendants of foreigners had no moral right to exclude later generations of foreign-born from the United States, especially since there was abundant land available. Finally, immigration restriction would become irrelevant if economic and social reform were carried out. Poverty resulted from monopoly and speculation, not from job competition; no man willing to work and earn his living could be the cause of another's poverty. Workers must therefore be liberated to use the abundant natural means of production which were being monopolized by a privileged few. "Get rid of the monopolist," said Labadie, "and the whole world could be dumped in America and America would be better for it."[36]

Probably only a minority of Knights shared Labadie's and Grenell's attitudes. Yet many who favored tighter controls on induced immigrants would not countenance total exclusion of all immigrants from Southern and Eastern Europe. They sought a rationale for restriction which could be reconciled with solidaristic and libertarian ideals.

The difficulty of this task led some to explore ways of limiting immigration without recourse to legislation at all. One proposal was to revert to the policy of the 1860s of encouraging voluntary controls on emigration by European trade unions. It was suggested that labor organizations on both sides of the Atlantic should cooperate to assemble and disseminate accurate information about the level of economic activity in the United States. One labor leader expressed the hope that "friendly relations and mutual correspondence between workmen of all countries" would place a check on the transportation of labor from one country in order to cheapen it in another at the behest of capital. Powderly himself, though favoring the bill to exclude alien contract labor, supported a propaganda campaign in Europe to counter the false claims of labor agents about the state of the American job market and to press the advantages of agitation and organization in achieving improvements in working conditions in Europe.[37]

However, these attempts to avoid the need for legislation were half-hearted and perfunctory, not least because labor organizations barely existed in those regions from which the new European immigrants came. Restrictionists came to believe that legislation was inevitable if the problem of unskilled, impoverished, and induced immigration from Southern and Eastern Europe was to be solved. Total exclusion of immigrants from this region would not conflict with internationalism if it could be shown that all such immigrants were under employer or agency inducement. This was unlikely to have been the case, and the example of immigrants from this region who became gold trade unionists and showed solidarity in strikes seemed to show as much. Powderly himself could not deny that some of the immigrants from Southern and Eastern Europe had emigrated without the inducement of agents and conceded that a total ban on immigration from this region would infringe traditional ideals in immigration policy. Powderly's commitment to unrestricted immigration from Northern and Western Europe was almost total, and he went to absurd lengths to defend the resourcefulness of the "old immigration" in finding the means "of increasing the facilities for obtaining employment."[38] His identification with this type of immigration was closer than that of Sylvis and Cameron in the 1860s, who recognized that it might be harmful in certain circumstances. Obviously perspectives had changed; there could be no talk of stricter measures against the old immigrants whilst much less desirable immigration from other regions of Europe went untouched.

It should now be clearer why the Knights supported the Alien Contract Labor Law of 1885. Although they were inhibited from adopting a total exclusion law, the majority believed some legislation was necessary if the problem of induced immigration was to be solved. Some were confident that the proposed law would be effective; other were sceptical but offered their backing because there did not seem to be an available alternative, particularly one that was as widely supported in Congress. There was, in short, a strong need to believe in the law as the only available means of reconciling restriction with the traditional internationalism.

It did not take long for labor leaders to recognize that the law was ill-suited to the task of excluding the so-called induced immigrants from Southern and Eastern Europe. Nevertheless, they turned their attention to tightening it up, still working on the assumption that induced immigration could be identified and prohibited. A decade later, after several unsuccessful attempts to make the act work in the way they wanted, spokesmen for organized labor were still claiming that proper administration of the law would ensure its success. There was, clearly, a marked reluctance to embark on the course of framing alternative measures to keep out undesirables. There were obvious difficulties in devising tests which could identify, at the port of entry, those immigrants who would break strikes and undercut wages, introduce crime and degradation, and refuse to assimilate. Labor was convinced that most of these immigrants came from the South and East of Europe, but it needed a test which would weed them out without being overtly discriminatory against the new immigration. Less than five years after the 1885 act was passed, the idea of a literacy test was floated by Edward Bemis. Some labor leaders appreciated that this offered them the chance to reconcile the conflicting claims of solidarity and self-protection in immigration policy.

NOTES

1. For a general introduction to the Knights of Labor, see Norman J. Ware, *The Labor Movement in the United States, 1860–1895: A Study in Democracy* (New York: Appleton and Co., 1929); Gerald N. Grob, *Workers and Utopia: A Study of Ideological Conflict in the American Labor Movement, 1865–1900* (Evanston, Ill.: Northwestern University Press, 1961).

2. Grob, *Workers and Utopia*, pp. 39–40; see also Gerald Rosenblum, *Immigrant Workers: Their Impact on American Labor Radicalism* (New York: Basic Books, 1973), pp. 113–14.

3. Grob, *Workers and Utopia*, pp. 35, 38; Rosenblum, *Immigrant Workers*, p. 110; Paul K. Crosser, *Ideologies and American Labor* (New York: Oxford University Press, 1941), p. 117.

4. *Records of Proceedings of the General Assembly of the Knights of Labor of America*, 4–20 October 1886 (hereafter referred to as Knights of Labor, *Proceedings*); Philip Taft, *The A.F. of L. in the Time of Gompers* (New York: Harper, 1957), p. 21; John R. Commons et al. *History of Labor in the United States* 4 vols. (1918; rpt. New York: Augustus M. Kelley, 1966), Vol. 2, p. 335.

5. Nathan Fine, *Labor and Farmer Parties in the United States, 1828–1928* (New York: Rand School of Social Science, 1928), p. 118; Richard Oestreicher, "Socialism and the Knights of Labor in Detroit, 1877–1886," *Labor History* 22, No. 1 (Winter 1981): 19.

6. *Detroit Labor Leaf*, 31 March 1886; see also Bureau of Labor Statistics of Illinois, *Fourth Biennial Report*, p. 161.

7. Ware, *Labor Movement*, pp. 29, 40; Henry Pelling, *American Labor* (Chicago: University of Chicago Press, 1960), p. 64.

8. See Powderly's comment quoted in Richard T. Ely, *The Labor Movement in America* (1886; rpt. New York: Arno Press, 1967), p. 78n.

9. Pelling, *American Labor*, p. 66; Ware, *Labor Movement*, pp. 50, 69–72; Grob, *Workers and Utopia*, p. 43; Illinois Bureau of Labor Statistics, 1886, p. 169; *Report of the Second Annual Convention of the Michigan State Assembly of the Knights of Labor*, 3–4 June 1885, pp. 17–18.

10. Ware, *Labor Movement*, pp. 158–61; Illinois Bureau of Labor Statistics, 1886, p. 169.

11. Commons et al. *History of Labor*, vol. 2, p. 336.

12. Fine, *Labor and Farmer Parties*, pp. 118–19; Oestreicher, "Socialism and the Knights of Labor in Detroit," pp. 23–24, 28–29.

13. See Chapter Three.

14. Pelling, *American Labor*, pp. 59, 65; Kinghts of Labor, *Proceedings*, 1883, 1884, and 1885; Charlotte Erickson, *American Industry and the European Immigrant, 1860–1885* (Cambridge, Mass.: Harvard University Press, 1957), p. 154.

15. Erickson, *American Industry*, pp. 109, 110, 115; Commons et al. *History of Labor*, Vol. 2, p. 372; *The Craftsman*, 25 October 1884; Knights of Labor, *Proceedings*, 1–10 September 1884; Select Committee on Existing Labor Troubles in Pennsylvania, *Investigation of Labor Troubles in Pennsylvania* (50 Cong., 2 Sess., H. Rept. No. 4147), pp. 8–12, 43, 49, 101–2, 165; *Report of the Committee on Labor* (48 Cong., 1 Sess., H. Rept. No. 444), p. 5.

16. Select committee on Existing Labor Troubles, pp. 252–53, 354–67; *Testimony* taken by the Senate Committee on Education and Labor, Vol. 1, 1885, pp. 810–11.

17. Erickson, *American Industry*, pp. 127–28, 132–34; *Testimony* taken by the Senate Committee on Education and Labor, Vol. 1, 1885, pp. 279–82, 1139; *Testimony Taken by the Select Committee of the House of Representatives to Inquire into the Alleged Violation of the Laws Prohibiting the Importation of Contract Laborers, Paupers, Convicts and Other Classes* (50 Cong., 1 Sess., H. Misc. Doc. No. 572), Vol. 15, pp. 392–401 (hereafter referred to as the Ford Committee).

18. Yet by no means all recent immigrants were strikebreakers, nor were they as pusillanimous in engaging in industrial action as was sometimes averred. See Erickson, *American Industry*, p. 121; Pennsylvania Secretary of Internal Affairs, *Annual Report 1887*, pt. 3 Vol. 15, pp. F4–F14.

19. Bureau of Statistics of Labor of Ohio, *Thirteenth Annual Report*, 1889, pp. 55–57; *Testimony* taken by the Senate Committee on Education and Labor, Vol. 1, 1885, p. 680; Vol. 2, pp. 5–9; *Report of the Committee on Labor* (48 Cong., 1 Sess., H. Rept. No. 444), pp. 5–9; Ford Committee, Vol. 15, pp. 497–501; Connecticut Bureau of Labor Statistics, *First Annual Report (Second Series)*, 1885, pp. 62–63.

20. *Testimony* taken by the Senate Committee on Education and Labor, Vol. 3, 1885, p. 580; Ford Committee, Vol. 15, p. 399; *The Craftsman*, 18 August 1888; Knights of Labor, *Proceedings*, 1–10 September 1884 (address of T. V. Powderly).

21. *Iron Molders' Journal*, August 1888.

22. Erickson, *American Industry*, pp. 33, 45.

23. Ibid., pp. 72–82.

24. *Bulletin of the Department of Labor* No. 9, March 1897: 114–15.

25. Ford Committee, Vol. 1, pp. 39–45, 57–59, 61, 67, 81–82, 94–103, 114–20,

127–31, 155–79; *Bulletin of the Department of Labor* No. 9, March 1897: 117–19; Erickson, *American Industry*, pp. 103–4.

26. *Bulletin of the Department of Labor* No. 9 (March 1897): 114–15.

27. Ford Committee, Vol. 1, pp. 70–154 passim; Erickson, *American Industry*, pp. 68, 86.

28. Ford Committee, Vol. 1, pp. 40, 57, 189.

29. Erickson, *American Industry*, p. 156; *Report of the Fifth Annual Session of the Federation of Organized Trades and Labor Unions*, 1885, p. 8 (comment by the Secretary, G. Edmonston).

30. *Testimony* taken by the Senate Committee on Education and Labor, 1885, Vol. 1, p. 337.

31. Grob, *Workers and Utopia*, p. 85; Erickson, *American Industry*, pp. 159–61; see also *Liberty*, 1 April 1882.

32. Erickson, *American Industry*, p. 157; Report of the Committee on Labor (48 Cong., 1 Sess., H. Rept. No. 444), p. 4.

33. Bureau of Statistics of Labor of the State of New York, *Third Annual Report*, 1885, pp. 479–85; *Iron Molders' Journal*, November 1888; *Cigar Makers' Official Journal*, March 1884; *The Advance and Labor Leaf*, 21 July 1888 (reprinted from the *Union Printer*).

34. *Testimony* taken by the State Committee on Education and Labor, Vol. 1, 1885, pp. 520–21.

35. *The Journal of United Labor*, 12 March 1887, 26 September 1889 (quoting from the Grand Rapids *Workman*).

36. *Detroit Labor Leaf*, 9 September 1885, 27 January 1886; *The Advance and Labor Leaf*, 27 August 1887, 25 February 1888.

37. Knights of Labor, *Proceedings*, 1–10 September 1884, 4–20 October 1886; *John Swinton's Paper*, 8 February 1885; Erickson, *American Industry*, p. 151.

38. Ford Committee, Vol. 15, pp. 502–5.

5

The American Federation of Labor, Induced Immigration, and the Literacy Test

One of the major problems associated with the writing of labor history is how to identify the opinions and attitudes of the rank and file. The overwhelming majority of employees in the American manufacturing, mining, transportation, and service industries in the period 1880 to 1914 were not unionized and did not articulate opinion through trade unions or other labor organizations. It is unwise to assume, therefore, that the official views either of the national and local trade unions or of central and state labor federations accurately reflected the opinions of the industrial workforce. Less suspect, but still to be treated with caution, is the supposition that trade unions voiced the sentiments of the majority of their members. This was more likely to have been true in respect of wages and conditions, on which the members were well informed and had a direct interest in ensuring that the leadership was responsive to their wishes. On questions of a broadly political nature, however, where the rank and file were less well briefed and less confident in their judgments, there was a strong possibility of divergence between the official line and the sometimes amorphous and ill-defined sentiments of the union members.

Despite these qualifications about the representativeness of official union policies, the necessary first step in determining opinion among the working class, certainly in the nineteenth century, is to ascertain and evaluate the views of the trade unions and the labor federations. Since the question of immigration was important to the trade union movement in general, as well as to individual unions, and since it did not come within the sphere of collective bargaining, the major forum for debates on this issue was the annual conventions of the American Federation of Labor (AFL), the organization which succeeded the Knights of Labor after 1887 as the most important central labor body in the United States. Accordingly, the primary aim of this chapter is to discuss labor's policy on the issue of European immigration from the standpoint of the AFL, noting how its policy evolved in the dozen years after the agitation for the Alien Contract Labor Law in 1885. However, as a necessary preface to this discussion, there will be a brief analysis of the somewhat complex meaning which the trade unions attached to the term contract labor. In the following chapter an attempt will be made to probe more deeply into opinion within the affiliated trade unions and in other organizations claiming to represent labor opinion, as well as among rank-and-file workers and influential individuals in the labor movement. In other words, the central problem of establishing the representativeness of the AFL's policy by identifying the opinion of ordinary working people will not be shirked, though the difficulties in the way are formidable.

The discussion which follows should establish that in the decade after 1885 organized labor took steady, undramatic, and cautious steps in the direction of tighter immigration controls. But in 1896 an extended debate on a new measure of restriction, the literacy test, took place at the AFL's annual convention, to be followed in 1897 by the adoption of the test as the cornerstone of the federation's immigration policy. This decision represented a quite radical change of direction, though it was also the culmination of many previous attempts to solve the specific problem of unskilled immigrant workers from Southern and Eastern Europe. The new policy, as we shall see, was designed to be both restrictive and discriminatory, but above all, it shifted the focus of the discussion about undesirable immigrants from the employers to the immigrants themselves, no longer assuming that the so-called undesirables were invariably under contract or inducement from American businessmen.

Although the AFL's decision in 1897 did not, in our view, command majority support in the ranks of organized labor, still less among unorganized workers, there is little doubt that within a further decade the AFL's commitment to this policy received firm backing from the vast majority of its affiliated trade unions. Consequently, in succeeding chapters we need to look beyond the annual or periodic fluctuations in labor opinion in order to account for the steady movement over two decades in the direction of tighter controls, considering such possible causal factors as the effects of technological change, economic fluctuations, the transformation in the ethnic composition of the immigrants, and, finally, the weakening of socialism in the AFL. But our immediate task is to establish the nature and direction of labor opinion on the immigration question as expressed by the AFL in the decade or so after 1885.

Following the decline of the Knights of Labor after 1887, the AFL became the most prominent national labor organization. Founded in 1886 in reaction to the breakdown of negotiations between leaders of important national trade unions and the Knights, it grew steadily for the next few years. Perhaps its earliest major achievement was simply to survive the acute economic depression which began in 1893, when many workers dropped out of its affiliated unions as a result of unemployment or a fall in wages. Its continued existence under these unfavorable conditions ensured that once the economy began to recover in 1898 there was a firm base for the organization and recruitment of new union members. One of the major differences between the AFL and earlier central labor organizations like the National Labor Union and the Knights of Labor was the dominant role the national trade unions occupied within it at the expense of city central labor bodies, workingmen's reform organizations, mixed local unions, and the adherents of a variety of radical causes. The national unions were determined that the federation would dance to their tune, answer to their needs, and fulfil only those limited tasks which they allotted to it. "The autonomy of the member unions," wrote Gerald Grob, "quickly became the most fundamental principle of the Federation."[1]

Consistent with this basic autonomy, the AFL was granted only limited powers by the jealous national unions which established it, the most important of which were the furtherance of trade union organization, the formation of city and state labor federations, and the promotion of legislation in the labor interest. The AFL had an extremely limited conception of its political role, particularly in this early period, and in this it reflected the preferences and convictions of its member unions, which were most forcibly and eloquently expressed by Samuel Gompers, the first president of the AFL.[2] It is important to understand what may be termed the philosophy of the AFL because of its implications for labor's policy on immigration.

In essence, this philosophy gave highest priority to improving the living standards of trade union members by means of worker self-help, craft solidarity, and collective action. Most of the early national unions within the AFL were craft unions aiming for stability through a policy of high dues, high benefits, and solidarity based on craft identification.[3] They had rejected the neo-Lassallean emphasis on political action through an independent political party of the working class in favor of collective bargaining with the employers. It was accepted that the ownership of the means of production and distribution would continue to be in private hands, but within the structure of capitalism unions would fight hard to improve the wages and conditions of their members. One of the most influential advocates of this line, Adolph Strasser, a close associate of Gompers, argued that trade unionists had "no ultimate ends" in the sense of restructuring society, but were going on from day to day fighting for immediate objects. It is arguable that this so-called "pure and simple unionism" or "business unionism" was "an affirmation of the aspirations of the rank and file" which reflected the individualist and materialist values of the American middle class.[4] Certainly a solidarity based on craft identification weakened the emergence of a wider class solidarity; but craft unity was only one obstacle in the way of the achievement of class consciousness to add to those based on ethnicity, religion, and language.

Craft unions were united, not only by a common attachment to self-help, but by a positive distrust of the broader collectivism implied in party political activity. Government, whether at the federal or state level, was an object of suspicion. Many of the early leaders of the AFL had served apprenticeships in politics, not as professional politicians but as politically active trade unionists and as reformers seeking to achieve changes in social and economic conditions in the interests of laboring men. Many had drawn unfavorable conclusions from their experiences, and these became transmuted into fixed principles. Consequently, the AFL was from the outset "more interested in avoiding the pitfalls of politics than in capitalizing upon the advantages of direct political action."[5] There were two exceptions to this general rule. Political action was necessary first to acquire and preserve the legal rights underpinning successful collective bargaining, and second to solve the handful of problems which were not susceptible to solution by collective bargaining and industrial action.

The AFL probably reflected the aspirations of the majority of its members on most issues in the decade and a half before 1900. It found a leader in Gompers who profoundly shared, and indeed helped to shape, its dominant philosophy and articulated it clearly and convincingly. "His success," Grob remarked, "lay in the fact that he could understand his constituents and formulate policy accordingly."[6] Occasionally his touch deserted him and there would be an embarrassing divergence between his policy and that of the rank and file; the political program of 1893 and 1894 was a case in point. Despite this, Grob concluded that the AFL became "the recognized spokesman of the working class" and reflected "the interests of its constituents." Whilst we cannot accept the first assertion—the AFL represented primarily its constituent, mainly craft unions and barely at all semi-skilled and unskilled workers, who were largely unorganized—we can assume that the federation represented fairly accurately the sentiments of its member unions. Later on we shall have to question this assumption in respect of immigration policy.[7]

Immigration was one subject which thrust the AFL into pressure group politics, owing to the inability of collective bargaining to solve the problems arising from it. Since these problems affected a large proportion of the ALF's affiliated unions, a collective response through the AFL seemed most appropriate. It is apparent that the philosophy underlying craft unionism was fundamentally antipathetic to at least certain types of immigration. For example, in seeking to work within capitalism for their own members' advantage, craft unions were compelled to strengthen their bargaining position in the marketplace by controlling the supply of labor. A contemporary report explained that the "trade-union is essentially exclusive, seeking to promote the material interests of a select few engaged in a specific calling and aiming to limit the number who shall be admitted to their craft or the privileges of their order."[8] Obviously a flow of skilled craftsmen from abroad tended to weaken a union's control over labor supply, although the damage might be limited if the influx was not excessive and if the immigrants had already been members of trade unions in their home countries. Furthermore, craftsmen who were themselves immigrants or the sons of immigrants might be unwilling to restrict immigration of other craftsmen, particularly if they originated from the same areas of Europe. In this way craft and ethnic identification helped to limit tendencies to restriction in the 1860s.

By the 1880s the ethnic origins of immigrants were beginning to change, the proportion with a trade union background was falling, and absolute numbers were increasing dramatically. In view of the craft unions' determination to strengthen their members' position in the marketplace, immigration represented a major threat to working conditions and living standards. Moreover, the introduction of new machines manned by unskilled workers was undermining the employment of craftsmen whose skills became wholly or partly redundant. Self-interest demanded opposition both to the machines and their operators, and this opposition was heightened when the machine minders were foreign-born, as they increasingly were. Only those trade unions which rejected the craft unions' philosophy and aimed to destroy the capitalist marketplace and to substitute for it a new order of society based on collective ownership of the means of production were inclined to accept notions of class conflict and the brotherhood of all wage earners, irrespective of ethnic or occupational differences or geographic origins. Such "revolutionary" unions were only a small minority in the AFL, the craft unions being firmly in the saddle for almost the whole of the period.[9] Consequently, the AFL's philosophy predisposed it to regard immigration as a danger to its members and acted as a counterweight to the internationalist traditions in the workforce.

This expectation of the probable consequences of pure and simple unionism for immigration is confirmed by a study of AFL conventions in the two decades after 1886, the year of its foundation. In two respects the AFL's immigration policy was clear-cut and undeviating throughout the period. It firmly adhered to the policy of its direct predecessor, the Federation of Organized Trade and Labor Unions, by supporting the exclusion of Chinese coolies under the act of 1882. Secondly, it supported the ban on entry of certain categories of immigrants regarded as particularly harmful and degrading, notably convicts, lunatics, idiots, paupers, and persons liable to become a public charge.[10] The AFL worked assiduously to ensure that the legislation was maintained, rigorously administered, and extended to cover new categories of immigrants with allegedly similar disabilities or handicaps. There is little room for debate about these aspects of AFL policy.

There is, however, less agreement about organized labor's attitude to the problem of alien contract labor. Of course, the AFL supported the Foran Act of 1885, which made it an offense for any person or corporation to assist the importation of any foreign laborer into the United States under contract to perform labor or service of any kind.[11] It was instrumental in obtaining successive amendments to the law in order to tighten up its administration and to block a number of loopholes. Disagreement arises about its precise objectives in opposing foreign contract labor. Did it aim to exclude skilled or unskilled immigrant workers, or both? A clear answer to this question, on which depends a correct understanding of labor's attitudes to immigration in the decade after 1885, cannot be obtained without analyzing the meaning which the term contract labor held for union members in the 1880s.

The main target of the craft union leaders, according to Charlotte Erickson, was the skilled workers imported to break strikes and to overcome labor shortages. In seeking amendments to the 1885 act the AFL aimed "to make the act serve the purpose for which they had intended it, that of excluding skilled contract labor." Erickson conceded that during the hearings on the bill in the House of Representatives and in the subsequent debate, the prime target of labor witnesses and sympathetic congressmen was the importation of cheap unskilled labor from Italy and Hungary.[12] However, the only hard evidence presented on the existence of contracts came from members of the skilled union of Window Glass Workers, who were seeking to prevent the recruitment under contract of skilled European (largely Belgian) glass workers. Erickson assumed that the Glass Workers' attitudes were typical of skilled unions as a whole. Of course, in seeking to arouse congressional support for the bill, labor had appealed to ethnic prejudice among the legislators by attacking the pauper and servile immigration from Southern and Eastern Europe and allowing it to be thought that this, too, was under contract. But for Erickson this criticism of unskilled immigrants by skilled American workers was mainly a means of excluding skilled contract labor from abroad. Unskilled immigrants, she believed, offered no threat to the jobs of skilled workers; indeed they took jobs "which the craftsmen who formed the bulk of the A.F. of L. membership would have scorned."[13]

However, Erickson conceded that AFL support for the literacy test, which became increasingly solid in the first decade of the twentieth century, apparently contradicted her interpretation of the federation's immigration policy as being directed mainly at skilled immigrant workers under contract. She admitted that the literacy test was designed quite unequivocally to restrict entry of the unskilled, allegedly servile, labor of Southern and Eastern Europe and was so understood by the craft union leaders. She explained this apparent *volte-face* on the part of the craft unions by reference to the "frustrations and disappointment" with the anti–contract labor laws which made "simpler, more direct" methods of limiting immigration more attractive, and to a more general concern for the maintenance of Anglo-Saxon culture without dilution.[14] She concluded that there was a general hardening of the position of the AFL leadership between 1900 and 1914 and that the ethnic prejudices evoked in 1885 as the means to an end were, in later years, largely formative of labor's attitudes to immigration.

Professor Erickson's interpretation of the aims of the labor movement in supporting the Foran Act raises important questions. Is she correct in believing that American craft unions, which dominated the AFL, mainly intended to exclude skilled immigrant labor under contract? If that is the case, was labor's criticism of unskilled immigrant workers mainly a tactical ploy as she believed, to whip up support in Congress by arousing ethnic prejudice? Finally, can we accept her method of reconciling labor's alleged opposition to skilled alien contract labor with its mid–1890s hostility to the unskilled foreign-born, as exemplified in its support of the literacy test? Clearly our answers to these questions will determine our understanding of labor's attitudes to European immigration in the two decades after the passage of the Foran Act.

The interpretation which follows is based on rather different answers from those suggested by Erickson. In the first place, it is arguable that skilled workers, from the mid–1880s onwards, profoundly objected to the importation of unskilled, as well as skilled, immigrant workers. They were, it is true, under the misapprehension that unskilled laborers were brought in under the same type of formal contract as skilled operatives like the glassworkers. Nevertheless, this does not detract from their substantive arguments against unskilled immigrant workers which they invoked to support the passage of the Foran Act of 1885. Second, although the prejudices of the legislators were played upon by labor witnesses at hearings before congressional committees, there is convincing evidence that the witnesses themselves shared these prejudices to a considerable degree. Ethnic prejudice was not merely functional to the passage of the law to keep out skilled contract labor of Northwest European origin, but was itself part of the motivation for excluding unskilled contract labor from Southern and Eastern Europe.

Finally, there is no disagreement that the legislation of 1887 and 1888 was designed to tighten up the Foran Act and, as Erickson argued, to make it serve the purpose for which the skilled workers had intended it. However, careful study of the arguments advanced by craft unions in favor of these legislative amendments makes it clear that the aim of the changes was at least as much to reduce the flow of unskilled immigrants as it was to restrict entry for the skilled. Moreover, craft unions embraced the literacy test in

the 1890s out of understandable frustration at the Foran Act's inability to
limit the influx of unskilled workers. The decade after 1896 did indeed mark
a turning point in the AFL's approach to immigration, but not as much in
objectives as in methodology. That is to say, from the passage of the Foran
Act in 1885 American craft unions attempted to limit the immigration of
unskilled as well as skilled workers by a succession of measures of which
the literacy test was the culmination. This is not to argue that the adoption
of the literacy test was not a radical new departure; rather, its novelty
consisted in its method and in its implications in tackling a decade-old
problem. To substantiate this interpretation we need only refer to the terms
of the Foran Act of 1885, to the motives and assumptions of craft union
leaders, and to labor's thinking in the 1890s.

The terms of the Foran Act of 1885 were quite compatible with the
exclusion of unskilled workers if it is assumed, as it was by labor lobbyists,
that unskilled workers were brought in under a form of contract. This
means that there was nothing in the act itself to support the contention that
it was only skilled labor that was under challenge. The central section of
the act laid down that it would be

unlawful for any person, company, partnership or corporation in any manner what-
soever to prepay the transportation or in any way assist or encourage the importation
or migration of any alien or aliens, any foreigner or foreigners, into the United
States . . . under contract or agreement, parol or special, express or implied, made
previous to the importation or migration of such alien or aliens, foreigner or foreigners, to perform labor or service of any kind in the United States.[15]

The act may be construed to mean that all immigrants who were encouraged
or assisted to migrate under contract or agreement, with the exception of
specifically excluded categories, were ineligible for entry into the United
States. Since unskilled workers were not excluded from the operations of
the act, it may be assumed that it was the intention of the legislators to
exclude any persons who could be proved to be under contract or agreement.
Additionally, the terms of the act were sufficiently inclusive to attempt to
regulate the flow, not only of immigrants under formal written contract,
but of those whose agreements were merely implied and informal, provided
they were made prior to entry into the United States.

Turning now to the motives and aspirations of the craft unions, we
recognize that skilled craftsmen felt increasingly threatened by the employment of unskilled immigrants in operating the new machines which were
spreading in a wide range of industries and destroying many of the old
crafts. They particularly objected to the use of foreigners as strikebreakers
since this represented a direct challenge to the attempts of employees to
control the terms and conditions of employment. Furthermore, the unskilled
immigrants aroused distinct ethnic prejudices among skilled American

workers owing to their, in the main, different regional and ethnic origins and their distinctive religious, linguistic, and cultural backgrounds.

A useful source of evidence about labor attitudes is the testimony taken by the Senate Committee on Education and Labor from some of the delegates to the 1883 Federation of Organized Trades and Labor Unions' Convention in New York City. It is evident that what trade union witnesses meant by contract labor was something more than skilled workers from Northwest Europe. What they had in mind, as was noted in Chapter Four, was a state of dependence on an employer following an inducement to travel to the United States to take up a job. Such inducements were offered to skilled and unskilled workers alike, but these witnesses particularly condemned the imported unskilled workers for the damage they inflicted on working and living standards. One of the earliest and most passionate opponents of imported unskilled labor was Peter McGuire, secretary of the Carpenters' Union and later a vice-president of the AFL. In his long evidence to the committee he anticipated most of the criticisms which, as time went by, became increasingly prominent. McGuire and other witnesses compared the imported Europeans with the Chinese, an analogy taken up by the editor of the *Cigar Makers' Official Journal*, who spoke for a union with the longest firsthand experience of Chinese coolie competition.[16]

It seems reasonably clear, therefore, that craft unionists were alarmed at the importation of cheap unskilled labor and, believing it to be under contract with employers or their agents, sought an end to it, as well as to the importation of skilled labor, by means of the Alien Contract Labor Law. However, an awkward question remains: is it plausible to accept that trade union leaders really believed that imported unskilled labor came in under formal contract or agreement? Or that a bill largely devised by a skilled craft, the glassworkers, to meet the specific needs of their own industry, would be effective in solving the very different problem of unskilled immigrant labor? No doubt some officials and rank-and-file members did so out of naïveté or a simple lack of precise information in an area where information was difficult to acquire. But the majority, it would appear, wanted to believe for ideological reasons. Committed to equality and individualism, they could not accept that what they termed "free" immigration—the immigration of self-motivated individuals seeking economic, political, or religious opportunity—was capable of inflicting damage on American workers. Nor could they recognize any justification for denying these opportunities to men and women whose ambitions duplicated those of earlier generations of immigrants from Europe. Hence, when they saw examples of immigration which had adverse consequences for the wages and conditions of employment, they had no choice but to define it as "unfree" or "servile," the product of the machinations of capitalists and totally under the latter's control. If not imported under contract, such labor had at least been induced, tempted, or persuaded to go to the United States by business interests, steamship lines, or labor agents. It seems that the motives of the craft unions in supporting the passage of the Foran Act were similar to those of the Knights of Labor in their aim of restricting the flow of "imported" or "dependent" labor, whether skilled or unskilled. Hence the unions were forced, through misunderstanding and ideology, to support a measure which, if adequate at all, was suited only to the exclusion of skilled workers under contract.

We come, finally, to the question of whether the 1890s were a turning point in labor attitudes in the way Professor Erickson suggested. In approaching this problem we must try to understand labor's aims in pressing amendments to the Foran Act and, in the end, seeking alternatives to it. Experience of its operation soon brought to light cases of skilled workers under contract evading its provisions, confirming suspicions that the act might not be very effective, even though it was a step in the right direction. There was, in addition, a growing number of complaints about the failure of the act to limit the inflow of unskilled workers from Southern and Eastern Europe. Consequently craft unions made repeated attempts through the AFL to improve the existing law, and these bore fruit in 1887 and 1888.[17]

Despite these improvements, Gompers complained to a sympathetic AFL convention in 1889 that the law was being evaded and that its casual administration by officials was bringing it into disrepute. In the next two years debates at union conventions and in the labor press took place against a background of widespread and intensive discussion in the country and in Congress on what to do about immigration. A select committee of the House of Representatives, known as the Ford Committee, had been established in 1888 to examine charges that the 1885 act, as amended, was being extensively evaded. It concluded, inter alia, that the contract labor law was easy to violate and that convictions under it were hard to secure. It recommended that the federal government take over direct administration of the Immigration Acts, that the number of excluded categories be increased, and that the period during which deportation of an illegal immigrant could take place be extended from one to two years after entry.[18] These recommendations were referred to committees of both the Senate and the House, and in the course of the next two years these committees produced a number of reports based on extensive evidence from interested parties. The testimony offered by the representatives of craft unions to these various congressional committees throws additional light on the expectations which organized labor had of the 1885 act.

It is apparent, for example, that there was widespread disappointment at the failure of the immigration laws to exclude the assisted immigration of unskilled workers or, in the words of Gompers, "to close the flood gates for hordes of laborers . . . brought to this country like slaves under contract." If disappointment is an index of expectation, then the act had regrettably failed to do what had been intended of it. In Gompers's opinion, contract laborers came in the category of stimulated immigration as compared with those who left their homelands on their own initiative. "It is the difference," he asserted, "of [sic] a horde of conscripts from a company of volunteers." He described the "involuntary" immigrants as "the criminal classes who are assisted from Europe to America," paupers, similarly shipped off, the "beguiled poor allured by false promises," and contracted laborers, that is, those on formal, written contracts. For Gompers, contract laborers included all those who were assisted to migrate to the United States by individuals or companies who stood to gain materially from the migration.[19] Gompers asked why such people were permitted to enter the United States. His answer was predictable: the contract labor law had not been properly enforced. This violation of the law had resulted, according to one union journal, in the increased immigration of that "degrading, debauching, labor-destroying element whose lives, habits and language are alien to the American people," in short, the "Continental Chinese." Their social degeneracy, asserted David Black of the Iron Molders, was the result of centuries of tyranny and unrestrained despotism. This, surely, is a far cry from the protests of the Window Glass Workers in 1885 against the importation, under written contract, of skilled but relatively low-paid glassworkers from Belgium, but it is not essentially different from the words of McGuire and other craft union leaders who, also in the mid–1880s, condemned the importation of unskilled workers from Southern and Eastern Europe. And just as McGuire hoped that the Contract Labor Law would be effective against the immigration of such workers, so the AFL in 1890 was still confident that the law was in the right direction and would fulfill its purpose if properly amended and administered.[20]

By 1891 the congressional committees had reported that there was a widespread demand for stricter enforcement of the immigration laws, though not for a radical change in their character. Consequently, the Immigration Act of 1891 consolidated and improved the existing legislation. Among its more important clauses, it added to the excluded categories polygamists and persons with loathsome or dangerous contagious diseases, and strengthened the Contract Labor Law by making it an offense to assist or encourage the immigration of any alien by promise of employment through advertisements published in any foreign country. Any alien travelling to the United States as a result of such advertisements would be treated as if under contract. Finally, the administration of the law was placed under the federal government with the creation of the office of Superintendent of Immigration.[21]

The revised immigration law still did not satisfy delegates to the AFL convention in 1892. Gompers alleged that employers importing foreign-born workers were coaching them to answer the immigration officials' questions. It was also difficult to obtain convictions against employers who broke the law because a prime witness, the contract laborer himself, was

immediately deported and was consequently unable to give evidence. Moreover, in a letter to the secretary of the treasury, Gompers asserted that there
were too few inspectors on duty at Ellis Island who were "earnestly devoted
to the Alien Contract Labor Law."[22] Yet again Gompers suggested amendments to the law and again the convention supported him. As a result
Gompers wrote a letter to Senator David Hill, chairman of the Senate
Committee on Immigration, which leaves us in no doubt that he equated
the importation or inducement of immigrants by "bankers" or labor agents
with contract labor. Legislation was indeed passed in 1893, but whether it
met the requirements of the AFL is uncertain. However, the delegates were
undeniably pleased by the evidence of more rigorous administration of the
law by the officials concerned. Henceforth their attention is absorbed, not
by alleged deficiencies in law enforcement, but by consideration of the best
way for the law to fulfil its purpose.[23]

Whilst the majority of craft unions continued to be fertile in suggesting
legislative amendments concerning contract and assisted immigration, some
concluded that the law itself was deeply flawed and incapable, however
amended or however well administered, of adequately restricting the flow
of undesirable immigrants. This theme emerges in the next three conventions of the AFL, which were held during the severest economic depression
of the nineteenth century.[24] One might have expected, in these circumstances, that vitriolic denunciation of these foreign-born competitors for
scarce jobs would have reached a climax, but, instead, criticism was com-
paratively muted. This was mainly attributable to two factors. The first
was that immigration had declined as a result of the depression, a fact which
Gompers noted in his speech to the AFL conventions in 1893 and 1894, and
there was also substantial remigration during these years. Second, the controversy over the socialist political program at the 1893 and 1894 conventions distracted attention from the immigration problem and placed
immigration in a new economic context. Debate about the necessary measures for the reconstruction of society and for the transfer of the ownership
of productive capital to the community could only highlight the fact that
responsibility for economic hardship lay with the capitalist system itself.
Tampering with the free movement of labor, whilst leaving the central
institutions of capital untouched, could not solve the problems of unemployment and periodic depression which were endemic to capitalism. Consequently, whilst the debate over the political program continued,
immigration was inevitably downgraded to being merely one of the symp-
toms of the capitalist malaise. It is therefore no surprise to discover the 1894
AFL convention concurring in a resolution that further restrictions on immigration were unnecessary.[25]

As to the alleged weakness of the existing law, delegates were exhorted
to cooperate fully with the authorities in order to bring about convictions
for violations. Gompers's successor, John McBride, reaffirmed that gov-

ernment officials were performing their duties conscientiously, but to be really effective they needed more help and cooperation from labor organizations in providing detailed evidence about infractions of the law. Yet it was realistic of the trade unions to conclude that any improved administrative procedure was likely to founder on the rock of judicial interpretation. The Commissioner-General of Immigration recognized the problem in his 1908 report when he wrote: "It is very difficult to secure evidence in such a form as will be sufficient in detail to enable suit to be brought under the penal provisions of the act." Under the law the importer was given the benefit of every doubt, since the courts held the law to be highly penal, arguing that it must be so construed "as to bring within its condemnation only those who are shown by direct and positive averments to be embraced within the terms of the law." Nothing was to be left to inference or conjecture. For example, specific evidence had to be adduced that a contract had actually been drawn up in a foreign country precisely designating the period of time during which employment was to continue and the rate of wages to be paid. Furthermore, the importer could not be convicted unless the contract had been completed and the immigrant laborer had actually set foot on American soil, after passing through immigration control.[26]

By the mid–1890s, the various difficulties in the way of excluding contract laborers by legislation and by better administration of the law had convinced many labor leaders that they had come to the end of that particular road and must set off on a new track. Why did it take the majority so long to accept what was obvious to some of their number in the early 1890s, namely that the alien contract labor law was incapable of fulfilling the purposes for which it had been enacted? It was not simply a case of obtuseness or a deficiency in comprehension. If an ordinary rank-and-file member of the Carpenters' Union could testify before the Committee on Immigration and Naturalization in 1890 that nothing could be done under the contract labor law because "it was necessary to prove a close contract," which was a perfectly accurate understanding of the case, it is difficult to argue that the persistence of craft union leaders in seeking to improve the law was due, in the main, to a lack of perceptiveness. On the contrary, they had been committed to the law owing to their distaste, not to say repugnance, for the canvassed alternatives. There were broadly two choices open to them. They could accept, as the carpenter witness did, that since there was no possibility of preventing foreign-born laborers migrating to the United States, the only way of maintaining living standards for American workers was by admitting to unions all competent workmen "of good moral character" in order to maintain bargaining strength with the employers. Whilst this might have been a feasible solution for the carpenters (though the national leadership of that union did not agree), most newcomers from abroad were unable to enter a union even if they wished to, because the occupations they tended to enter were not usually unionized. Furthermore, native-born workers had no confidence that unskilled immigrants from Southern and Eastern Europe would be willing to join even the few appropriate unions in more than token numbers.[27]

The alternative was to adopt a more restrictive immigration policy involving perhaps a total prohibition of immigration for a period of years, or an increased head tax, or a literacy test. The latter course was advocated by Charles Litchman, once a prominent official of the Knights of Labor. In his opinion the best way of restricting the volume of immigration was to exclude the least desirable immigrants. Litchman believed that labor organizations were unenthusiastic about the literacy test in the early 1890s because they were afraid of being called Know-Nothings. Furthermore, the majority of craft union leaders were either foreign-born or the children of parents born abroad, and were naturally reluctant to bar the way to opportunities from which they themselves had benefitted. Most important of all, the strong internationalist traditions in the labor movement inhibited labelling immigrants as undesirable unless they were under inducement from employers or agents.[28] In that tradition "voluntary" immigrants were to be welcomed, either on the democratic grounds of equality of opportunity or in the cause of offering asylum to the victims of oppression. It would, therefore, have been a quite fundamental, indeed painful, departure from existing traditions of freedom in immigration policy to adopt the literacy test as a method of restriction. This objection to it was advanced by, among others, Samuel Gompers, the man who shortly afterwards was to become one of its strongest advocates. "I have always felt," he wrote, "that restricting opportunities for others is a grave responsibility . . . America is the product of the daring, the genius, the idealism of those who left homes and kindred to settle in the new land. It is an ideal typifying a haven and an opportunity." Literacy could not be construed as an index of knowledge or character.[29]

Gompers was to find himself in a dilemma, however. If his recommendations for tightening up the Alien Contract Labor Law proved ineffective, what other course was open to him? Surely a total ban on all immigration would prove unacceptable since it would exclude the desirable along with the undesirable. Some solution was required that excluded most of those immigrants who were under inducement and whom the contract labor law was failing to keep out. This conclusion was strengthened by the conviction that a substantial proportion of recent immigrants were, at best, unassimilable in the short term and, at worst, no more assimilable than the Chinese in the long run. All amendments to the existing law had failed to solve the problem, and it was understandable that some restrictionists, including Gompers himself, should be attracted by the quite new approach contained in the literacy test, which promised greater effectiveness in excluding "involuntary" or induced immigrants.

This approach raised severe problems of its own. This category of immigrants had been described by its opponents as degraded, servile, and unassimilable, but it was questionable whether this equation was perfect. Were all induced immigrants unassimilable and degraded? Conversely, were all unassimilable immigrants actually imported? In view of evidence about the increasingly large numbers from Southern and Eastern Europe who migrated in response to the promptings of relatives and friends already in the United States, by no means all immigrants from that region could be described as imported, and a new restrictive measure would have to take account of that fact. The literacy test was an imperfect and undiscriminating measure in this respect. Its advocates made the shaky assumption that literacy was some kind of guarantee of sound human qualities.[30]

The test also failed to distinguish between imported and "voluntary" immigrants, abolishing the distinction which had been the norm for the previous thirty years. Under the proposed new test, the motive for emigrating from Europe became subordinate as a criterion for entry to that of the capacity to assimilate, to "identify with American life and purposes," which, its sponsors believed, was measurable by literacy. Such a bill was evidently discriminatory on the grounds of geography and ethnicity, owing to the high levels of illiteracy in Mediterranean and Slavic countries. The test would have excluded a number who, though illiterate, were highly motivated and might have been capable of fairly rapid assimilation. By the same token it would not have excluded those who were under employer inducement to migrate to the United States and were fortunate enough to be literate.[31]

The proposed law, then, did not solve the problem of how to discriminate effectively between voluntary and induced immigration, though it went some way towards it. But, in its favor, it was believed to provide the American government with the means of excluding unassimilable immigrants who originated in disproportionate numbers from Southern and Eastern Europe. Small wonder, then, that some prominent trade union leaders seized on the literacy test as a more effective means than the Alien Contract Labor Law of excluding imported unskilled workers. But, equally, we should not be surprised that the test was bitterly opposed within the labor movement, given labor's long tradition of welcoming voluntary immigrants.

Such opposition was no doubt anticipated by the supporters of the literacy test, but in view of the anxiety over immigration among trade unionists and the uncertainty about how next to proceed, conditions were not totally unpropitious for convincing the membership that the test was the answer to their prayers. Seizing the opportunity provided by the obvious popularity of the literacy test in the U.S. Congress, where, in 1896, it was embodied in the Corliss-Lodge Bill, Gompers initiated what turned out to be a dramatic debate on immigration policy at the AFL convention in 1896. Reports of the debate reveal that, whilst some delegates had thrown overboard the

long-standing traditions of hospitality regarding immigration, others insisted on remaining faithful to the old distinction between "dependent" and
"voluntary" immigrants. They continued to assume that voluntary immigrants identified with American ideals—indeed, that was one of the major
reason for their migration—and as a result could easily be assimilated. Since
the debate was something of a turning point in labor's approach to immigration, it deserves further consideration.

Gompers initiated the debate by drawing the delegates' attention to the
immigration bills before Congress, and asserting that the convention could
not remain neutral on such an important public issue. Taking his advice,
the convention agreed to refer the question of immigration to a special
committee under the chairmanship of Peter McGuire, secretary of the Carpenters' Union and an articulate and convinced restrictionist. The recommendations of this committee were an interesting mixture of old and new.
It promptly endorsed the Corliss-Lodge Bill but reverted to the old rhetoric
of condemning "artificial" immigration, which was "encouraged by avaricious steamship lines and corporations," and approved the stricter enforcement of the existing law by immigration officials. The committee
offered a cluster of proposals for the tighter control of immigration, including a so-called "consular clause" under which American consuls at
foreign ports would play a greater role in enforcing the restrictions on
criminal and pauper immigration, and a "naturalization clause" by which
there would be stricter civil and educational qualifications for naturalization
and a requirement that every immigrant on landing should express his
intention to become a U.S. citizen within a year.[32]

It was poor tactics to present a package containing so many different and
controversial proposals. This served to increase opposition to the report
from delegates who had little in common except hostility to one section or
another of the committee's recommendations.[33] As a result, supporters of
the report were comfortably outnumbered by its critics, many of whom
simply denied that the true cause of the social and economic malaise from
which the country was suffering lay in immigration. In the circumstances,
the authors of the report were no doubt relieved to avoid a vote, accepting
a compromise resolution to submit the "entire matter" to affiliated unions
so that they could mandate their delegates to the following year's convention. All in all, it appears to have been a good day for the traditional freedoms
in immigration policy. However, a word of caution is in order. Reports of
the debate suggest that the delegates were unwilling to make a snap decision
on a number of diverse and fairly novel proposals. They needed more time
for reflection. Moreover, the most radical of the committee's recommendations, the literacy test, stood a better chance of ultimate endorsement by
the AFL than some of the more modest proposals, simply because it was
so popular in Congress and seemed politically practicable to the legislators.

While the recommendations of the special committee were being considered by the affiliated unions, both houses of Congress passed the Corliss-Lodge Bill, which was subsequently vetoed by President Cleveland at the end of his administration in March 1897. Consequently, when the next AFL convention met later in the year, the issue of immigration was receiving less public attention and the popular tide in favor of the bill had begun to ebb. Gompers, anxious to resuscitate the bill with a kiss of life from organized labor, urged the delegates to throw their weight behind the movement to gain "legislative relief," reminding the convention that the AFL's affiliated unions had been requested to instruct their delegates on the immigration issue.[34] The delegates soon had an opportunity to exercise their mandate when a series of motions was placed before the convention. One supported the literacy test, one proposed the total suspension of immigration for five years, and one, from the Bakers' Union, opposed any further restriction of immigration. In considering these varied, indeed diametrically opposed, points of view, a convention committee prefaced its recommendations to the convention by referring to the serious divisions on the immigration question among trade unions and labor organizations. However, these divisions did not inhibit it from giving its approval to the literacy test, on the ground that the replies to the questionnaire submitted to affiliated unions showed a majority in favor of restriction.[35] Once again, more than half the speakers in the debate opposed the recommendations, using similar arguments to those of the previous year. Against this weight of strong feeling, the supporters of the test had little to offer but their votes. Their speeches were few in number and, judging from the reports, feeble in content. Yet they won the day by more than two to one on the delegate vote and by five to one on a card vote. Opinion among the delegates seems to have been transformed in the course of a single year.[36]

The year 1897 therefore appears to be a turning point in AFL attitudes to immigration. It accepted an ethnically discriminatory restrictive measure and never reversed that decision, though in the immediately succeeding decade it was notably unenthusiastic about it. This coolness arouses suspicion about the meaning of the 1897 vote. Almost certainly the vote was based on a misunderstanding of the decisions of individual unions. Moreover, organized labor in 1897 was far more divided, confused, and unhappy about the Corliss-Lodge Bill than the voting figures at the AFL convention imply. Indeed, widespread acceptance of the principle of ethnic discrimination in immigration law as applied to Europeans was not achieved for a further decade.

Nevertheless, although the 1897 decision was probably unrepresentative of rank-and-file trade union opinion, as we shall see in the next chapter, it was quite consistent with the successive attempts made over the previous decade to restrict the inflow of what was customarily described as cheap, imported, servile, and degraded foreign unskilled labor, or in common parlance, contract labor. In that sense, 1897 saw the climax of an old campaign rather than, as Erickson suggests, a new departure.

Yet, in another sense, 1897 marked out a new course for the federation. Its formal approval of the literacy test, whatever the doubts about the representativeness of the decision, did in fact end the long-held distinction between voluntary and induced immigration, owing to the incapacity of the literacy test to make that distinction. Furthermore, the principle of ethnic discrimination was adopted as the basis for proposed changes in the immigration law, reflecting the narrowing gap, as labor saw it, between European and Chinese immigrants. The inference now was that the AFL regarded illiterate Southern and Eastern Europeans as no more capable of assimilation than the Chinese. However, the distinction was not obliterated altogether. Unlike the Chinese, these Europeans were not considered the prisoners of an inferior genetic endowment, locked into their biological cells for eternity. For them, there remained the hope of self-improvement and the possibility, one day, of obtaining the coveted prize of entry into the land of opportunity.

NOTES

1. Gerald N. Grob, *Workers and Utopia: A Study of Ideological Conflict in the American Labor Movement, 1865–1900* (Evanston, Ill.: Northwestern University Press, 1961), p. 140.

2. Gompers was President of the AFL from its foundation in 1886 until his death in 1924, with a break of one year in 1894–95.

3. In this they modeled themselves on the British craft unions which grew to maturity between 1850 and 1880.

4. Marc Karson, *American Labor Unions and Politics, 1900–1918* (Carbondale: Southern Illinois University Press, 1958), pp. 117–19.

5. Grob, *Workers and Utopia*, p. 163.

6. Ibid., p. 145.

7. See Chapter Six.

8. Bureau of Labor Statistics of Illinois, *Fourth Biennial Report*, 1886, p. 161.

9. The Brewery Workers, the Boot and Shoe Workers, and the Bakers were among the most prominent of the internationalist or "revolutionary" unions in the first half of the 1890s.

10. The law excluding them was also passed in 1882.

11. *American Federationist*, December 1895, p. 173.

12. Charlotte Erickson, *American Industry and the European Immigrant, 1860–1885* (Cambridge, Mass.: Harvard University Press, 1957), pp. 157–58, 165.

13. Ibid., p. 185; see also p. 165.

14. Ibid., p. 185.

15. Quoted in Samuel P. Orth, "The Alien Contract Labor Law," *Political Science Quarterly* 22 (1907), p. 51.

16. Senate Committee on Education and Labor, *Testimony Relative to Labor and*

Capital, 4 vols. (Washington, D.C., 1885), Vol. 1, 1884, pp. 337, 583, 680; *Cigar Makers' Official Journal*, March 1884, p. 1.

17. American Federation of Labor, *Report of the Proceedings of the Third Annual Convention, 1888*, p. 10 (hereafter referred to as AFL, *Proceedings*); *Report of the Immigration Commission* (61 Cong., 3 Sess., S. Doc. No. 747), Vol. 2, p. 569; Erickson, *American Industry*, p. 168; Orth, "Alien Contract Labor Law," p. 51.

18. AFL, *Proceedings*, 1889, pp. 15, 19, 24; *Reports of the Immigration Commission*, Vol. 2, p. 570.

19. *Proceedings of the Committee on Immigration and Naturalization* (51 Cong., 2 Sess., H. Rep. No. 3472), Vol. 2, pp. 93, 101; *Testimony Taken by the Select Committee of the House of Representatives to Inquire into the Alleged Violation of the Laws Prohibiting the Importation of Contract Laborers, Paupers, Convicts and other Classes* (50 Cong., 1 Sess., H. Misc. Doc. No. 572), Vol. 15, p. 401.

20. *Iron Molders' Journal*, November 1888, May 1896; AFL, *Proceedings*, 1890, pp. 33–34.

21. *Reports of the Immigration Commission*, Vol. 2, p. 571; *Iron Molders' Journal*, May 1897.

22. Samuel Gompers to the Hon. Charles Foster, 18 July 1892, Samuel Gompers Letterbooks (microfilm, Library of the State Historical Society of Wisconsin, Madison).

23. AFL, *Proceedings*, 1892, p. 30; Samuel Gompers to Senator David B. Hill, 23 January 1893, Samuel Gompers Letterbooks; *American Federationist*, March 1917, pp. 189–95; *Iron Molders' Journal*, May 1897; *Reports of the Immigration Commission*, Vol. 2, p. 573.

24. ALF, *Proceedings*, 1893, 1894, and 1895.

25. Ibid, 1893, p. 13; 1894, pp 12, 47.

26. Ibid., 1893, pp. 13 and 42; 1894, p. 12; 1895, pp. 14, 63; *Reports of the Immigration Commission*, Vol. 2, pp. 377, 380, 382; *Reports of the Industrial Commission* (57 Cong., 1 Sess., H. Doc. No. 186), Vol. 15, Section LIX; Orth, "Alien Contract Labor Law," pp. 53, 57.

27. *Proceedings of the Committee on Immigration and Naturalization* (51 Cong., 2 Sess., H. Rept. No. 3472), Vol. 2, pp. 631–32.

28. Ibid., p. 319; William Weihe, President of the Amalgamated Association of Iron, Steel, and Tin Workers, was convinced that "good labor" would not allow itself to be imported. See Senate Committee on Education and Labor, *Testimony*, Vol. 2, p. 7.

29. Samuel Gompers, *Seventy Years of Life and Labour* 2 vols. (London: Hurst and Blackett, 1925), Vol. 2, p. 154; *Proceedings of the Committee on Immigration and Naturalization*, Vol. 2, p. 96.

30. *Reports of the Industrial Commission*, Vol. 15, Section LX.

31. Gompers, *Seventy Years*, Vol. 2, p. 151; *Reports of the Immigration Commission*, Vol. 1, p 99.

32. AFL, *Proceedings*, 1896, pp 24, 49, 81–82.

33. Andrew Furuseth, of the Seamen's Union, disliked the committee's proposals on consular inspection and compulsory citizenship and opposed the report. In the following year he voted in favor of the literacy test. AFL, *Proceedings*, 1896, p. 82; 1897, p. 94.

34. Ibid., 1897, p. 23.

35. Ibid., p. 88. Note that the committee was careful not to say that the majority favored the literacy test.

36. Ibid., pp. 91, 94. The reasons for that apparent change of heart will be discussed in Chapter Six.

6

Labor and Immigration in the 1890s: A Reassessment

It is now time to consider whether the AFL articulated working-class opinion in the 1890s, and if so, to what extent. Despite assertions to the contrary, it could hardly claim to represent the mass of semi-skilled and unskilled workers, who were largely unorganized. It may be more reasonable to assume, however, that decisions reached at AFL conventions accurately reflected the sentiments of the majority of trade union members. We now have to question that assumption in relation to the decision taken at the 1897 convention to endorse the Corliss-Lodge Bill, which favored, *inter alia*, the imposition of a literacy test for immigrants entering the United States. It appears that this decision was an aberration induced by a peculiar combination of circumstances. It represented a deviation both from a conventional set of attitudes and, in the precipitate way in which it was taken, from the gradualist methods by which the AFL had determined its policies on a number of important public issues. Furthermore, post–1897 conventions of the AFL either ignored the question of European immigration or endorsed policies adopted in the first half of the 1890s, as though the year 1897 was a forgotten and perhaps even shameful interlude.

However, after 1900, the AFL began to move slowly towards readopting its earlier line on the literacy test, although it was several years before it finally did so. There is much stronger evidence that by then its policy was more representative of general opinion among ordinary trade union members than was the case in 1897. At that time there was little or no recognition in the labor movement that the literacy test was the appropriate solution to the problems associated with immigration. It is therefore surprising to find the 1897 AFL convention endorsing a measure which had little popular support among the union membership, and equally surprising that so few historians have questioned the representativeness of the decision.

This interpretation of events conflicts with widely accepted opinion on the significance of the 1897 vote. Prominent contemporary figures in American labor organizations, for example, concluded that the AFL's decision commanded majority support among trade unionists.[1] Most labor historians have tacitly accepted this conclusion by merely noting the AFL's decision and by making no attempt to test its accuracy.[2] Philip Foner alone has argued that the votes was a triumph for the skilled leadership of the AFL officers at the convention.[3] This general acceptance of the vote at its face value has misled some historians into supposing that the decision symbolized the erosion of idealism and brotherhood by the swelling tide of racism, already at full flood in the Chinese exclusion movement.[4]

The purpose of this chapter, therefore, is to assess the degree of support among rank-and-file union members for the Corliss-Lodge Bill. Our conclusion is that labor was split far more evenly than the vote implies and that resistance to discriminatory restrictionist legislation was substantial. If that was so, how were the convention delegates persuaded to vote so overwhelmingly for the Corliss-Lodge Bill? The answer is to be found in the manipulation of an ill-informed and uncertain convention membership by a determined and unscrupulous leadership. We differ from Foner in believing that most delegates, far from being resolutely opposed to the literacy test, were in an acute dilemma over the immigration problem and in their confusion proved receptive to management by the leadership. We disagree with Alexander Saxton's assertion that racism had overcome idealism in the reception of European immigrants by the mid–1890s; *that* victory would be delayed for another decade and even then would be incomplete.

The belief that there was little enthusiasm for the tests is justified by a careful examination of the direction and quality of opinion in the ranks of organized labor. By quality of opinion is meant, for example, whether opinion had crystallized or was in a fluid state, how strongly it was held, and how well informed it was. By using a systematic methodology proposed by Lee Benson, it is possible to identify past public opinion more reliably and precisely. The results attained by this method are, Benson argues, more generally acceptable than those which depend on intuitive judgments by historians and on criteria of evaluation usually left implicit and vague.[5]

In order to establish the direction of opinion, Benson suggests the use of various "historical opinion indicators," which are, in order of importance: actions or events; expert estimates of the distribution of opinion; and expressions of opinion by representative or influential persons. In the category of "actions or events" two kinds of activity which indicate opinion are included: (1) official actions of institutions or groups such as resolutions, voting, platforms, and so on; and (2) individual or spontaneous acts such as demonstrations, acts of violence, and strikes.[6] Each of these will be considered in turn.

In attempting to determine the direction of opinion on the literacy test within unions through an examination of official union actions, a check on the voting records of individual unions on the questions submitted to them by the AFL in 1897 would be desirable. However, only in a few cases are such voting records available. To supplement them there are, in a minority of cases, accounts of debates and votes at union conventions taking place immediately before or after 1897 on immigration restriction proposals. In the main, however, we have had to try to reconstruct opinion by indirect methods. The results of this process are summarized in Table 1. Material relating to 31 of the largest and most important trade unions was examined.[7] The results of votes either by referendum or at convention on the desirability of further restriction were recorded in column (a). In the majority of cases there is no record of a vote, and hence tentative estimates were made of the probable vote, had one been taken. These estimates are to be found in column (b). If it appeared that the membership was evenly divided or had good reason for voting either way, this was denoted as "equivocal." Similarly, the results of votes on the literacy test were recorded in column (c) and tentative estimates of probable opinion, where no record of a vote exists, in column (d). These estimates were derived from studying the response of individual unions to immigration in the period immediately before and after 1897. How, for example, did union delegates vote at AFL conventions in the 1890s on immigration resolutions? What was the attitude of the unions to the admission of immigrants into membership? Was immigration identified as one of the causes of insecurity in the trade? What was the extent of socialist influence in the union? And what sentiments were expressed in the editorials and correspondence columns of the union journal? In the majority of cases, enough evidence is available to permit fairly confident replies to the questions and to make plausible estimates of the direction of opinion on the literacy test. This process of creating profiles of union attitudes in order to make plausible inferences about opinion on a specific issue is illustrated by the following brief case studies of some of the more important unions. Similar profiles have been created for all the unions in the table, but it is unnecessary to present each of them here, since the methods employed should be amply demonstrated by the examples chosen.

As early as 1879 the secretary of the Iron and Steel Workers' Union wrote to the Amalgamated Iron Workers' Society of Great Britain expressing concern over the influx of ironworkers to the United States when there was little chance of employment for them. In response to this influx and the importation of contract laborers, the iron and steel workers joined other unions in the campaign to obtain an alien contract labor law. Concomitantly, the union began to stiffen its regulations for the admission of immigrant

Table 1

Opinions of Membership of Selected Trade Unions on Restriction of European Immigration: 1896–1897

Trade Union	Opinion by vote on further restriction (a)	Estimated probable opinion on further restriction (b)	Opinion by vote on literacy test (c)	Estimated probable opinion on literacy test (d)
Barbers	NK	A	NK	E
Boot & Shoe Workers	A[1]	-	NK	E
Brewery Workers	NK	N	NK	N
Bricklayers & Masons[2]	NK	A	NK	N
Carpenters	A[3]	-	A[3]	-
Cigar Makers	A[1]	-	NK	A
Coopers	NK	E	NK	E
Electrical Workers	NK	E	NK	E
Engravers	NK	N	NK	N
Glass Bottle Blowers	A[3]	-	N[3]	-
Granite Cutters	NK	E	NK	E
Hatters	A[3]	-	NK	E
Horseshoers	NK	E	NK	E
Iron Molders	NK	A	NK	E
Iron, Steel & Tin Workers	NK	A	NK	A
Knights of Labor[2]	A[3]	-	A[3]	-
Locomotive Engineers[2]	NK	A	NK	A
Locomotive Firemen[2]	NK	A	NK	E
Machinists	NK	E	NK	E
Meat Cutters	NK	A	NK	E
Mineworkers (UMWA)	A[3]	-	NK	N
Plumbers	NK	E	NK	N
Piano Workers	NK	A	NK	E
Stonecutters	NK	A	NK	E
Tailors	NK	A	NK	E
Textile Unions	NK	E	NK	N
Typographers	NK	E	NK	E
United Garment Workers	A[3]	-	A[3]	-
Western Federation of Miners	NK	N	NK	N
Woodworkers	NK	N	NK	N

SOURCE: Space forbids a full and detailed citation of sources here, but they include federal and state government reports and a comprehensive selection of union journals and union and labor histories.

ABBREVIATIONS: A = Affirmative   N = Negative
                E = Equivocal   NK = Not Known

1. By referendum vote.
2. Not affiliated to AFL.
3. By convention or General Assembly vote.

workers.[8] By the early 1890s the union was an exclusively craft organization. After 1894 its membership declined as a result of unsuccessful strikes, an employer counteroffensive, and the concentration of the industry into larger production units.

Moreover, the adoption of new technology reduced the proportion of skilled men in the workforce and stimulated the employment of unskilled immigrants from Southern and Eastern Europe with no experience in the iron and steel industry. Instead of attempting to recruit these workers to strengthen their bargaining position, the union accused them of collaborating with the employers to undermine skilled trades within the industry. In addition, union members were dismayed by the prospect of closer association with recent immigrants.[9] A refusal to open its own doors implied support for closing the doors of the United States. By 1903 the editor of the union's journal was calling for stricter immigration legislation. However, there is no hard evidence about membership views on the issue of immigration restriction in the 1890s. It is true that at the AFL conventions in 1896 and 1897, the union's president, M. M. Garland, spoke in support of the literacy test, but it is unclear whether the union's national convention had debated the questions submitted to it by the AFL in 1897.[10] Nevertheless, in view of the hostility of union members to immigration from the 1890s and the total absence of support for immigrants in the union's journal, the membership would almost certainly not have opposed the literacy test had that appeared to be an effective means of keeping out unskilled immigrants from Southern and Eastern Europe. Therefore the iron and steel workers can be placed, with some confidence, among supporters of the Corliss-Lodge Bill.

By contrast, the delegates of the Brewery Workers of the 1897 AFL convention voted against the proposals to tighten controls on immigration. They appear not to have been instructed to do so by their union, since its Boston convention "omitted to define its position in this question." The union journal, however, was confident that the majority of union members would not support further restrictions on immigration. From its foundation in 1886, the union had been dominated by German-born socialists, though the Irish- and native-born constituted a growing minority of the membership. Attachment to the principle of working-class solidarity was demonstrated by the organizing policy of the union. Its aim was to recruit all the trades in and around the breweries—teamsters, coopers, engineers, firemen, and maltsters. Adoption of the industrial rather than the craft form of organization "encouraged the growth of class rather than job consciousness" and stressed the need for solidarity. This all-inclusiveness predisposed the union to protect itself against the economic consequences of immigration by recruiting the immigrants rather than by restricting their entry by law. Accordingly this union has been placed in the ranks of those opposing the literacy test.[11]

The Boot and Shoe Workers' Union falls into the equivocal category. It was reported as having voted in favor of restriction in its response to the AFL questionnaire in 1897. Accordingly, its delegate to the AFL convention supported restriction and voted for the literacy test, albeit against his own convictions. In doing so he reversed the union's role at the convention of the previous year. It might appear that the leadership changed its vote on immigration restriction in response to an expression of opinion from the union.[12]

However, the vote of the union is not free from ambiguity. On the one hand, as Horace M. Eaton, the union secretary, testified, whenever the question of immigration restriction was submitted to the rank and file, in New England at least, they voted for it. Union members clearly identified immigration as one of the major causes of increasing unemployment and declining wage levels. Nevertheless, union affirmation of support for general restriction in 1897 did not entail a specific endorsement of the literacy test, and there can be no assurance, consequently, that in casting his vote to endorse the Corliss-Lodge Bill at the AFL convention the union delegate was accurately representing the opinion of the membership.[13]

The ambiguity of the delegate's vote is heightened when we consider the differential impact of immigration on the union's membership and the changing political and industrial strategy of the union itself. Evidence that union members resented immigration was drawn mainly from the New England and New York regions, which were the first to feel the impact of immigration from Southern and Eastern Europe. Elsewhere the effects of job competition from recent immigrants had barely been registered. In the United States as a whole the ethnic composition of the work force in the footwear industry remained largely unchanged between 1880 and 1900. About one-third of the workers were foreign-born, and among these the Germans and the Irish predominated in 1900 as they had in 1880. It was only in the 1890s that the industry's labor force began to be recruited principally from the countries of Southern and Eastern Europe.[14] Clearly, evidence about feelings of hostility to immigration taken from regions suffering most acutely from the influx of Southern and Eastern Europeans would be unrepresentative of the attitudes of workers in other areas where this form of competition was insignificant. Hence the precise meaning of votes registered by union members in favor of a greater degree of restrictiveness in immigration legislation might have varied from region to region. In other words, support for restriction need not have implied an endorsement of the literacy test, and the further members were from the cities and towns of the Northeast, the less likely that the restrictionists would support such a novel and "radical" proposal.

The political and tactical context of the 1897 vote also requires comment. In the 1890s there was a strong socialist influence in the union, despite its Irish leadership. Its two chief officers, John F. Tobin and Horace M. Eaton, were both socialists, and their economic policies owed much to Socialist Labor Party influence. They disdained the high dues and benefit systems of most contemporary craft unions and pursued a policy of frequent strikes and support for local militancy. Though an endorsement of the Socialist Labor Party was defeated at the union's 1897 convention, a new Marxist preamble to the constitution was adopted, albeit narrowly. The socialist influence, though arising from the severe effects of mechanization in the industry and not from ideas of solidarity derived from the industrial form of organization, nor from Marxist internationalism, may nevertheless be interpreted as having had a softening effect on attitudes towards immigrants. However, after 1899 the union began to substitute for its socialist-inspired industrial policies the traditional craft union recipe of high dues and high benefits, and to concentrate on using the union stamp as a means of maintaining wages. It then became more exclusive in its policies, devoting its major efforts to the minority of workers in the industry who had attained a contract with the employers on the basis of the union stamp. "Organized selfishness" of this type implied diminishing sympathy for outsiders, including immigrants. Intolerant comments on recent immigrants in the union journal in 1903, which compared immigrants to rotten apples, reflected this new exclusiveness. Consequently it comes as no surprise to learn that Italian and other recent immigrants working in the shoe industry turned to a newly formed rival organization, the United Shoe Workers' Union, for protection and support.[15]

It seems abundantly clear, then, that the union's vote on immigration in 1897 took place in a period of transition, both in the ethnic composition of the industry's work force and in the policy and tactics pursued by the union. The leadership was coming to recognize the inadequacy of socialist-inspired industrial policies, though still paying lip service to the need to establish a socialist commonwealth. It is a matter of judgment whether this transition had gone far enough by 1897 for us to interpret the union's support for the literacy test at the AFL convention as truly representatiive of rank-and-file opinion. Consequently the union has been placed in the company of those whose policies on immigration could not be precisely defined.

The woodworkers present a more straightforward case of opposition to the literacy test. In the three decades before 1900 the furniture and woodworking industries had undergone a revolution. The introduction of labor-saving machinery in the 1870s and its diffusion in the subsequent decades, the development of factory production, and the influx of unskilled, mainly immigrant workers to operate the machines, made the old crafts obsolete. In New York, competition from the machine transformed the "once flourishing craft [of cabinetmaking] into a small remnant," and only the older craftsmen remained.[16] The furniture workers, though a union of their trade existed in the 1870s, were insufficiently organized to resist the innovations or control the pace and manner of their introduction. Consequently, as

Gompers testified to the Ford Committee in 1888, their wage fell by between 20 and 50 percent between 1882 and 1886.[17]

The union of the workers in the industry in 1897 was the Amalgamated Woodworkers' International Union, formed in 1896 out of an amalgamation of the Machine Woodworkers and the Furniture Workers. There is no record in the union journal of a vote of the membership on the AFL's questionnaire. It is known, however, that Thomas I. Kidd, the union's secretary and delegate to the 1896 and 1897 AFL conventions, voted against the literacy test proposal and contributed a number of powerful editorials in the union journal attacking the policy of increased immigration restriction.[18] His vote and his published views probably reflected the opinion of both actual and potential members of his union. The woodworkers were mainly unskilled immigrant laborers operating machines. According to a survey published by the Immigration Commission, out of a sample of employees in the furniture industry, about 60 percent were foreign-born and another 20 percent were native-born of foreign parentage. On the other hand, woodworkers in the planing mills were mainly native American, and a higher percentage of them were organized. Wage levels were higher than in the furniture industry and foreign-born workers were zealous in seeking to maintain wage levels.[19] It is unclear what the attitude of the mill workers was to further restrictions on immigration, though it is at least arguable that stronger union organization in the mills protected them against the worst effects of immigration and hence moderated their position on restriction. It is therefore quite plausible that Kidd's hostility to the literacy test at the 1896 and 1897 AFL conventions would be popular with native-born as well as foreign-born members of his union.

Allowing for some unavoidable error in the creation of these profiles of union attitudes and in the inferences to be drawn from them, we can still find little evidence of enthusiastic support for the literacy test among union members. It is undeniable that one-quarter of the unions noted in the table voted in favor of further restriction. If we add the unions estimated to have been favorable to further restriction, then one-half of the unions in the sample would have supported additional immigration restrictions. If one further assumes that half the "equivocal" unions would have chosen further restrictions, then about two-thirds of the total sample could be classed as restrictionist.

However, the important question, given the doubts about the representativeness of the 1897 vote, is how many of these restrictionist unions supported the literacy test. It would appear that about one-fifth of the total sample were supporters or probably supporters of the test, whilst about one-third opposed or probably opposed it. The rest, about half the total number, were undecided or confused, and their votes could have gone either way. On the assumption that one-half of the equivocal unions would have opted for the literacy test, the total number of unions then in favor of it would still have been slightly less than a majority of the sample. The even division of opinion noted here was reflected in the debate and voting at the 1897 AFL convention but clearly does not explain the 1897 vote. If these tentative estimates of opinion are approximately correct, it would be unwise to argue that the vote resulted from a ground swell of support from union membership.

Further evidence about opinion on immigration among rank-and-file union members has been obtained from the minutes of a small sample of union locals and trades councils in the state of Wisconsin.[20] In addition, the state's Bureau of Labor and Industrial Statistics, in its report for 1887–88, surveyed the opinion of employees on the question of immigration, asking specifically whether immigration was harmful to the trade or industry in which the respondents were employed. About 60 percent of the respondents thought that immigration harmed them, but the replies also showed that workers in only about 40 percent of the trades and industries considered themselves adversely affected by immigrant competition.[21] If this report is to be taken seriously as an index of opinion, it seems that a substantial proportion of the labor force in Wisconsin (and, by the commission's own comparison, in the rest of the United States) considered immigration to be detrimental to its interests. What the report does not tell us is the degree of alarm with which immigration was regarded by workingmen, and whether they ranked it as a major grievance calling for remedial legislation. If, as Benson argues, opinion is perhaps best indicated by actions or events, some insight into the depth of feeling on the immigration question in the state may be obtained from the proceedings of local branches of trade unions, or local labor federations. Do these show that resolutions hostile to immigration were passed spontaneously by the local unions for transmission to the union's headquarters or to the state federation of labor or other bodies? Or was the subject of immigration largely ignored in the activities of local unions or treated routinely and in a formal way without real commitment? The minutes of a small sample of union locals and trades councils covering the period from the late 1880s to the 1900s may supply an answer.[22]

The most important finding is that local unions paid little attention to issues which could be resolved only by changes in the law at a state or federal level, for example the eight-hour day, child labor, immigration, and so on. Locals were absorbed by routine matters of organization and relations with local employees. The carpenters and the painters and decorators of Lake Geneva, Wisconsin, for example, devoted almost the whole of their local union meetings to such matters as local elections in the union, income and expenditure, fines on members, the wording of contracts with employers, payment of sickness benefits, and regulations regarding apprentices. Other locals of carpenters, trainmen, bricklayers, and typographers were equally absorbed in local minutiae.[23] Only on rare occasions were members of locals motivated to pass resolutions on wider issues which could not be resolved at a local level. The railroad trainmen of Baraboo, Wisconsin, for instance, were worried over the effects on the train service of bills before the state legislature.[24] But perhaps union members did not regard the local branch meeting as the appropriate forum for the discussion of issues of general importance. The absence of resolutions on immigration should not, therefore, be interpreted as evidence of indifference to the problem.

On the other hand, time was occasionally taken up at these locals' meetings by discussion of general issues referred to them by other bodies, their national union, for example, or the AFL or the State Federation of Labor. Members of the locals clearly thought there was no incongruity in taking up these questions, and therefore a general issue with local implications and capable of arousing strong feeling would have been open for discussion at local union meetings. Often items were placed on the agenda of the local trades councils as the result of prior decisions taken at meetings of affiliated local unions; delegates would be expected to convey the sentiments of their locals or to report back the item for further discussion. For example, the Coopers' Union in Superior, Wisconsin, requested the Trades and Labor Assembly to memorialize Congress on the need to suppress convict labor. This request was approved and delegates were instructed to report the matter to their local unions, where opportunity for discussion existed.[25] If this was the normal procedure and if immigration was a subject which aroused strong feelings among rank-and-file members, it is reasonable to suppose that discussion about this and the other emotive issues would have taken place at local union meetings, with the full recognition that whilst the local itself might have little weight, its concern in the form of a resolution would be passed on to a body capable of wielding wider influence.

It may still be objected that the very small sample of local unions whose records have been examined precludes any generalization about the intensity of feeling among workingmen in general in Wisconsin. This objection has obvious force, and it would be incautious to advance any but the most tentative conclusions. Nevertheless, Wisconsin's Bureau of Labor Statistics noted that carpenters and bricklayers felt themselves to be among the most badly injured by immigrant competition. In their locals, above all, one might expect to come across signs of hostility to immigration. But in none of the carpenters' and bricklayers' locals whose minute books were available were resolutions against immigration passed, except at the behest of some other organization.[26] This finding leads to the inference that the intensity of opinion against immigration within the trades of carpentry and bricklaying was insufficiently great to stimulate spontaneous action against it. This is not to say that, if requested by their national union or local trades council or state federation, locals in these trades would not pass resolutions condemning immigration.[27] But the passage of such resolutions tells us no more than the report of the Bureau of Labor Statistics about the strength of local feeling, and nothing about the kind of restriction favored by the rank and file. These examples of endorsements of decisions taken elsewhere are paralleled in the case of the trades councils in the state. Initiatives taken by these bodies were generally limited to local matters, and only on very rare occasions did they originate a resolution about national issues. Their normal procedure was to receive correspondence from a variety of outside bodies and to take action on the proposals contained therein.

Given the small sample, and the need for caution in making deductions from the limited evidence available, are we justified in concluding that the alleged concern of Wisconsin workers over immigration was too shallow to lead to a spontaneous outpouring of indignation among the local trade union and labor organizations? The evidence suggests that, for the rank-and-file trade union member, what mattered above all was the improvement of local wages and conditions and the strengthening of the local union organization as a means to that end. Immigration restriction was either peripheral to these major objectives or possibly regarded as a breach of traditional policy. Nowhere do we find records of discussions on alternative methods of immigration restriction or ways of making the law more effective. There is nothing in the minutes of these local unions to lead us to modify our earlier conclusion that the 1897 vote at the AFL was not the product of a substantial shift of opinion among ordinary trade union members.

Is this conclusion corroborated by examination of the less ordered, extraparliamentary actions of union members in the form of demonstrations and strikes? Careful examination of strike statistics lends no credence to the view that feeling among trade unionists in the 1890s was greatly aroused over the immigration issue.[28] The proportion of strikes in the last two decades of the nineteenth century caused by opposition to immigration was minute. Attempts to increase wages, to reduce hours, or to prevent wage reductions and the lengthening of hours accounted for the overwhelming majority of strikes. Strikes called explicitly against the employment of particular categories of workers were a tiny minority, and of these, strikes specifically directed against the employment of foreigners occurred on extremely rare occasions. A more detailed analysis of major strikes bears out these findings. Of course, the element of uncertainty affecting these conclusions due to unconscious motivation on the part of the strikers cannot be removed. However, it is probable that strikes were a better indicator of discontent in the 1880s and 1890s than they have been in the twentieth century because of their greater spontaneity and lower degree of management by union officials.[29] Again, while workers may have considered that strikes were an inappropriate means of combatting immigration, such rational calculation could have been expected only in cases where indignation and stress levels were fairly low. Profound discontent about immigrants would almost certainly have shown itself in industrial action in the same way that workers struck against convict labor, another "evil" which they otherwise sought to remove by remedial legislation.[30] Finally, the strike statistics do not show any increase in the number of strikes against particular categories of workers during the 1890s, a time when, if we are to believe in the "conversion" of 1897, such strikes should perhaps have been on the increase. Whilst we should be cautious in drawing conclusions from these strike statistics, taken in conjunction with the other evidence they offer no support for the idea that there was a swelling tide of indignation at recent immigration which was reflected in the 1897 vote.

This view is reinforced by estimates of labor opinion made by government officials or by private individuals whose position enabled them to make an informed assessment of current opinion. The best-informed public officials were the federal and state commissioners of labor, charged with reporting to the legislatures on the conditions and opinions of laboring men. Much of the evidence presented in their reports is in the form of replies to questionnaires which had been submitted to labor organizations or to individuals. In the period from 1886 to the early 1890s opinion was, in the main, lukewarm towards further restriction, though a strong minority of replies were firmly in favor of strengthening the immigration law, since some immigration was felt to be harmful.[31] For the mid- to the late–1890s we are dependent on the reports from one state, New York, and although they are thorough and wide-ranging, they cannot be regarded as expressing the direction of worker opinion in the United States as a whole.

Nevertheless, two features of these reports stand out. First, immigration was a cause of serious and increasing concern among wage earners, and this was reflected in the growth of restrictionist views between 1894 and 1896. In 1894, for example, trade union locals throughout the state were invited by the Bureau of Labor Statistics to recommend issues requiring legislation. The respondents placed immigration restriction in an important but not pre-eminent position. No radical measures for solving the problem were proposed, emphasis being on the proper enforcement of the Contract Labor Law.[32] In the following year the bureau drew the public's attention to labor's major complaint in respect of immigration, the large number of seasonal workers from Europe, the so-called "birds of passage." These constituted a major problem for New Yorkers, even though a large proportion of them originated in the British Isles, Belgium, Holland, Switzerland, and other parts of Northwest Europe. These transients provoked New Yorkers to scornful denunciation of their practice of accumulating savings for the subsequent consumption of "porridge, bloaters, maccaroni and sauerkraut" on the other side of the Atlantic.[33]

Yet this was hostility to a particular category of immigrant and does not prepare us for the assessment in the 1896 report that foreign labor competition was, in the eyes of workingmen, the greatest difficulty that organized labor had to contend with, calling for urgent amendments to immigration law.[34] However, the bureau's own evidence, published subsequently, contradicted its earlier conclusion. After a survey of opinion among more than one thousand local labor unions in New York State, the bureau estimated that three-quarters of the locals, having about 60 percent of the total membership, had not been adversely affected by immigration, either through displacement or lower wages. The remaining organizations, with about 40 percent of the membership, reported that they had been "directly and detrimentally affected" by immigrant labor.[35] In view of this it is implausible to contend that immigration was organized labor's greatest problem.

Nevertheless, those union members whose employment was so far unaffected were undoubtedly apprehensive about future threats to their welfare and status from immigrant competitors. Others, like one Brooklyn Bricklayers' local, supported restriction "on general principles," even though the members were not directly affected by competition from foreigners.[36] Assessment of the degree of unease about immigration on the basis of replies to questions about existing adverse economic consequences may underestimate the importance of the issue to workingmen. There can be little doubt that it loomed larger in their consciousness than it had two years earlier and that more of them than hitherto were prepared to adopt a radical solution to the problem.

However, and this is the second conclusion to be drawn from these reports, the radical solution actually adopted was not the literacy test. Instead, the 1897 resolution of the New York State Federation of Labor, adopted by referendum vote of affiliated unions, recommended a law suspending immigration for five years or until labor demand had caught up with supply.[37] It is noteworthy that the federation's chosen method of restriction was suspension of immigration from whatever source, and not the literacy test, which would have discriminated along ethnic lines and would not have prevented migration of most "birds of passage" from Northwest Europe. It thus appears that in New York, arguably the state most affected by immigration, a harder line on restriction among workingmen did not result in support for the policy expressed by the AFL. This serves to deepen scepticism about the representativeness of the 1897 decision.

Other well-informed observers offered contradictory evidence on the direction of opinion. Speaking about Indiana, where he was labor commissioner, Lycurgus P. McCormack emphasized that he came across little restrictionist sentiment either in the labor press or at the numerous union conventions he attended. In flat denial of this, David Black, of the Iron Molders' Union, claimed to detect widespread support for the exclusion of illiterate immigrants.[38] Perhaps the most reliable evidence on this score came from two socialist trade unionists, P. J. Conlon and Horace Eaton, who, though antirestrictionist themselves, had to admit that restrictionist attitudes were widely held.[39] Such general sentiments, though, were quite compatible with opposition to the literacy test, a point specifically made by J. G. Schonfarber, a Knights of Labor official. So far as he could see, restrictionists were unable to agree on the form new restrictive legislation should take. There may also have been a division of opinion between the majority of labor leaders and the rank and file. According to Mrs. T. H. Symonds, a trade unionist and labor editor, ordinary union members were far less happy about restriction, particularly as so many were foreigners themselves and felt guilty about erecting barriers.[40]

Finally, we must turn to the opinions of elected officials of trade unions. These are important because they reflect powerful rank-and-file views or indicate the possible evolution of the public mind in the future. Their position may fit them to perceive, more clearly than the men they represent, the development of certain kinds of danger to their members' interests. Samuel Gompers, for example, wrote that because of his familiarity with Castle Garden and with areas of immigrant concentration in New York City, he "appreciated the seriousness of the immigration problem in advance of many of the other trade unionists."[41] This different perspective, and the influence these men wielded as representatives, conferred on them a degree of authority to form public opinion not granted to ordinary trade union members. This influence could not easily be exerted when it was opposed by aroused and well-informed rank-and-file opinion, but where the ordinary members were indifferent, confused, or not immediately and adversely affected by events, leaders would have considerable power to shape opinion.

What, then, were trade union leaders advising their members about immigration restriction in the late 1890s? Out of a sample of 15 prominent officials, two-thirds supported additional immigration restriction of some kind. They included powerful figures like M. M. Garland of the Iron and Steel Workers, James Duncan of the Granite Cutters, John Mitchell of the Mineworkers, Peter McGuire of the Carpenters, George Perkins of the Cigar Makers, and of course Gompers himself.[42] This group divided over the method of restriction to be adopted. More than half, but a minority of the total sample, advocated the literacy test. Men like Gompers, Duncan, and McGuire supported it because it would cut levels of immigration substantially and attract the support of a majority of members of the U.S. Congress. But presumably it also had the advantage of appearing to be nondiscriminatory whilst in practice striking disproportionately at immigrants from particular ethnic groups.[43] Other restrictionists in the group, however, opposed the literacy test because, they said, illiteracy could not be equated with foolishness, knavery, or inferiority. But what alternative restrictive measures did they commend to their members? Here their solutions were diverse, impractical, and confused. They ranged from George Perkins' suggestion of consular inspection to make the numbers admitted to the United States proportional to the number of jobs available, to John

Mitchell's prescription of total prohibition of immigration and, three years later, his acceptance of the nebulous concept of restricting immigration to those able to command the union rate of wages. For restrictionists, there was no single, obvious alternative to the Corliss-Lodge Bill. Of course, opponents of any further restriction like Eaton of the Boot and Shoe Workers, John McBride of the Mineworkers, and Kidd of the Woodworkers were relatively untroubled by these doubts and hesitations. For them, restriction was merely "puttering with the effects of capitalism" and "assisting our political opponents to spring another senseless, hypocritical and barbarous political issue."[44]

If the majority of trade union leaders were advising their members to support restriction, if not the literacy test, advice being received from people who sympathized with the aspirations of labor in the 1890s and who occupied positions of real or potential influence as journalists, clergymen, or politicians tended in the opposite direction. Slightly under half of this group argued for restriction but opposed the literacy test. They included influential figures like Henry D. Lloyd, John P. Altgeld, and George E. McNeill. Lloyd was extremely persuasive, emphasizing out of his own knowledge and experience the dangers to society from the rule of wealth, and stressing that capitalism, not immigration, was at the root of social ills. The only immigrants he would attempt to keep out were those under contract, who were "used by capital as a club to knock out the brains of working men." The antirestrictionists were mainly socialists or anarchists, like Daniel De Leon, Eugene Debs, Max Hayes, and Benjamin Tucker. From this group came some of the most scathing criticism of the literacy test which members of labor organizations were likely to meet.[45] Out of the entire sample of 18, only 3 urged their readers to support further restriction by means of the literacy test. Clearly, then, neither among trade union leaders nor among influential figures in, or on the fringe of, the labor movement was there anything like unanimous support for the Corliss-Lodge Bill.

This examination of the direction of opinion amply confirms the doubts expressed initially about the representativeness of the 1897 vote. These doubts are further reinforced when we ask whether the opinion expressed in that vote could be characterized as, for example, firm or fluid, convinced or uncertain, ignorant or well informed. Now while it is evident that the representatives of organized labor in the 1890s were moving towards tougher restriction, they were as yet unprepared for a discriminatory measure like the literacy test and revealed a good deal of uncertainty in developing their position. Compare this uncertainty and the sudden, even precipitate, endorsement of the test in 1897 with the steady pursuit over a long period of time of the eight-hour day, child labor legislation, and other measures where opinion was well thought out and firmly held.

Again, interesting light is shed on the quality of the opinion expressed in 1897 by determining how important the immigration question was to members of labor organizations. If a problem is only of moderate importance, the possibility of radical remedial measures emerging must be remote. Hence it is important to relate labor opinion on immigration restriction and the literacy test to opinion on other issues affecting the lives of workingmen, and to attempt to place these concerns in order of priority. Among demands made on the legislatures, those calling for tougher immigration restriction occupied a subordinate position. It is difficult to accept that organized labor as a whole attached major significance to the immigration issue before the 1897 vote. A moderate commitment to immigration restriction was unlikely, therefore, to have generated a sudden, spontaneous, and overwhelming endorsement of a radical method of dealing with the problem.[46]

As to the intensity of opinion on this issue, it is arguable that a favorable vote of five to one indicated a current of strong feeling in the ranks of organized labor. It is equally possible that it mainly represented reluctant acquiescence. If enthusiasm there was, it was not sustained. This is borne out by the fate of the literacy test resolution at the AFL conventions in the following decade. According to Foner, from 1897 onwards the AFL "called for more and more stringent legislation to restrict immigration."[47] Yet, in fact, it was not until 1905 that another resolution endorsing the literacy test was carried by an AFL convention. In the intervening period, interest in European immigration was perfunctory, and there was no enthusiasm for re-endorsing the literacy test. The tentative way in which the literacy test was reintroduced into AFL conventions testified to the lack of confidence among the members of the Executive Council that it commanded majority support. Such groping and hesitant movement is the very opposite of the picture drawn by Foner. Even if the vote of 1897 had been representative, it had ceased to be so shortly afterwards and remained a minority view for almost another decade. In other words, opinion favorable to the literacy test, if such it was, was of short duration and less likely to have had deep roots and firm support.

We assume, finally, that informed opinion tends to be stronger and more durable than uninformed. If so, whilst it is impossible to determine accurately how knowledgeable convention delegates were on the question of immigration restriction, we may doubt whether the majority were well informed on the pros and cons of the debate and on the practical political possibilities. There had been very little time for the education and conversion of the rank and file by restrictionist leaders. In comparison with the major planks of the AFL's legislative program in the late 1890s, the literacy test had a short history and a dubious pedigree. In the circumstances, we may agree with Jacob Schonfarber of the Knights of Labor, who doubted whether the people understood the literacy test well enough to pass judgment on it.[48]

If opinion on the literacy test was as lukewarm as this, we have now to try to explain the decisive vote in its favor in 1897. It seems probable that the restrictionist leadership of the AFL used its position to manipulate the convention delegates and that they in turn, for a variety of reasons, proved responsive to this pressure. The first stage in the process of creating an opinion favorable to the literacy test occurred when the Executive Council of the AFL failed to carry out the instructions of the 1896 convention to refer the "entire matter" of immigration restriction to affiliated unions. Instead, the circulated questionnaire omitted all reference to the literacy test as a method of limiting immigration, a serious and deliberate omission.[49] It is clear from Gompers's correspondence at the time that he was interested in obtaining a vote not for or against the literacy test but for or against further restriction. His awareness of the implications of probable voting patterns and of the procedure to be followed at the convention in the light of the referendum result is evidence that he had given careful thought to the form in which the questionnaire should be submitted.[50]

Omission of the literacy test, then, was not an error but the result of careful calculation about how best to obtain a vote in its favor at the next convention. It will readily be appreciated that, in the absence of a question specifically on the literacy test, unions could not mandate their delegates either for or against. This is precisely the result Gompers and his associates had sought. To have submitted a question on the test would have run the risk of unions voting against it and thus hamstringing the subsequent convention. As it was, Gompers could plausibly argue that the delegates would have *carte blanche* to determine the most appropriate means of implementing the general restrictionist sentiment, and the leadership a clear field in which to exercise its persuasive talents.

In embarking on this campaign of persuasion, the leadership had a stronger hand than in the previous year. In the first place, it had on its side most of the delegates from the large unions. It is clear from the voting figures on the literacy test resolution that the block vote of the large unions was responsible for the size of the majority in support of the literacy test. On a delegate count, there was little more than a two to one majority in favor, which was boosted to five to one on the card ballot.[51] The "conversion" of these delegates, and no doubt some from smaller unions as well, can be at least partially explained by a recognition of the following factors.

In 1896 the literacy test had been only one of a number of quite controversial recommendations for limiting immigration which were presented to the convention as a unified package. Some delegates supported the literacy test but opposed other provisions in the package like consular inspection and stricter civil and educational qualifications for naturalization.[52] However, in 1897, support for the literacy test was not split in this way since the resolution before the convention simply invited endorsement of the Corliss-Lodge Bill.

Second, the leadership was able to deploy an argument, unavailable in the previous year, that the referendum result virtually bound the delegates to support the literacy test. Andrew Furuseth of the Seamen's Union argued that the resolution expressing support for the Corliss-Lodge Bill was as near as the delegates could get to meeting the instructions of their unions.[53] In thus invoking popular support, Furuseth was either very ill-informed or disingenuous in the extreme, for the delegates, as we have seen, had not been mandated at all on the literacy test as a result of the referendum. But that fact itself gave the delegates room for maneuver and placed no restriction in their way in responding to the argument of popular support.

Third, in the interval between the conventions, both the Senate and the House of Representatives had passed the Corliss-Lodge Bill and the House had repassed it over Cleveland's veto. Both Gompers and the convention committee reporting on immigration referred to this, assuming that delegates would be impressed by the large congressional majorities and by the politically practical nature of the literacy measure. No alternative restrictionist proposal commanded as much political support at this time.

The precise influence which swung the delegates into the literacy test lobby in 1897 is unclear, since we have only the barest account of the speeches at the convention and no knowledge of what went on behind the scenes. The factors outlined above may have been enough to persuade the undecided and wavering delegates of 1896 to give a massive vote for the literacy test the following year. But it is also highly probable that Gompers and his close associates in the AFL hierarchy, McGuire, Duncan, Garland, and Henry White, engaged in powerful lobbying on its behalf. The conditions for successful horse-trading were present. Historians have testified to the immense personal authority of Gompers in the trade union movement and to the resourceful way in which his regime "imposed upon the loose federation almost a personal dictatorship" in nontrade matters. The organizing activities of the AFL had been extremely useful to individual unions in recruiting members; indeed, some unions had come into existence as a result of the initial efforts of AFL organizers.[54] The credit which Gompers had accumulated in this and other ways could be called upon at AFL conventions when he needed it, with the following provisos: that his proposals did not breach a union's autonomy in matters connected with its own trade or industry; that they did not intrude into very sensitive and divisive areas like partisan politics; and that they did not conflict with a firm position to which delegates had been committed by their unions. All these provisions were satisfied on this occasion. Consequently, though it is impossible to prove the case, it is likely that Gompers was able to reap the benefit of past services and present influence in winning votes for the literacy test.

In these circumstances, delegates took the easiest course open to them and endorsed what they had hitherto resisted or ignored. The failure of delegates to recommit themselves to this policy for almost another decade is, in part, testimony to the shallowness of their conviction in 1897. The AFL's vote, accordingly, did not represent a strong commitment to the literacy test, or a triumph for racism over idealism in the approach to immigration. Within ten years, however, egalitarian and humanitarian sentiments in the organized labor movement had been weakened sufficiently for the AFL to begin to give continuous and enthusiastic support for the literacy test, embodying in immigration legislation for Europeans the same principle of ethnic discrimination which had been applied earlier to the Chinese.

NOTES

1. See, e.g., David Black in *Iron Molders' Journal*, March 1898.

2. Philip Taft, *The A.F. of L. in the Time of Gompers* (New York: Harper, 1957), p. 306; Lewis L. Lorwin, *The American Federation of Labor: History, Policies, and Prospects* (Washington, D.C.: The Brookings Institution, 1933), p. 53; Henry Pelling, *American Labor* (Chicago: University of Chicago Press, 1960), p. 102.

3. Philip S. Foner, *History of the Labor Movement in the United States*, 4 vols. (1947; rpt. New York: International Publishers, 1962), Vol. 2, pp. 363–64.

4. Alexander Saxton, "Race and the House of Labor," in Gary B. Nash and Richard Weiss, eds., *The Great Fear: Race in the Mind of America* (New York: Holt, Rinehart and Winston, 1970), pp. 115–16.

5. Lee Benson, "An Approach to the Scientific Study of Past Public Opinion," *Public Opinion Quarterly* 31 (1967): 526–29. Note also the view of Harry Braverman that "interpretation of the opinions, feelings, sentiments and changing moods of the working class is best accomplished by experienced and well-attuned observers and participants" who at their best "convey a solidity, a depth and subtlety of observation . . . that is entirely absent from the tabulations of sociology." Harry Braverman, *Labor and Monopoly Capital: The Degradation of Work in the Twentieth Century* (New York: Monthly Review Press, 1974), p. 30.

6. Benson, "Approach," pp. 557–58.

7. Space forbids a full and detailed citation of sources here, but they include federal and state government reports and a comprehensive selection of union journals and union and labor histories.

8. Jesse S. Robinson, *The Amalgamated Association of Iron, Steel, and Tin Workers* (Baltimore: Johns Hopkins Press, 1920), p. 44; Gerd Korman, *Industrialization, Immigrants, and Americanizers* (Madison: State Historical Society of Wisconsin, 1967), p. 51.

9. *Report on Conditions of Employment in the Iron and Steel Industry in the United States*, Vol. 3, *Working Conditions and the Relations of Employers and Employees* (62 Cong., 1 Sess., S. Doc. No. 110), pp. 31–37, 149–51; David Brody, *Steelworkers in America* (1960; rpt. New York: Harper Torchbooks, 1969), pp. 119–21.

10. American Federation of Labor, *Report of the Proceedings of the Sixteenth Annual Convention*, 1896, p. 82 (hereafter referred to as AFL, *Proceedings*); AFL, *Proceedings*, 1897, p. 90; *Reports of the Industrial Commission* (56 Cong., 2 Sess., H. Doc. No. 495), Vol. 7, pp. 86, 392–94.

11. *Brauer-Zeitung*, 23 April 1891, 4 December 1897, 25 December 1897; AFL, *Proceedings*, 1897, p. 91; John H. M. Laslett, *Labor and the Left: A Study of Socialist and Radical Influences in the American Labor Movement, 1881–1924* (New York: Basic

Books, 1970), pp. 13, 16–17; Herman Schlütter, *The Brewing Industry and the Brewery Workers' Movement in America* (Cincinnati, 1910), p. 134.

12. *Reports of the Industrial Commission,* Vol. 7, p. 371; AFL, *Proceedings,* 1896, p. 82.

13. *Reports of the Industrial Commission,* Vol. 7, p. 371; Bureau of Statistics of Labor of the State of New York, *Sixteenth Annual Report,* 1898, pp. 1072–74; *The Shoe Workers' Journal,* July 1903.

14. *Reports of the Immigration Commission,* 41 vols. (61 Cong., 2 Sess., S. Doc. No. 633), Vol. 12, pp. 225–27; Edwin Fenton, "Immigrants and Unions, A Case Study: Italians and American Labor, 1870–1920" (Ph.D. diss., Harvard University, 1957), pp. 305–7; *Reports of the Industrial Commission,* Vol. 15, Section 37.

15. Laslett, *Labor and the Left,* pp. 66–91, 96 n. 61; *The Shoe Workers' Journal,* July 1903.

16. Clyde Griffen, "Workers Divided: The Effect of Craft and Ethnic Differences in Poughkeepsie, New York, 1850–1880," in Stephan Thernstrom and Richard Sennett, eds., *Nineteenth-Century Cities: Essays in the New Urban History* (New Haven: Yale University Press, 1969), p. 84; Walter E. Weyl and A. M. Sakolski, "Conditions of Entrance to the Principal Trades," *Bulletin of the Bureau of Labor* No. 67 (1906): 690, 719; *Reports of the Industrial Commission,* Vol. 15, Section 37.

17. *Testimony Taken by the Select Committee of the House of Representatives to Inquire into the Alleged Violation of the Laws Prohibiting the Importation of Contract Laborers, Paupers, Convicts and Other Classes* (50 Cong., 1 Sess., H. Misc. Doc. No. 572), Vol. 15, p. 397.

18. *International Woodworker,* December 1890, January 1896, July 1896, December 1896, July 1897, December 1897, January 1898; AFL, *Proceedings,* 1897, p. 94.

19. *Reports of the Immigration Commission* (61 Cong., 3 Sess., S. Doc. No. 747), Vol. 1, p. 307; Weyl and Sakolski, "Conditions of Entrance," p. 690; *International Woodworker,* December 1897.

20. Wisconsin Bureau of Labor and Industrial Statistics, *Second Biennial Report,* 1885–86, Part 9, pp. 416–26.

21. Ibid., *Third Biennial Report,* 1887–88, pp. xxv, 1–14.

22. These minute books are to be found in the United States Labor Collection, State Historical Society of Wisconsin, Madison.

23. Brotherhood of Painters, Decorators and Paperhangers of America, AFL Local 104, Lake Geneva, Wisconsin, Minutes of Meetings, 1908–13; United Brotherhood of Carpenters and Joiners, AFL Local 290, Lake Genenva, Wisconsin, Minutes of Meetings, 1899–1910.

24. Brotherhood of Railroad Trainmen, Local 177, Baraboo, Wisconsin, Minutes, 1885–89.

25. Superior Trades and Labor Assembly, Minutes, 10 June 1894.

26. Wisconsin Bureau of Labor and Industrial Statistics, *Third Biennial Report,* 1887–88, p. xxvi; Bricklayers', Masons' and Plasterers' International Union, Local 15, Eau Claire, Wisconsin, Minutes, 1902–10; Local 14, Waukesha, Wisconsin, Papers, 1902–10; United Brotherhood of Carpenters and Joiners, Local 314, Madison, Wisconsin, Minutes, 1899–1910; Local 755, West Superior, Wisconsin, Minutes, 1901–10; Local 161, Kenosha, Wisconsin, Minutes, 1897–1910.

27. Carpenters Local 314, Minutes, 25 February 1902, 27 January 1903; Carpenters Local 161, Minutes, 9 November 1905.

28. *Reports of the Industrial Commission*, Vol. 17, p. 652; Arthur Kornhauser, Robert Dubin, and Arthur M. Ross, eds., *Industrial Conflict* (New York: McGraw Hill, 1954), p. 64.

29. *Reports of the Industrial Commission*, Vol. 17, p. 652–55; Commissioner of Labor, *Sixteenth Annual Report*, 1901, *Strikes and Lockouts* (57 Cong., 1 Sess., H. Doc. No. 18), pp. 41, 357ff.; an analysis of 44 major strikes between 1880 and 1900 with descriptions drawn from John R. Commons et al., *History of Labor in the United States*, 4 vols. (1918; rpt. New York: Augustus M. Kelly, 1966), Vols. 2 and 4, and Foner, *History of the Labor Movement*, Vol. 2; Kornhauser, Dubin, and Ross, *Industrial Conflict*, p. 24.

30. Commons et al., *History of Labor*, Vol. 2, p. 498.

31. See, e.g., New Jersey Bureau of Statistics of Labor and Industries, *Ninth Annual Report*, 1886, p. 181; Connecticut Bureau of Labor Statistics, *Third Annual Report*, 1887, pp. 286–346; Pennsylvania Secretary of Internal Affairs, *Annual Report*, 1889, Vol. 17, Pt. 3.

32. Bureau of Statistics of Labor of the State of New York, *Twelfth Annual Report*, 1894, pp. 372–431.

33. Ibid., *Thirteenth Annual Report*, 1895, pp. 383–92; *Sixteenth Annual Report*, 1898, pp. 1025–26.

34. Ibid., *Fourteenth Annual Report*, 1896, p. 798.

35. Ibid., *Sixteenth Annual Report*, 1898, p. 1036.

36. Ibid., p. 1041.

37. Ibid., p. 1030.

38. *Reports of the Industrial Commission*, Vol. 14, pp. 56–57; *Iron Molders' Journal*, March 1897.

39. *Reports of the Industrial Commission*, Vol. 7, pp. 370–71; *Monthly Journal of the International Association of Machinists*, September, 1897.

40. *Reports of the Industrial Commission*, Vol. 7, pp. 435–37; Vol. 14, pp. 263–65.

41. Samuel Gompers, *Seventy Years of Life and Labor*, 2 vols. (London: Hurst and Blackett, 1925), Vol. 2, p. 158.

42. The sample also includes Thomas Schaffer of the Iron and Steel Workers, Peter J. Conlon of the Machinists, August C. McCraith of the Printers, and Henry White of the Garment Workers.

43. AFL, *Proceedings*, 1896, p. 24; Samuel Gompers to P. J. McGuire, 22 February 1898, Samuel Gompers Letterbooks (microfilm, Library of the State Historical Society of Wisconsin, Madison); *Report of the Committee on Immigration* (54 Cong., 1 Sess., S. Rep. No. 290), Vol. 2, pp. 2–6.

44. *Reports of the Industrial Commission*, Vol. 7, pp. 160–80; Vol. 8, p. 51; John Mitchell, *Organized Labor* (Philadelphia: American Book and Bible House, 1903), pp. 182–83; Samuel Gompers to Max Hayes, 7 July 1897, Samuel Gompers Letterbooks (quoting the Cleveland Central Labor Union).

45. *Report of the Committee on Immigration and Naturalization* (51 Cong., 2 Sess., H. Rept. No. 3472), pp. 611–18; *Liberty*, 13 June 1896; *St. Louis Labor*, 11 January 1896; David Herreshoff, *American Disciples of Marx: From the Age of Jackson to the Progressive Era* (Detroit: Wayne State University Press, 1967), p. 169. Other members of this group of "influentials" included D. D. Wilson (editor of the *Monthly Journal of the International Association of Machinists*), John Swinton, George A. Schilling

(of the Chicago *Arbeiter Zeitung*), David Black, and Edward McSweeney (an assistant commissioner of immigration).

46. Pennsylvania Secretary of Internal Affairs, *Annual Report*, 1889, Pt. 3, *Industrial Statistics*, Vol. 17, pp. E1–E58; Bureau of Statistics of Labor of the State of New York, *Twelfth Annual Report*, 1894, pp. 372–431; Thomas W. Gavett, *Development of the Labor Movement in Milwaukee* (Madison: University of Wisconsin Press, 1965), p. 89; Foner, *History of the Labor Movement*, Vol. 2, pp. 287–88.

47. Foner, *History of the Labor Movement*, Vol. 2, p. 364.

48. *Reports of the Industrial Commission*, Vol. 7, p. 435.

49. Circular to the Executive Council, 11 May 1897, and Samuel Gompers to P. J. McGuire, 24 May 1897, Samuel Gompers Letterbooks.

50. Circular to the Executive Council, 11 May 1897, and Samuel Gompers to Max Hayes, 19 July 1897, Samuel Gompers Letterbooks.

51. AFL, *Proceedings*, 1897, pp. 91, 94.

52. Ibid., pp. 81–82.

53. Ibid., p. 91.

54. Mark Perlman, *Labor Union Theories in America* (Evanston, Ill.: Row, Peterson and Co., 1958), p. 113; Norman J. Ware, *Labor in Modern Industrial Society* (New York: Heath and Co., 1935), pp. 263–64; Bernard Mandel, *Samuel Gompers: A Biography* (Yellow Springs: Antioch Press, 1963), pp. 101–2; James O. Morris, *Conflict within the A.F.L.: A Study of Craft versus Industrial Unionism, 1901–1938* (Ithaca, N.Y.: Cornell University Press, 1958), p. 8; Taft, *The A.F. of L.*, pp. xi, xii.

7

The Undermining of Solidarity in the Labor Movement, 1880–1914

A major purpose of the study of past public opinion is to establish what that opinion was and how it evolved over a period of time. In the absence of opinion polls, historians are compelled to rely on a variety of imprecise and impressionistic indicators which invariably raise doubts about their conclusions. In Chapter Six an attempt was made to apply a more systematic method of opinion testing in order to overcome some of these problems.

Further difficulties arise from historians' attempts to analyze the reasons for these changes in opinion: the subjective assessments of members of the group whose opinion is being measured frequently diverge from those of contemporary observers and subsequent students. The availability of new evidence and the broader, less partisan, perspectives of later scholars can significantly alter the analysis of those who participated in, and indeed helped to shape, public events.

The main aim of this chapter is to identify and assess the long-term factors responsible for the sustained trend towards immigration restriction in the labor movement in the three decades before 1914. Some of these factors had an immediate and direct impact, others operated slowly and subtly over a lengthy period; some were based on accurate information, others on misperceptions and misapprehensions. Whatever their nature, they all served to undermine internationalist and solidaristic sentiments and to weaken the "compelling sense of commonality of experience."[1] Among the most important were the following: fluctuations in the economy, particularly the depressions of 1893–97 and 1907–9; the long-term trends in real wages; the volume and character of immigration; technological innovation and the revolution in managerial techniques; and the erosion of community feeling.

These factors were, in the main, undramatic, cumulative in effect, and sometimes only dimly perceived by members of the labor movement. For example, few labor spokesmen could clearly articulate the connection between the introduction of modern technology and the growing desire in labor's ranks to cut immigration. This failure to relate changing opinion to some of the significant socioeconomic developments is understandable in view of the complexities of opinion formation. Of course, opinion developed on the basis of misapprehension and error is no less a motivator of behavior than opinion resulting from accurate perceptions of reality. Still, historians must recognize that a study of labor opinion using labor sources only is likely to reflect the prejudices and misperceptions, as well as the insights, of contemporaries. It is therefore unsatisfactory simply to report labor's interpretation of events, important though that may be for the record; the use of other evidence permits a more balanced and complete explanation of what occurred. In confining oneself to labor sources only, never far from one's mind are the questions, How true are these statements? Do they accord with reality? What important factors do they omit? Hence the second purpose of this chapter is to question the factual accuracy of some of the information on which labor opinion relating to immigration was based.

Discussion of opinion formation in the labor movement reasonably begins with economic fluctuations. The ups and downs of the economy, the level of real wages, and the degree of short-time working and unemployment affected workers so directly that they were able to make quite plausible connections between their experience and the level of immigration. It is important, therefore, to try to establish the long-term trends in real wages and the impact of economic fluctuations on employment.

Between 1865 and 1890 workers in the manufacturing industry improved their standard of living. Despite the doubling of the labor force, real wages and earnings rose by a half from their 1860 level.[2] However, the increase in real wages was concentrated in the 1880s, when immigration was at a postwar peak.[3] Whilst immigration may have prevented wages rising as high as they might, the depressant effect was insufficient to prevent a fairly substantial improvement in living standards, at least for those in employment. By contrast, in the two decades after 1890, the employed made only insignificant gains in real wages, hourly earnings rising by a mere 7 percent between 1890 and 1914. When allowance was made for a decrease in the number of hours worked, real average weekly earnings in manufacturing in 1914 were found to be about 5 percent below the average for 1890–99.[4] Paul Douglas attributed this decline to three factors: the ending of the frontier, the deceleration in the pace of technological change, and the rapid increase in the flow of immigrants to the United States.

More recent estimates of real wages in these prewar decades are less pessimistic than those of Douglas. Albert Rees, for example, estimated that real hourly earnings of manufacturing workers rose by 37 percent between 1890 and 1914, but he noted that this rate of increase was lower than estimates for the 1860–90 and post–1914 periods, concluding "that the closing of the frontier and the high level of immigration did have some effect in holding down real wages, though not nearly so large as had previously been believed." The wave of heavy immigration beginning in 1900 coincided with a sharp rise in the rent index, and real wages in a number of industries remained depressed below previous peaks for several years. Immigration, Rees concluded, "was probably an important factor in keeping both the rate of increase in real wages and in productivity during this period below the rate achieved more recently."[5]

Leaving aside the question of whether wages stagnated, or increased steadily albeit at relatively slow rates, we must recognize that levels of employment were left out of account in these calculations. When they are included, the real earnings of the wage-earning class demonstrate "a much more violent fluctuation from year to year with the business cycle than do earnings of workers who continue to be employed throughout the period." Douglas calculated that whilst the real earnings of those in employment fell by only 8 percent between 1892 and 1894, the real earnings of the group "attached to industry" decreased by no less than 20 percent. The recovery of this group was equally marked when employment began to rise temporarily in 1895.[6]

Accordingly, attempts to establish an accurate picture of trends in working-class living standards must give due weight to levels of unemployment. These were most severe during the depression which began in 1893 and continued, despite a temporary and incomplete recovery in 1895, into the late 1890s. Recovery after 1897 was slow, and most sections of the economy did not reach the capacity levels of the 1892 peak until 1901 or 1907. Unemployment shot up again during the depression in 1907–9. In 1893 production in a wide range of industries declined by about 20 percent between June and December. Wages, prices, and employment fell correspondingly. By August 1894, the low point of the first part of the depression, employment was almost 15 percent below that of January 1893. From this trough to the next peak in November 1895, unemployment declined from around 17 percent of the labor force to around 13 percent, at which point it began to rise until it touched about 15 percent in 1896. Even in 1899, when recovery was well under way, unemployment was still almost 8 percent.[7]

These aggregate statistics conceal the very much worse unemployment figures in certain industries and regions of the country. Charles Hoffmann's calculations put the unemployment level in September 1893 at 22 percent in Massachusetts and 44 percent in Michigan. In December 1893, it was 35

percent in New York; in January 1894, it was more than 20 percent in
Connecticut. Similarly, estimates of unemployment in particular industries
show that workers were especially hard hit in the iron industry, where, at
one point in 1893, 40 percent of the labor force was unemployed. Furthermore, in the woollen and carpeting industries of Massachusetts the highest
unemployment figures in 1893 were 31 percent and 62 percent respectively.[8]

In view of these figures, working-class discontent in the 1890s and the
fierce industrial conflicts of 1893–94 are unsurprising and explicable. Almost
three million families were in acute distress through the unemployment of
a wage earner, and many others suffered from wage cuts or short-time
working. Those still in work were increasingly conscious of their vulner-
ability and swelled the protesters against social and economic conditions.
The acute discontent, suffering, and deprivation of these years cannot be
ignored when we analyze labor's response to the flow of European immigrants. A particular example of how economic developments affected attitudes to immigration comes from the textile town of Fall River in
Massachusetts. The loss of markets and the decline in profitability resulted
in speed-ups, job competition, and occupational insecurity. This in turn led
to a refusal by the working class of the town to accept newly arrived
immigrant workers as part of the community. In the economic circumstances of the 1890s it was unrealistic to expect that internationalism and
solidarity in regard to immigrants would survive unscathed.[9]

Labor was indeed receptive to allegations that immigration was at the
root of its economic problems. Trade union leaders provided their members
with accurate information about the volume and distribution of immigration, which in itself gave pause for thought. However, they also relayed
charges about the social characteristics of the newest immigrants, emphasizing qualities of criminality, pauperism, insanity, and illiteracy. These
charges were at best misleading, and at worst malicious, but they tended
to carry conviction to the beleaguered workers of the 1890s, particularly
since they reflected a broad consensus of opinion. Hence labor's attitude to
immigration appears to have been shaped, not only by a largely accurate
understanding of the very large numbers involved, but also by the changing
ethnic composition of the foreign-born and by the apparent social characteristics of these newcomers. Our purpose is to determine which of these
aspects of immigration constituted a genuine cause for apprehension among
the skilled working class during the period.

The totals of immigration by decade are set out in Table 2. These figures
vary directly with the level of activity in the American economy. The total
for the 1880s reflects the economic prosperity of that decade and that for
the 1890s is evidence of the declining attraction of the depressed American
economy to potential immigrants. The annual figures of Polish immigration
in the 1890s indicate a close correlation between immigration and annual
fluctuations in the economy (Table 3).

Table 2
Immigration by Decades: 1820–1910

Decade	Total	Decade	Total
1820-30	151,824	1871-80	2,812,191
1831-40	599,125	1881-90	5,246,613
1841-50	1,713,251	1891-1900	3,687,564
1851-60	2,598,214	1901-10	8,795,386
1861-70	2,314,824		

SOURCE: Reports of the Immigration Commission (61 Cong., 3 Sess., Senate Doc. 747), Abstracts of Reports, vol. 1, p. 57.

Table 3
Immigrants from Poland: 1891–1898

Year	Total	Year	Total
1891	27,497	1895	790
1892	40,536	1896	691
1893	16,374	1897	4,165
1894	1,941	1898	4,726

SOURCE: Report of the Commissioner-General of Immigration, Year ending June 30, 1905, in Bulletin of the Bureau of Labor, No. 72, Sept. 1907, p. 407.

This reduction in annual totals understates the impact of the depression on the foreign-born worker since there was considerable remigration during this decade. The rapid economic growth of the first decade of this century is reflected in the immigration figures, which were 60 percent greater than the previous highest decadal total. However, here again, the two depression years beginning in late 1907 produced a fall in immigration of between one-third and one-half.[10]

Despite these decadal fluctuations, there was a long-term upward trend in immigration between 1880 and 1914 which was apparent to contemporaries and influenced public opinion. Receiving considerably less attention was the fact that the proportion of the foreign-born in the total American

Table 4
Immigration as a Percentage of U.S. Population: 1850–1910

		Immigration		
Year	Population (1,000s)	Decades	Total (1,000s)	Percentage of population at previous census
1850	23,192	1851-70	5,019	21.2
1870	38,558	1871-90	8,059	20.9
1890	62,622	1891-1910	12,483	19.9

SOURCE: Isaac A. Hourwich, Immigration and Labor: The Economic Aspect of
European Immigration to the United States (New York: Putnam, 1912),
p. 101.

population remained remarkably stable, varying between 13.3 percent and
14.7 percent between 1880 and 1910. Similarly, the ratio of immigration to
population in the period 1850 to 1914 stayed relatively constant (Table 4).

If these figures had been widely understood, they might have reassured
the increasing number of trade unionists who were anxious about immigration. But there were other aspects of the problem which caused concern
and underpinned the impressionistic evidence that many relied on.

First, the birth rate of the foreign-born was high enough to increase the
proportion of the foreign stock (that is, the foreign-born and their children)
to the total white population from around 34 percent in 1880 to almost 40
percent in 1910.[11] Second, the majority of the immigrants from Southern
and Eastern Europe in the period 1890–1914 were young men who were
either unmarried or migrating without their families. This meant that immigration contributed more to the growth of the labor force than it did to
the growth of the population as a whole. Even in the depressed 1890s
immigration was responsible for 10 percent of the total growth of the labor
force. In all, between 1890 and 1910 the foreign-born constituted more than
one-fifth of the workforce. But in the manufacturing industry the foreign-
born were about 30 per cent of the workforce between 1870 and 1910, and
in particular industries this proportion was exceeded. There were, for example, twice as many foreign-born as native-born in the ready-made clothing industry in 1910 and more than half as many in blast furnaces and rolling
mills, public works construction, and maintenance of way. In Pennsylvania
41 percent of all employees in the iron and steel and coal industries in 1905
were Italians, Slavs, or Hungarians. Consequently, the foreign-born com-

Table 5
Nativity of the Foreign-Born Population: 1880, 1910

Nativity	Percentage of total foreign-born	
	1880	1910
German birth	29.4	18.5
Irish birth	27.8	10.0
English birth	9.9	6.5
Russian and Finnish birth	0.5	12.8
Austro-Hungarian birth	2.0	12.4
Italian birth	0.7	9.9

SOURCE: Grace Abbott, The Immigrant and the Community (New York:
         The Century Co., 1917), p. 288.

peted more intensely with native labor in mining and manufacturing than
their proportion in the total population indicates.[12]

Moreover, the geographical origins and the ethnic character of the European immigrants in this period were transformed. In 1882, 87 percent of
European immigrants originated in Northern and Western Europe. By 1895
the proportion had declined to about one-half, and a decade or so later
immigrants from the South and East of Europe constituted just over 80
percent of Europe's total.[13] Table 5 shows the declining importance of
Western Europeans in American immigration. One of the major consequences of this was that native-born Americans and the foreign-born originating in Western Europe had the task of coming to terms with economic
competitors from abroad whose ethnic, cultural, linguistic, and religious
characteristics were decidedly alien from them. The maintenance of a sense
of community, which was a precondition for harmonious integration of
the newcomers into the labor force, became increasingly arduous and finally,
in many cases, impossible. The sense of commonality and shared identity
was further attenuated by the circulation of statistical information which
indicated that recent immigrants from Southern and Eastern Europe possessed lower standards of occupational skill, literacy, physical and mental
health, and respect for the law. This information was utilized by the anti-
immigration lobby to strengthen its case for tighter controls on immigration. However, many of the inferences drawn from this material were
inaccurate and misleading. Close analysis shows how little immigrants from
Southern and Eastern Europe differed from their Western European predecessors in important economic and social characteristics.

Distribution of immigrants among broad occupational categories remained fairly stable between 1880 and 1910, despite the dramatic changes
in the ethnic composition of the immigrants. In 1880 immigrants were

concentrated in personal services, trade and transportation, and manufacturing. By 1900 there had been some expansion of employment in trade
and transportation, but the concentration in manufacturing remained steady
despite changes in individual industries. No significant change had occurred
by 1910.[14]

But what truth is there in the graver allegation that in the period 1899–
1909 only half as many of the "new" immigrants were skilled compared
with their fellow newcomers from Western Europe? There were, it is true,
fewer professional people and farmers within their ranks and far more farm
and common laborers. However, these calculations excluded Jews, the most
highly skilled of the new arrivals, from the total of recent immigrants, with
an obviously distorting effect. Moreover, it was inappropriate to compare
the skill composition of the two streams of immigration within the same
period. Arguably a more accurate comparison would be between a period
when Northern and Western Europeans were predominant in the immigrant
stream and one during which Southern and Eastern Europeans constituted
the overwhelming proportion, for example, between the decade 1871–81
and the decade 1899–1909. If this comparison is made, 18 percent of the
new immigrants with occupations were skilled, compared with about 23
percent of the Western Europeans. If, however, the calculation is made on
the basis of total immigrant numbers, then there was a higher proportion
of skilled workers among the more recent immigrants.[15] Furthermore, these
comparisons were made on the basis of the occupations the immigrants
claimed to have had in their home countries. If the occupations followed
by immigrants in the United States are used as the basis for comparison,
then the new immigrants turned out to be both more skilled and more
unskilled than the old. The reason for the latter was the fall in the proportion
of proprietors, managers, and officials, which included farmers, however
humble. In fact, since farmers were generally unskilled in an industrial sense,
their diminishing proportion in the immigrant workforce did not represent
a genuine decrease in the proportion of skilled craftsmen among the new
immigrants. These findings raise doubts about the assertions of scholars
like J. W. Jenks and W. Jett Lauck in respect of the occupations and skills
of the new immigrants and weaken the case for restriction in so far as it
was based on them.[16]

The alleged decline in skill was not the only ground for charges that
recent immigrants were less assimilable with the American population than
previous generations of the foreign-born. Attention was also drawn to the
allegedly higher proportion of criminals, paupers, and the insane among
them. Whereas earlier immigrants had come "from countries renowned for
their educational development, strict morality and sturdy independence of
spirit," the new immigrants emerged from "the scum and social entrails"
of the "least civilized" parts of Europe, too many of them being paupers
and criminals whom their governments wished to get rid of. As a result,

they filled American hospitals, jails, and insane asylums at the expense of the American taxpayer.[17] It was claimed, for example, that the proportion of the foreign-born insane to the total number of insane persons in the United States was one and three-quarter times the proportion of the foreign-born in the total population, and that foreign-born paupers were three times that proportion. There was also a disproportionate number of foreign-born criminals. Figures collected by the Immigration Commission and the Industrial Commission seemed to show as much.[18]

Yet there was a great deal of misunderstanding about the significance of the crude statistics. If crime was largely a function of urbanism and of the proportion of male members of the community between the ages of 15 and 30, then recent immigrants with their high urban concentration and large share of young males would inevitably produce a disproportionate number of criminals. Hence when the crime rates of the foreign-born and native-born populations between the ages of 20 and 45 are compared, it turns out that immigrant criminalty was only slightly higher than that of native Americans. Furthermore, evidence exists that in certain areas immigrant criminality was lower than that of the native-born. In the County of New York, convictions of foreign-born at the Court of General Sessions between 1904 and 1908 were low relative to the share of immigrants in the population.[19] Even if it is admitted, despite some ambiguity in the statistics, that the foreign-born population was relatively more criminal, this tells us nothing about the kind of offenses for which the foreign-born were convicted in comparison with the native-born.

The claim has been made that the foreign-born committed proportionately more than their share of homicides and crimes of violence, but less, proportionately, of "gainful offences." Furthermore, in "offences against public policy" like disorderly conduct, drunkenness, malicious mischief, and violation of city ordinances, the foreign-born were in the lead. But a more balanced picture must take into account that homicides were overwhelmingly urban in incidence and that the foreign-born population was heavily concentrated in cities. Then, in respect to offenses against public policy, a large part of the so-called criminality of the foreign-born consisted merely of the violation of city ordinances which were offenses only because the persons committing them were not naturalized.[20]

A further distinction needs to be made between the different ethnic groups constituting the foreign-born. The implication of the criticism directed at the criminality of the foreign-born was that the new immigrants from Southern and Eastern Europe were mainly responsible. Yet in cases of drunkenness and disorderly conduct, the highest number of convictions was to be found among the Irish and Scots; for gainful offenses, the English and Germans were at the top of the ladder. In a long-term perspective it is probable that the crime rate of the foreign-born had been falling steadily since the 1850s. The ratio of foreign-born prisoners to foreign-born population in that decade was more than five times that of native prisoners to native population, but by the 1890s the gap between the ratios had dramatically narrowed.[21] There is, in fact, little to show that the new immigrants were unique in their criminal propensities. The Immigration Commission wisely qualified its own statistics by commenting that "no satisfactory evidence has yet been produced to show that immigration has resulted in an increase in crime disproportionate to the increase in adult population."[22]

Another common charge against the new immigrants was the high proportion of paupers and those unable to support themselves. The 1910 census showed that the ratio of foreign-born paupers to the foreign-born population was four times as great as the ratio of native-born paupers to the native-born white population. However, this ratio appears much less unfavorable if it is placed in a long-term context. For example, during the period 1880–1910, when the proportion of new immigrants in the total immigration was rising rapidly, the relative amount of pauperism among the foreign-born was decreasing. In fact, the more recent immigrants from Russia, Austria-Hungary, and Italy had a far lower ratio of almshouse pauperism than the Irish, the British, the Scandinavians, and the French Canadians.[23]

Part of the explanation for this lies in the age structure of the recent immigrants: the concentration in the age range 15 to 45 reduced the danger of pauperism, whilst the older immigrant groups had a larger proportion of their members unfit to work by reason of age, disability, accident, and industrial disease. The proportion of paupers among foreign-born white men under 45 was comparable to the figure for native-born whites, but for those over 45 there was a much larger proportion of pauperism among the foreign-born. This undoubtedly reflected the lower capacity of the foreign-born to save for retirement or sickness owing to their less secure and well-paid positions in the occupational hierarchy. Possibly, too, they had a smaller circle of relatives and friends in the United States to help to care for them.[24]

A further criticism of the new immigrants was directed at the higher incidence of insanity among them in comparison with the native-born. The 1910 census showed that the ratio of foreign-born whites in insane hospitals in the United States was more than twice as high as the ratio for native whites. However, this proportion had not increased during the previous twenty years at a time when immigration from Southern and Eastern Europe had been exceptionally heavy. In 1890, when most European immigrants still originated in Western Europe, the foreign-born furnished one-third of the total number of insane persons despite constituting only one-seventh of the total population.[25]

Thus the new immigration contributed relatively little to the total of the foreign-born insane between 1890 and 1910. The figures of the insane in each ethnic group in 1910 show that the Italians, Russians, and Austro-Hungarians had only half the average number of insane of all foreign-born.[26] Furthermore, the disparity between the insanity rates of the foreign- and native-born is virtually eliminated when age and the urban-rural ratio are held constant. One would expect to find a larger percentage of industrial workers in insane asylums than any other class in the population. "The foreigners," wrote Peter Roberts, "work in dangerous places, get the lowest wage, suffer from intermittent labor, and many of them are under a serious strain in the conflict for subsistence." There seems, in fact, to be a correlation between the incidence of insanity and "general economic conditions."[27] This implies that the foreign-born insane were the victims of life in the United States, a plausible conclusion in view of the exclusion of insane persons by the immigration laws.

The repeated allegations that the foreign-born had higher levels of crime, pauperism, and insanity have been shown to be at best misleading and at worst gravely inaccurate. But one charge that carries greater weight is that immigrants were less literate than the native-born. The literacy levels of immigrants began to receive widespread publicity in the mid–1890s as a result of the congressional efforts to enact a literacy test for immigrants. Both the Industrial and Immigration Commissions drew attention to the relatively low levels of literacy among the new immigrants. Figures published by the Immigration Commission showed the following levels of illiteracy for different ethnic groups: Portuguese, 70 percent; Southern Italians, 54 percent; Lithuanians, 49 percent; Russians, 38 percent; Poles, 35 percent; Hebrews and Greeks, 26 percent; and Slovaks, 24 percent. By contrast, immigrants from the countries of Western Europe had an illiteracy rate of less than 5 percent.[28] The argument that a truer comparison between the "old" and the "new" immigrants would result from eliciting the illiteracy rates of Western European immigrants in the 1870s is acceptable in principle. However, it is impossible to apply it owing to the unavailability of literacy figures for the 1870s. Nonetheless, it may be inferred that literacy levels of old immigrants would have improved substantially between the 1870s and 1890s owing to the advances in the provision of primary education in the countries of Western Europe. It may therefore be assumed that a comparison using the 1870s as a base for Western European immigrants would be much more favorable to the new immigrants than that of the Immigration Commission.

The undesirable social characteristics attributed to the new immigrants by the labor leadership on the basis of official statistics do not, in general, conform to the facts. Undoubtedly such beliefs about the foreign-born were influential in molding labor opinion on the immigration question. Even more important in this respect was labor's conviction that unemployment and stagnant living standards were closely connected with high levels of immigration. Yet the proportion of the foreign-born in the population hardly changed in the period; perhaps more significant was the concentration of the foreign-born in particular regions and industries. Yet even this was probably not decisive in turning opinion. Attitudes to immigration depend fundamentally on the ethnic, linguistic, and religious characteristics of the immigrants in relation to the host population. The decisive question is whether, given the same economic and social conditions in the United States in the period 1880–1910, an immigrant stream composed almost exclusively of Western Europeans would have received the same response from American public opinion as that given to the new immigration. In all probability, it would not, even though pressures towards restriction in some form would have existed. A nation of immigrants cannot easily deny to latecomers the opportunity so eagerly grasped by their forerunners unless its ideals of solidarity have been attenuated by the radically different character of the new arrivals. Incomprehensible languages and customs, different forms of religious observance, and alien manners and strange forms of behavior were crucial in severing the bonds of sympathy and in inhibiting the will to overcome economic problems by common action. Ultimately it seemed easier for labor to attempt to ease the strains of economic life by rejecting the immigrants. The changing ethnicity of the newcomers gave the trade unions the chance to blame them for labor's problems rather than to grapple with the fundamental causes of working-class discontent. The most significant of these, possibly, were the consequences of technological and managerial innovation in American industry, which were unprecedentedly intense and disruptive between 1880 and 1914.

The impact of technical change was heightened through its coincidence with fundamental changes in industrial organization, such as the rise of the large corporation and the giant factory unit. Under the stress of these dislocating and disorienting forces, labor sought ways of resistance, perhaps through trade union action, or through maintaining control of the work process, or by means of political mobilization. The growing hostility towards new immigrants was further intensified as they became identified in the popular mind with the subverting process of technical change. It was their misfortune to be the agents of modernization.

Machinery affects labor in a variety of ways: it may reduce wages, create unemployment, lower the value of skill, and lead to displacement of the most directly affected workers. Displacement does not necessarily imply immediate redundancy. It has been satisfactorily defined as "the loss of the opportunity to sell acquired skill at the rate of remuneration which would have been received if the machine had not been introduced."[29] The extent of the loss of opportunity varied according to circumstances; in some industries affected by technological change, for example the softstone industry, displacement might be very extensive, in contrast to the limited effects in the printing industry. But between these two extremes "displaced" workers could expect declining opportunities to market their skills, leading to lower wages, unemployment, and perhaps permanent idleness in the case of those restricted by age and immobility.[30]

Of course, the adverse consequences of technological change may affect only a limited section of the population, while the benefits of such changes will be shared among the whole society. It is also true that in an expanding economy, like the American in the three decades before 1914, some of those displaced by technical change will have the opportunity to rise to supervisory and planning positions at lower management levels. The proportion of those able to take advantage of this opportunity varied from industry to industry and region to region, but probably only a minority of the skilled workforce could reasonably expect such upward mobility. And although the benefits of technical change were widely diffused, the major sufferers from the introduction of new machines were the skilled workers, who were well aware that what they might gain as consumers was far outweighed by the destruction of their craft.[31] As the skill involved in the process of production became increasingly part of the machine, erstwhile skilled workers tended to become machine minders. Profitable enterprise implied "that the capitalist would dissociate labor from the productive process and reintegrate the two on his own terms, in such a way as to maximize the surplus value produced by the labor force."[32]

Displacement and deskilling brought about by technological change had material consequences for wages, employment, and conditions of work; it also made a considerable impact on the collective mentality of the skilled working class, which was demoralized by the weakening of its control over the productive process. In most industries it seemed impossible to avoid the inexorable progress of machine technology, which shattered the carefully constructed edifice of craft control and destroyed the position of the "autonomous craftsman." The full impact of this process on the collective psychology of the skilled workers can only be understood if the extent of workers' self-determination in the premachine age is fully recognized.

The idea of labor's rights, which in origin were indissoluble from the rights of Jacksonian "producers," lay in the conviction that hard work and skill were the measure of virtue. The possession of skill, itself a guarantee of social status, also held out the promise of upward mobility into the small master or employer class. A community of virtuous producers implied equality of opportunity and of rights, the elimination of monopoly and privilege, and the freedom of workers to reap the rewards of their abilities. Accordingly there was no place for class distinctions between masters and journeymen. The factory system, developing apace in the post–Civil War period, and the widespread introduction of machines collided with this traditional value structure.[33]

In the first place, machines destroyed or reduced skill, damaging the self-esteem and social status of skilled workers and undermining social equality. Furthermore, since the machines were owned and controlled by capital, the balance of power between workers and owners shifted in the latter's favor. In the handicraft era, capital had had to deal with independent and individualistic workers who successfully fought off its attempts to exercise complete control, even when they had lost the ownership of the means of production. Control of the productive process required the displacement of the worker's technical knowledge as well, which was only made possible by the introduction of the machine. Naturally, capital was enthused by machinery's capacity to cut costs and increase productivity, but it also had the inestimable advantage of securing output from the whim of the skilled workers.[34]

Inevitably, given the skilled workers' pre-industrial value structure, there emerged a stubborn resistance to the insatiable appetite of capital for control over the process of production. The code of the craftsman demanded "manliness" in relation to the boss, a determination to preserve workers' dignity and to resist any suspicion of servile behavior. At the center of this resistance was the attempt to preserve worker autonomy by reliance on the workers' superior knowledge of the techniques of production. But where this failed, under the constant pressure of new technology, workers set informal output quotas to avoid the indignity of speed-ups and to maintain a comfortable pace of work to prevent exhaustion at the end of the day.[35]

The success of worker resistance varied from industry to industry. Grim and resourceful defense could only achieve so much in the face of overwhelming advantages supplied to capital in some industries by the efficiency of the new technology. The dimensions of the threat to skilled workers can only be appreciated by recalling the pace and extent of technological change in the three decades after 1880. Of the more prominent American industries two, boots and shoes and coopering, had passed through the first stage of displacement of skilled craftsmen before 1880. Others experienced far-reaching technological change after 1880, with serious adverse effects for skilled workers. Industries in this category included stonecutting, textiles, iron and steel, cigar making, machinery, woodworking, garment making, coal mining, and sections of the glass industry. Two industries, granite cutting and printing, experienced technological change, but its impact on skilled workers in the industry was softened by mitigating factors. Yet here, too, workers experienced anxiety and had to adapt their work patterns.

The textile industry was a good example of the way in which machines served to deskill and intensify labor and to strip craftsmen of status and independence. Skilled workers were replaced by the semi-skilled or unskilled, often foreign-born newcomers, and only those with scarce skills, like loomfixers and mule spinners, remained in the industry.[36] The introduction of the Northrop loom, the Industrial Commission reported, enabled weavers to produce five times as much cloth as they had forty years earlier. Similarly the ring spindle, using only semi-skilled, mainly immigrant labor, had widely replaced the mule, which produced only half as much and required highly-skilled mule spinners for its operation. However, mule spinners might be tolerated if they allowed their wages to fall to the point where they became competitive with ring spinners.[37]

The garment trades represented an equally barren area for skilled artisans. Here machinery had been introduced early; the sewing machine was perfected in the 1850s and rapidly introduced after the Civil War. Cutting machinery was brought in in the mid–1870s and the mechanical presser around the turn of the century. Each of these inventions produced its casualties among skilled operatives, but the major inroad in skill in the last two decades of the nineteenth century was achieved by the minute subdivision of the craft skills of operator, baster, and presser into a large number of component parts, each part performed by low-paid, unskilled, immigrant labor, mainly Russian Jews and Italians. Only two kinds of skilled workers were able to survive this fierce low-wage competition: the cutter, whose skill and judgment was still required in all branches of the trade, and the journeyman tailor, employed in the relatively less important custom tailoring side of the industry.[38]

A similar pattern of displacement or dilution of skills can be found in the iron and steel industry, where new machinery or plant permitted the employment of low-paid, unskilled, immigrant labor. Each new machine tended to displace either skilled men at the top of the job hierarchy or unskilled men at the bottom, where brute labor power was replaced by automatic hoists and loading equipment. Fortunately, the number of skilled workers in the steel industry increased owing to the growth of the industry, though they constituted a diminishing proportion of the total workforce. Even so, the most highly skilled workers experienced wage reductions in the period 1892–1910, and the wages of the skilled and semi-skilled remained stationary.[39]

A comparably rapid expansion in the bituminous coal industry cushioned the effects of technological change on the skilled labor force. The skilled hewers or pickmen, who were independent craftsmen working largely without supervision, found their skills at a lower premium after the introduction of blasting and machine cutting. By 1913, half the soft coal produced in the United States came from mines using undercutting machines. The pick miners' tasks were further subdivided into shot-firing, loading, timbering, and tracking. Miners' leaders recognized the real possibility of former skilled workers becoming simple coal shovellers, their only qualification being "a strong back and physical energy." Still, the rapid rate of growth of the industry moderated the painful effects of displacement.[40]

The impact of machines was also cushioned by the miners' union, which in Ohio and Indiana was able to set the rate for machine mining at between two-thirds and three-quarters of the rate for hand mining. This permitted higher earnings for machine operators and, by narrowing the differential between the two rates, reduced the incentive for the too-rapid introduction of machines.[41] Nevertheless, those who still wished to practise a traditional skill often had to uproot themselves from their homes and settle in another mining region. In the short term, at least, this process caused hardship and anxiety coupled with resentment at the threat to traditional skills. No doubt promotion to supervisory positions helped to salve the wounds of some displaced miners.

Two groups of workers suffered even more severely from technological innovation. In the softstone industry, a new type of planer was introduced in the 1880s and widely installed after 1895. By 1915 approximately 1,000 planers were in operation, replacing about 7,000 skilled stonecutters. In most places the policy of the union in trying to limit the use of planers was a dismal failure. After initial resistance it was forced to concede that only half the workers operating the planers should be skilled stonecutters, the other half being unskilled planer hands. They were lucky to obtain even this, since it was doubtful that training as a stonecutter was much advantage to a planerman. In any case the industry was in decline owing to competition from new products like concrete and terra cotta. Accordingly the number of skilled workers in the industry was halved between 1900 and 1915, resulting in serious unemployment.[42]

The second group of skilled workers in this category was the makers of glass bottles and jars. This industry provides an example of the differing degrees of displacement produced by different machines. The relatively mild and containable consequences of the semiautomatic machine of the 1890s for skilled workers compare favorably with the shattering blow to the craft inflicted by the Owens Automatic Bottle Machine introduced after 1905. Operated by unskilled workers, it reduced production costs to 5 per cent of their previous level. By 1917 the 200 machines in production were capable of producing as much as 10,000 hand blowers, and the 9,000 hand blowers of 1905 had been reduced to 2,000 in 1917, a figure which would have been much lower had not demand for bottles almost doubled in the period.[43]

In two industries, however, the displacing effects of machinery were less severe. The classic, often-quoted example of the printing industry shows that a combination of trade union resourcefulness and specific economic and industrial conditions could overcome the major problems connected with technical innovation. Circumstances favored the printers in that the very nature of the new linotype machine of the 1880s and the peculiar economic conditions in the printing industry limited the effects of displacement. It was quickly apparent that the machine could be operated most efficiently by skilled compositors. Moreover, the cheapness of machine composition reduced costs and prices and stimulated demand for printed matter, especially for newspapers. Though machines brought great advantages in speed to the newspaper industry, the union was able to extract concessions out of the owners' desires to meet deadlines and keep the presses running. Lastly, there was little to fear from the competition of immigrants as machine operators owing to their inability to read English. All these factors softened the impact of the new machine. The policy of the union skilfully exploited these advantages.[44]

Similarly, industrial conditions and trade union policy combined to reduce the impact of new machinery in the granite-cutting industry. In this case the union encouraged those of its members with "a taste and aptitude for machinery" to apply to employers for training on the new machines and in a number of other ways pursued a flexible and positive policy.[45] Nevertheless, the real strength of the granite cutters compared with most skilled workers was that for "the really fine work" of carving and lettering they were indispensable, and this gave them a strong bargaining position. Furthermore, the granite cutters became the most proficient operators of machines through their expert knowledge of granite. Overall the same combination of circumstances prevailed in granite cutting as in printing: the superior effectiveness of the skilled man as a machine operator; the actual or anticipated increases in demand for the product as a result of falling production costs; the flexibility of the trade union leaders; and the relatively mild challenge of immigrant workers.[46]

The two industries of printing and granite cutting show how the effects of new technology could be contained if the circumstances were favorable. But in most industries these "salvaging factors" were not present or not strong enough to prevent a quite serious displacement of skill, which took the form of lowered wages, longer hours, unemployment, or redeployment to machines which required lower levels of skill for their operation. For many the choice was often between continuing in a skilled position but at a lower wage or moving to the less skilled task of machine operation, also at lower wages.

Although machines had devastating effects on the economic position of most skilled workers, undermining their "autonomy" and social status at the same time, this was not the sum total of their impact on the lives of artisans. The possession of a skill signified "pride in work, interest and creative activity." With the wide dissemination of machine technology in the decades after 1880, craftsmen allegedly lost this personal satisfaction and sense of achievement, suffering in the process "cultural and psychological impoverishment." The machine left little room for the exercise of "every sense and faculty," killing "art and creativity" and offering the mindless performance of some narrowly standardized task. Hence work was degraded and jobs lost their meaning, becoming mere "random point[s] in a seemingly endless line." "The worker's needs for imaginative participation in his work and for seeing things as a whole [were] lost and the unity of production [was] shattered."[47] Demoralization was not confined to those actually experiencing displacement but was shared by those who expected their skills to be undermined in future. All skilled workers had an interest in defending skill whenever it was challenged; each new example of displacement could not fail to demoralize and concern those upon whom the axe had not yet fallen.[48]

Many craftsmen turned to their unions for advice and protection. But the realization dawned that the unions themselves were very vulnerable to technological change. Gompers and other trade union officials identified mechanization as a threat to craft unions through the training of unskilled or semi-skilled workers to do the craftsmen's work.[49] Furthermore, they recognized that the essential purpose of the new management methods was to destroy craft organizations. Because unskilled immigrants were not easy to recruit owing to the differences in language, culture, and previous work experience, unions often gave up the task or never even attempted it. They sought all the more desperately to maintain jobs for their members, either by opposing the machines or by obtaining the opportunity for them to work as semi-skilled machine operators. Moreover, there was an understandable temptation to join the call for immigration restriction. This would not necessarily prevent displacement but might delay it, or improve the terms upon which skilled workers would be asked to yield up their skill.

The undermining of skill by machines weakened the craftsmen's position in the labor process but did not destroy it. The degree of autonomy retained by skilled workers varied from industry to industry depending on the nature and pace of mechanization therein. But the trend was unmistakably in the direction of attenuating worker control and shifting the balance of power in favor of management. Moreover, the size of the workplace or factory grew substantially under the impact of modern technology, and workers increasingly felt themselves to be part of a labor army in which the individual's identity and function became submerged. With the increase of mergers and takeovers in the late 1890s the factory became further depersonalized and the sense of control over one's working life greatly diminished. "The human scale of nineteenth-century labor thus fell away," to use David Brody's words. In large mills there was "evidence of an irresistible power, baffling and intangible," deaf to the workers' voice and uncaring about their aspirations.[50] After 1900 the worker was entering the new world of modern industry, not only heavily mechanized, gigantic in scale, and impersonal, but also subject to new management disciplines and techniques. One of the major objections to the introduction of scientific management by labor was that it shifted the ownership of knowledge about the work process in the direction of the employer.[51]

The increased size and complexity of manufacturing operations intensified management's problem of achieving control of the work process in the factory. The heavy investment required by giant factories would only yield a satisfactory return if the plant operated at full capacity and maximum efficiency. Machinery, indispensable as it was for increasing employee power vis-à-vis skilled workers, provided "only islands of control in the flow of production." Management inevitably sought new methods of establishing order over the chaos of informal expedients which had grown up as the factory increased in size. It came to depend on an industrial bureaucracy developed by professional engineers who became deeply involved in management problems in the last two decades of the nineteenth century.[52]

The achievement of the bureaucracy was to introduce new methods of operation which increased the authority and control of management over production. Among these novel methods were cost accounting systems, production and inventory control, wage incentive plans, order and method in the acquisition and handling of materials, systematic inspection procedures, and printed job and instruction cards for workers. All served to further diminish worker autonomy, transferring important functions from foremen and workers to the emerging management bureaucracy, and subjecting the workers to "general rules and standardized terms of work."[53]

Among the new methods, piecework systems of wage payment were often strongly resisted by labor since they gave management the power to coerce labor to higher levels of output. Workers imposed maximum output levels on themselves, and tried to ensure that all piecework employees in a particular workplace earned the same amount. As a result, employers turned to the developing science of management as a means of accumulating all the workers' traditional knowledge in their hands.[54]

Scientific management differed in only one important respect from systematic management. Its most influential practitioner and theorist, Frederick W. Taylor, combined technical innovations, centralized planning, and the systematic routing of materials with his most original contribution to improved management, time study and the differential piece rate. Taylor's aim was to remove from workers their remaining control over the production process by creating a method by which management could "gather up" the great mass of traditional knowledge, learning what the workers already knew. This, he believed, was a precondition of adequate management, permitting the establishment of standard methods by which work was to be performed, and overcoming the systematic "soldiering" which he alleged was the basis of traditional working practices. Taylor's proposal to use time study methods to carry out systematic analysis of each distinct work operation and to use the results to impose a carefully constructed differential piece rate to ensure that work was done in the manner and at the pace laid down was peculiar to the scientific management movement.[55]

The application of Taylor's methods had fundamental consequences for craft workers. It represented for the craftsman the theft by his employer of his traditional skill. The theft was carried out by "arbitrary and pretentious men in white shirts" with no real understanding of the craft, let alone mastery of it. If Taylor's system were to be widely adopted, the balance of strength between management and workforce in the factory would be irreversibly shifted in management's direction. In effect, the system would remove from the workers the need to think and exercise initiative, and would transfer such functions to management. The system was wrong, one trade union official commented, "because we want our heads left on us."[56]

Taylor was well aware of what was involved. In its essence, he said, "scientific management involves a complete mental revolution on the part of workingmen." Among its consequences were higher levels of tension and insecurity among workmen. Men felt harassed and driven by the pace of work, became nervously exhausted and went home fatigued. Hugh Aitken concluded that the dominant theme in workers' evidence before the House committee on the Taylor system was one of distrust. They objected less to what had been done at that point than to what might be done in the future in the way of "mechanizing" the worker.[57]

The assessment is probably correct. Relatively few firms had introduced the Taylor system in its entirety; rather more had applied one or more features of the system.[58] However, knowledge of the system and an understanding of what it symbolized were fairly widely diffused. Taylor's *Shop Management* (1903) was read by union machinists and became a major source of evidence about the intentions of the employers. The molders' strike at the Watertown Arsenal in 1911 opened the eyes of many workers to what was at stake. Certainly the threat to skilled workers was well enough understood to ensure that a strike was called in the repair shops of the Illinois Central Railway in 1911 on the mere suspicion that time study was to be introduced.[59]

Though the revolutionary possibilities in scientific management were widely recognized in the labor movement, they remained for the most part possibilities rather than actualities before the First World War. The continuing impact of technological change remained the more immediate challenge to the majority of skilled workers. The problem which now has to be resolved is whether there was a connection between mounting dissatisfaction with immigration on the part of organized labor and the increasing alienation of craftsmen from the work process brought about by the "constant revolutionizing of production" and the changing methods of management.[60] An answer to this question involves the recognition that skilled labor identified semi-skilled and unskilled immigrant workers as accomplices or agents of the employers in the process of skill displacement.

During the nineteenth century a great gulf existed between the skilled craftsman and the unskilled laborer, reflecting differences in achievement, income, and status. The skilled workers saw themselves as an elite, sharing few interests with the laborers. They recognized that any economic advance on the part of the unskilled was likely to be at their expense. In particular, the new technology which was subverting craft skills was being operated by semi-skilled and unskilled workers. The displaced skilled workers had to forfeit their higher wages, their strong bargaining position, and their higher status. They keenly resented this decline in their fortunes.[61]

The division between skilled and unskilled was reinforced by the changing ethnicity of the work force. Much of the animosity directed at the machine and at the employers was diverted onto the newly arrived machine operators from Southern and Eastern Europe. This process was assisted by the employers who deliberately used immigrants to exacerbate the differences among the workforce and to break up any incipient solidarity. Strikes against technical innovation were frequently beaten by the introduction of immigrant workers to carry on production. The bitterness created by such actions was as frequently directed against the immigrant strikebreakers as against the employers, since the newcomers were "surrogates for management" and a logical object of attack, there being no more heinous offense in the labor movement than strikebreaking.[62]

Without the employment of immigrant labor, many skilled workers believed, the new machines would either have remained idle or have been operated by skilled workers on more favorable terms. This popular view of the relationship between immigration and mechanization received support from the Immigration Commission, which "tended to blame immigrants from Southern and Eastern Europe for bringing about increased mechanization." However, the commission did not agree that immigration caused mechanization, rather that the widespread introduction of machines was facilitated by the arrival of large numbers of unskilled European immigrants.[63] A different view was taken by the Industrial Commission, reporting a decade earlier. Technical innovation was only made possible by this immigration. "Many coal operators," for example, doubted whether machinery would have been introduced in bituminous coal mining had foreign labor not been available. The fact remains, however, that machine coal mining made the greatest advance in coalfields with the smallest percentage of Southern and Eastern Europeans in the labor force.[64] But it is immaterial to our argument whether immigration caused mechanization or whether mechanization facilitated immigration. It is indisputable that, for whatever reason or combination of reasons, new machinery tended to be operated by unskilled foreign-born workers who, from around 1890, constituted a rapidly growing section of the labor force.

It is, therefore, very probable that a strong connection existed between displacement and deskilling on the one hand and hardening attitudes to immigration on the part of the deskilled. However, the force of the connection varied with the existence and strength of other factors. If the working-class community could somehow maintain its communal solidarity and its self-identity, there would be less likelihood of a growth in restrictionist sentiment. In a solidaristic community the real enemy would have been identified as the employers or the capitalist class in general. If, however, there was a fragmentation of the working-class community, increased immigration would widen the cracks and lead to sections of the working class turning against the newcomers.

It is instructive to consider two contrasting working-class communities as a means of identifying the kinds of factors which mediated between displacement and the growth of hostility to immigration.[65] The two communities are Lynn and Fall River in Massachusetts, the former being mainly a shoe manufacturing and the latter a cotton textile town. Despite technical change, Lynn succeeded in retaining its communal cohesion and working-class solidarity in the face of immigration. By contrast, Fall River's working-class community fragmented under a variety of pressures, and its skilled workers came to see immigrants as a threat to employment in an increasingly unstable job market.

The different response to immigrants in different communities depended on a wide variety of factors. The most notable were: the location and size of the workplaces; the nature of the work; the degree of residential integration; the existence and strength of shared recreational institutions; the characteristics and volume of immigration; and the persistence of pre-industrial beliefs, attitudes, and traditions among the workforce.

In Lynn the factory system established itself very rapidly after the Civil War, and mechanization and the detailed division of labor were achieved by 1880, earlier than in most industries. This experience was demoralizing and caused regret for the passage of the old masters' shops. But communal bonds did not snap under the strain. The new factories were concentrated in the central district of the town and the shops themselves were relatively small, employing perhaps one hundred workers. This was small enough to avoid the impersonality and anonymity of very large factories, and the nature of the work permitted conversation and socializing. The workers congregated together in a tenement district known as the Backyard which was adjacent to the factory area. The residents were of different ethnic origins.

A succession of ethnic groups entered the workforce over a period of time. Yet the earliest immigrants to the city were native Americans, many of whom had worked in the old putting-out industry. Consequently, almost three-quarters of all the shoeworkers in Massachusetts in the 1880s were of native stock, and natives still predominated in the mid–1890s. The proportion of the foreign-born from Southern and Eastern Europe was minuscule in 1900 but rose quite rapidly after 1905. However, in contrast to the position in most industries, a considerable proportion of these newcomers had previous experience of the industry in which they were employed in the United States. For example, 49 percent of the Russian Jews and 88 percent of the Italians in Lynn had been shoemakers in their homelands; this provided a better basis for solidarity than a workforce totally without skills.

These circumstances permitted and encouraged the maintenance of shared recreational and welfare institutions, both formal and informal. The central location of workplaces and homes facilitated attendance by both native-born and foreign-born at lunch rooms, bars, and the union hall. This social interaction permitted the transmission to the newcomers of community values, of the meaning of unionisn, and of the importance of class solidarity. This was a process of integrating newcomers into the community and resisting the pressures for fragmentation and dissolution. It probably could not have succeeded without the existence of a succession of quite strong unions among the Lynn workforce. In the 1880s, when many industries were suffering the onset of mechanization and displacement, the shoe industry had already experienced that phase, and the workers were keen to form an industrial union, joining together all the workers in the industry. They were able to depend on a strong tradition of militant unionism, dating back to at least the 1860s, which emphasized the opposed interests of labor and capital and sought to maintain labor's position by encouraging work solidarity.

Fall River presented a striking contrast. Its social and occupational structure, urban topography, residential patterns, and the numbers and ethnicity of the immigrant part of the workforce were markedly dissimilar to Lynn's. Factories were widely dispersed around the city and residential areas grew up around them. This prevented concentration of settlement in the city center, discouraging residential integration of the foreign-born. The factories themselves employed a considerably larger number of people, and this, plus the noise of the machines and the constant speed-ups, prevented the sort of informal on-the-job socializing which was possible in the small shops of Lynn. The isolation of individual workers in the workplace was paralleled by the isolation of ethnic groups in their own neighborhoods around the factory sites. It was impossible to recreate or sustain the kind of communal institutions existing in Lynn, which catered for members of all ethnic groups. The pattern of immigration also differed from that of Lynn. English and Irish newcomers in the 1860s and 1870s, often skilled workers with a trade union background, were being joined by French Canadians in the 1880s. These latest arrivals created a bad initial impression by strikebreaking, by establishing residential segregation, and by maintaining a distinct ethnic culture. Mainly farmers or agricultural laborers, they had no previous experience of employment in the cotton textile industry. Such was the demand for labor, however, that their numbers rapidly increased until by 1896 they constituted 42 percent of the work force of Fall River. They had an advantage over succeeding immigrant groups in being able to speak English and being familiar with Anglo-Saxon political and legal institutions. Among later arrivals were the Portuguese, whose numbers in the community rose from 1,700 in 1895 to 7,020 in 1905. They too were unskilled and residentially segregated, possessing separate ethnic institutions. They shared these characteristics with the Poles, who arrived in substantial numbers after 1900.

The major difference in the position of the French Canadians from that of the Portuguese and the Poles was that the workforce and the trade unions gave them a more favorable reception. At first they aroused suspicion; but trade unions found it in their own self-interest to try to integrate the new arrivals into working-class institutions. Without the informal social connections of Lynn, this was not an easy task. But serious efforts were made to create working-class solidarity as a precondition for success in strikes. Employers' pressure for speed-ups forged a common sense of grievance among workers from all ethnic groups.

However, this major effort to resist the forces of fragmentation by integrating the Canadian immigrant into the working-class community was not repeated in the case of later arrivals. In the 1904 strike the trade unions abandoned their integrating role, refusing to accept the Portuguese and the Poles on the same terms as the French Canadians. There were several reasons for this. One was simple demoralization; having made great efforts to incorporate the French Canadians into the working-class community, the union members were dismayed by the need to repeat the process in the case of the later arrivals. Not speaking English, the Portuguese and the Poles were harder to organize and were less familiar with American ways than their predecessors. Furthermore, their physical characteristics were regarded as alien, and their customs and standard of living so radically different that the task of integration seemed dismayingly formidable. The sheer volume of the new arrivals was an additional obstacle; the proportion of foreign-born to native-born in Fall River was much greater than in Lynn. Finally, the economic depression in the Fall River textile industry after 1900, plus continued mechanical and organizational innovation, increased insecurity and encouraged the view that immigrants were responsible for displacement and unemployment. In these conditions the trade unions acted defensively, relying on skilled workers and renouncing any obligation to recruit the unskilled newcomers for common action in industrial disputes. Consequently the working-class community was fragmented, the integrating forces being too weak to withstand the enormous pressures for communal dissolution. Once the bonds of solidarity were broken, it was an easy step for unions to accept the need for tighter restriction of immigration. The disintegrating forces were many and various, and few unions were able to maintain their previous commitment to the open door.

The examples of Lynn and Fall River clearly illustrate the general factors contributing to the increase in restrictionist sentiment which have been the subject of this chapter. The selection of foreign-born newcomers as a major cause of the deterioration in working and living conditions and hence as a target for hostility depended on a prior failure to integrate them satisfactorily into the larger community. This failure was a consequence of a variety of factors which, combined together, appeared irresistible: the cultural differences of the later arrivals, their sheer numbers, the stagnation or worsening of living standards, occupational displacement, and the transformation of the factory environment. The pent-up frustrations and irritations resulting from profound social and economic change found an outlet in the movement for immigration restriction. Solidarity had become a victim of modernization.

NOTES

1. See John T. Cumbler, *Working-Class Community in Industrial America: Work, Leisure, and Struggle in Two Industrial Cities, 1880–1930* (Westport, Conn.: Greenwood Press, 1979), pp. 7, 23.

2. Clarence D. Long, *Wages and Earnings in the United States, 1860–1890* (Princeton, N.J.: Princeton University Press, 1960), pp. 109, 113. The share of the foreign-born in the labor force rose from just under one-fifth to slightly over one-fifth in the period 1860–90.

3. Long, *Wages and Earnings*, p. 115.

4. It should be noted that unemployment could bite savagely into gains in real wages. In the year 1886, the average worker was idle for about one-quarter of the possible working time. See Henry David, *The History of the Haymarket Affair*, 2nd ed. (New York: Russell and Russell, 1958), p. 20; see also Paul H. Douglas, *Real Wages in the United States, 1890–1926* (New York: Augustus M. Kelley rpt., 1966), pp. 108, 129; Everett J. Burtt, Jr., *Labor Markets, Unions, and Government Policies* (New York: St. Martin's Press, 1963), p. 311.

5. Albert Rees, *Real Wages in Manufacturing, 1890–1914* (Princeton, N.J.: Princeton University Press, 1961), pp. 5, 126. This ignores the possibility that the effects of immigration on the wage levels of the "pre-existing labor force" will be less than the real wage index implies, since immigrants become a significant part of the sample. See Oscar Handlin, "What Happened to Race?" in Oscar Handlin, ed., *Race and Nationality in American Life*, rpt. in S. Fine and Gerald S. Brown, eds., *The American Past* (New York: Macmillan, 1975), Vol. 2, p. 89.

6. Douglas, *Real Wages*, pp. 466–67.

7. Charles Hoffmann, *The Depression of the Nineties: An Economic History* (Westport, Conn: Greenwood Press, 1970), pp. 47–48, 66, 74, 79–87, 110.

8. Ibid., pp. 97, 104–6, 109.

9. Cumbler, *Working-Class Community*, pp. 199–206.

10. Peter Roberts, *The New Immigration* (New York: Macmillan, 1912), p. 162; *The Carpenter*, July 1914, quoting figures from the *Bulletin of the Bureau of Immigration*, March 1914; *Reports of the Immigration Commission*, 41 vols. (Washington, D.C., 1911), *Abstracts*, Vol. 1, p. 57.

11. E. P. Hutchinson, *Immigrants and Their Children, 1850–1950* (New York: Wiley and Sons Inc., 1956), p. 3. The pace of the increase was steady throughout the three decades including the 1890s.

12. Simon Kuznets and Ernest Rubin, *Immigration and the Foreign-Born* (New York: National Bureau of Economic Research, 1954), pp. 3, 42; Grace Abbott, *The Immigrant and the Community* (New York: The Century Co., 1917), pp. 200–202;

Bulletin of the Bureau of Labor 72 (September 1907): p. 414; *Reports of the Industrial Commission* (57 Cong., 1 Sess., H. Doc. No. 184), Vol. 15, p. 296.

13. *Reports of the Immigration Commission, Abstracts*, Vol. 1, p. 13.

14. Hutchinson, *Immigrants and Their Children*, pp. 100–101, 157–70, 216–17.

15. *Study of Methods of Americanization*, Bulletin No. 46, 10 September 1919, (Saposs Papers, Unprocessed Mss., State Historical Society of Wisconsin, Madison), quoting from an article by Paul Douglas, "Is the New Immigration More Unskilled than the Old?" *Publications of the American Statistical Association*, March 1919.

16. Joseph Schachter, "Capital Value and Relative Wage Effects of Immigration into the United States, 1870–1930" (Ph.D. diss., City University of New York, 1969), pp. 23–26; J. W. Jenks and W. Jett Lauck, *The Immigration Problem*, 6th ed. (New York: Funk and Wagnalls, 1926), passim.

17. *Advance Advocate*, August 1905; *Coopers' International Journal*, October 1905.

18. *Reports of the Industrial Commission*, Vol. 15, Section 10, pp. 287–88; Roberts, *New Immigration*, p. 167. A study of charity hospitals in New York City showed that 52.3 percent of the cases were foreign-born persons, 28.5 percent native-born of foreign parentage.

19. *Reports of the Industrial Commission*, Vol. 15, Section 10, p. 287; *Reports of the Immigration Commission, Abstracts*, Vol. 1, p. 33; Roberts, *New Immigration*, p. 234; see also Abbott, *Immigrant and the Community*, p. 111 (on Chicago).

20. Roberts, *New Immigration*, pp. 235–36; *Reports of the Immigration Commission, Abstracts*, Vol. 1, p. 33. Eighty-six percent of the crimes committed by Greeks in New York City consisted of a violation of a corporate ordinance.

21. *Journal of United Labor*, 25 June 1891.

22. Roberts, *New Immigration*, p. 235.

23. Abbott, *Immigrant and the Community*, pp. 190–91.

24. Ibid., p. 192.

25. Ibid., p. 188; *Reports of the Industrial Commission*, Vol. 15, Section 10, p. 288.

26. Abbott, *Immigrant and the Community*, p. 191.

27. Roberts, *New Immigration*, p. 167; Handlin, "What Happened to Race?" p. 93.

28. *Reports of the Immigration Commission, Abstracts*, Vol. 1, p. 99; see also Bureau of Labor Statistics of the State of New York, *Sixteenth Annual Report*, 1898, p. 1022.

29. Philip Taft, "Organized Labor and Technical Change: A Backward Look," in Gerald G. Somers, Edward L. Cushman, and Nat Weinberg, eds., *Adjusting to Technical Change* (New York: Harper and Row, 1963), pp. 27–28; George E. Barnett, *Chapters on Machinery and Labor* (Cambridge, Mass.: Harvard University Press, 1926), p. 117.

30. Frank Tannenbaum, *The Labor Movement* (New York: Putnam's, 1921), pp. 5–11; Taft, "Organized Labor and Technical Change," p. 29.

31. See, for example, Harry Braverman, *Labor and Monopoly Capital: The Degradation of Work in the Twentieth Century* (New York: Monthly Review Press, 1974), pp. 128–29.

32. Don Clawson, *Bureaucracy and the Labor Process: The Transformation of U. S. Industry, 1860–1920* (New York: Monthly Review Press, 1980), pp. 61 (quoting Marx), 62; John T. Cumbler, *Working-Class Community*, p. 15; David F. Noble, *America by Design: Science, Technology, and the Rise of Corporate Capitalism* (New York: Oxford University Press, 1979), p. 259.

33. Daniel J. Walkowitz, *Worker City, Company Town: Iron and Cotton-Worker*

Protest in Troy and Cohoes, New York, 1855–84 (Urbana: University of Illinois Press, 1978), pp. 41–42, 49.

34. Braverman, *Labor and Monopoly Capital*, pp. 193–95; Clawson, *Bureaucracy and the Labor Process*, p. 193; David F. Noble, "Social Choice in Machine Design: The Case of Automatically Controlled Machine Tools," in Andrew Zimbalist, ed., *Case Studies in the Labor Process* (New York: Monthly Review Press, 1979), pp. 31–32.

35. David Montgomery, *Workers' Control in America: Studies in the History of Work, Technology, and Labor Struggles* (Cambridge: Cambridge University Press, 1979), pp. 11, 13, 14; Clawson, *Bureaucracy and the Labor Process*, pp. 149–50.

36. Herbert J. Lahne, *The Cotton Mill Worker in the Twentieth Century* (New York: Farrar and Rinehart, Inc., 1944), p. 14; Walkowitz, *Worker City, Company Town*, pp. 153–54.

37. *Reports of the Industrial Commission*, Vol. 15, Section 36. See also Rowland T. Berthoff, *British Immigrants in Industrial America, 1790–1950* (1953: rpt. New York: Russell and Russell, 1968), p. 36.

38. *Testimony* taken by the Senate Committee on Education and Labor, Vol. 1, 1885, pp. 747–52; Edwin Fenton, "Immigrants and Unions, A Case Study: Italians and American Labor, 1870–1920" (Ph.D. diss., Harvard University, 1957), p. 458; *The Garment Worker*, 17 June 1904. There was a substantial advantage to the employer or subcontractor in adopting the subdivision of labor, using machinery whenever possible. A given quantity of vests could be made in one-quarter of the time required by hand labor, and jackets, trousers, and overalls in one-tenth of the time. See *Thirteenth Annual Report of the Labor Department, Hand and Machine Labor* (55 Cong., 3 Sess., H. Doc. No. 301), 1898–99, p. 122.

39. *Reports of the Industrial Commission*, Vol. 15, Section 38; Isaac A. Hourwich, *Immigration and Labor: The Economic Aspects of European Immigration to the United States* (New York: Putnam, 1912), pp. 399–404.

40. Keith Dix, "Work Relations in the Coal Industry: The Handloading Era, 1880–1930," in Zimbalist, *Case Studies in the Labor Process*, pp. 163–64; David Brody, *Workers in Industrial America: Essays on the Twentieth-Century Struggle* (New York: Oxford University Press, 1980), p. 4; Hourwich, *Immigration and Labor*, p. 420; Berthoff, *British Immigrants*, p. 55; *Thirteenth Annual Report of the Labor Department, Hand and Machine Labor*, 1898–99, p. 122; United Mineworkers of America, *Proceedings of the Twelfth Annual Convention*, 1901. It was calculated in 1912 that the development of mining in the South and Southwest since 1889 had been sufficient to create jobs for every wage earner who had been at work in the bituminous coal mines of Pennsylvania and the Midwest in 1889.

41. Walter E. Weyl and A. M. Sakolski, "Conditions of Entrance to the Principal Trades," *Bulletin of the Bureau of Labor* No. 67, (1906): 730.

42. Fenton, "Immigrants and Unions," pp. 430–33; Barnett, *Chapters on Machinery and Labor*, pp. 30–34; Weyl and Sakolski, "Conditions of Entrance," pp. 734–36.

43. Barnett, *Chapters on Machinery and Labor*, pp. 85–107.

44. Ibid., pp. 6, 27–28; Weyl and Sakolski, "Conditions of Entrance," p. 741.

45. *Granite Cutters' Journal*, April 1904, May 1904.

46. Ibid., April 1904; Fenton, "Immigrants and Unions," pp. 437–39.

47. Elting Morison, "This Uncertain Relation," *Daedalus*, Winter 1980, pp. 179–

84; David Montgomery, *Workers' Control in America*, p. 1; Edward Shorter and Charles Tilly, *Strikes in France, 1830–1968* (London: Cambridge University Press, 1974), p. 13; Gerd Korman, *Industrialization, Immigrants, and Americanizers* (Madison: State Historical Society of Wisconsin, 1967), p. 53; Frank Tannenbaum, *Labor Movement*, pp. 26–29; Peter N. Stearns, *Lives of Labor: Work in a Maturing Industrial Society* (London: Croom Helm, 1975), pp. 128–29.

48. Montgomery, *Workers' Control in America*, pp. 68–69; Clawson, *Bureaucracy and the Labor Process*, pp. 62–64; Braverman, *Labor and Monopoly Capital*, p. 73; see also Bureau of Statistics of Labor of Ohio, *Thirteenth Annual Report*, 1889, pp. 50–69.

49. Milton J. Nadworny, *Scientific Management and the Unions, 1900–1932: A Historical Analysis* (Cambridge, Mass.: Harvard University Press, 1955), p. 53.

50. During the last third of the nineteenth century, the "average" plant in 11 out of 16 major industries more than doubled in size. In 1870 there was only a handful of large factories, mainly concentrated in the textile industry, but by 1900 there were 1,063 factories with 50–1,000 workers and 443 more with more than 1,000 wage earners. See Daniel Nelson, *Managers and Workers: Origins of the New Factory System in the United States, 1880–1920* (Madison: University of Wisconsin Press, 1975), p. 4; David Brody, *Workers in Industrial America*, p. 8, in part quoting from John A. Fitch, *The Steel Workers* (New York, 1911).

51. Nadworny, *Scientific Management*, pp. 70–71.

52. Nelson, *Managers and Workers*, pp. 9, 48; Noble, *America By Design*, pp. 260–61; Clawson, *Bureaucracy and the Labor Process*, p. 167.

53. Nelson, *Managers and Workers*, pp. 50–54; Hugh G. J. Aitken, *Taylorism at Watertown Arsenal: Scientific Management in Action, 1908–1915* (Cambridge, Mass.: Harvard University Press, 1960), pp. 28–29; Brody, *Workers in Industrial America*, p. 10.

54. Clawson, *Bureaucracy and the Labor Process*, pp. 168–170, 180, 217; Montgomery, *Workers' Control in America*, p. 37.

55. Nelson, *Managers and Workers*, pp. 55–61; Nadworny, *Scientific Management*, pp. 52–53, 92; Braverman, *Labor and Monopoly Capital*, p. 98; Montgomery, *Workers' Control in America*, pp. 114–15.

56. Aitken, *Taylorism*, pp. 23, 173; Montgomery, *Workers' Control in America*, p. 117; Braverman, *Labor and Monopoly Capital*, pp. 107–13.

57. Nadworny, *Scientific Management*, pp. 51, 62; Aitken, *Taylorism*, pp. 25, 210–20.

58. It was the machinery and metalworking industries that were most affected. Contemporaries disagreed about the extent of the application of scientific management techniques. See Montgomery, *Workers' Control in America*, p. 33, and Nelson, *Managers and Workers*, pp. 69–70.

59. Montgomery, *Workers' Control in America*, pp. 116–17. For further discussion of workers' awareness of the system and its implications, see Nadworny, *Scientific Management*, pp. 51–56; Aitken, *Taylorism*, pp. 171–80.

60. Jean Monds, "Workers' Control and the Historians: A New Economism," *New Left Review* 97 (May–June 1976): 88–90.

61. Irwin Yellowitz, *The Position of the Worker in American Society, 1865–1896* (Englewood Cliffs, N.J.: Prentice Hall, 1969), pp. 29–30; Montgomery, *Workers' Control in America*, pp. 35, 119; Nadworny, *Scientific Management*, p. 53; Weyl and

Sakolski, "Conditions of Entrance," pp. 705–9; Korman, *Industrialization, Immigrants, and Americanizers*, p. 53.

62. Michael Harrington, *Socialism* (New York: Saturday Review Press, 1972), pp. 132–33; P. K. Edwards, *Strikes in the United States, 1881–1974* (Oxford: Blackwell, 1981), pp. 250–51; Daniel J. Walkowitz, *Worker City, Company Town*, pp. 227, 240–43.

63. Charlotte Erickson, *American Industry and the European Immigrant, 1860–1885* (Cambridge, Mass.: Harvard University Press, 1957), p. 124; *Reports of the Immigration Commission*, Vol. 1, pp. 494–95.

64. *Reports of the Industrial Commission*, Vol. 15, Section 34; Hourwich, *Immigration and Labor*, pp. 426–31.

65. For what follows I depend on John T. Cumbler's excellent *Working-Class Community in Industrial America*, passim.

8

Labor's Debate on Immigration:
Restrictionists versus Internationalists

From the mid–1890s until the establishment of the Immigration Commission by the U.S. Congress in 1907, the American labor movement debated the merits of tighter immigration controls. This debate differed from the discussions of the 1880s in that the focus of controversy shifted from the capitalist importers of cheap foreign labor to the foreign laborers themselves. These years therefore represent a crucial break with the past and establish a signpost for the future.

American workers and their representatives divided into two camps in this debate. In the one were those who contended for more restrictions on immigration, in the other those who favored keeping the law as it was. Of course there were disagreements between the protagonists on both sides. Not all restrictionists approved of the literacy test; not all opponents of further restriction wanted to maintain the existing laws. Nor did the arguments remain static over the whole decade. Some which received emphasis in the 1890s were less prominent by 1906 and others arose to take their place. The protagonists themselves modified their positions or found it expedient from time to time to keep silent until the climate of opinion altered to their advantage. Samuel Gompers, for example, spoke and wrote little about immigration between 1897 and 1902, admitting that "the number of unemployed was less than it had been for some years before and fellow wage earners had a less keen sense of the effects of admitting immigrants without discrimination."[1] But whilst Gompers' views remained unchanged, those of Douglas Wilson of the Machinists' Union evolved quite dramatically. In 1893 he lavished praise on the contribution of immigrants to the

building of America, asserting that only the most energetic and plucky of
the European populations tore up their roots and that those very qualities
of energy and courage guaranteed that immigrants would make good citizens. Drawing on the melting pot analogy, he argued that the mingling
of the blood of different breeds produced a more perfect civilization.[2]

By 1904 Wilson had joined the ranks of the fire-eaters, asserting that wage
laborers had much to lose from immigrant competition in the labor market.
Previous generations of immigrants were "of a higher type than is typified
in the hordes who crowd the steerages of incoming immigrant ships. . . .
[they had demanded] an American home, comfort, decent clothing, cleanliness, school privileges for [their] children and time for recreation for [them-
selves]," unlike the more recent arrivals. What had changed? In 1893 Wilson
had been just as critical, but his angry words were then reserved for contract
laborers and the "unscrupulous and unpatriotic" scoundrels who imported
them. But by the first years of this century Wilson had accepted that the
contract labor law was ineffective in excluding immigrants. Perhaps, after
all, the unthinkable was true: that undesirable immigrants had come of their
own volition and that some method of checking this type of immigration
was necessary.[3]

Despite the differences of emphasis there is a basic continuity in the
restrictionist case over the crucial decade. Almost all the charges and coun-
tercharges of 1905 found echoes in the earlier period, and arguments from
the mid–1890s persisted into the next decade. In 1905 J. W. Sullivan, editor
of *The Garment Worker*, made a speech to the National Civic Federation
entitled "What is to Be Done about Immigration?" In it he summarized the
reasons for further restrictive legislation and prophesied that maintenance
of the existing policy would result in

more rackrent for slum landlords, more dividends for foreign corporations subsi-
dized by European governments, more rake-offs for contractors, *padroni* and foreign
agents of transportation [companies], more voting cattle for our political stockyards,
more blood for real estate sharks, more non-unionists for manufacturing combines,
more outlay for every charitable and penal institution in the country, and incalculably
more misery for America's wage earners.[4]

Few of the restrictionists' charges of the previous decade were excluded
from Sullivan's list of evil consequences. For convenience of analysis this
restrictionist indictment may be examined in three sections: economic, political, and cultural.

The economic arguments against immigration bulked largest in trade
union and labor journals and in the proceedings of labor conventions. They
were advanced more frequently than other aspects of the restrictionist case
and were just as prominent at the end of the decade of debate as at the
beginning. This is not surprising. The overwhelming majority of male

immigrants at the end of the nineteenth century were manual workers offering direct competition to the existing labor force, which believed it could not escape the damaging consequences for wages, hours, and employment. The majority of new immigrants, thought one observer, had "had no experience but of privation, want, low wages and a repulsive diet," and inevitably they impoverished both labor and society. "There is no escape," said Judson Grenell in Malthusian tones, "the increase of population is the propagation of poverty." American workers, complained others, were beggaring themselves for the benefit of foreign nations, and every day the bread was grasped from their mouths by thousands of immigrants. Not all protests were phrased quite as melodramatically as these. More often the tone was restrained and apparently objective, and common sense was appealed to as detailed examples were given of the danger to the American standard of living posed by unrestrained immigration. Surely it was obvious that an influx of cheap immigrant workers tended to reduce wages (or at least to limit their rate of increase), to swell the ranks of the unemployed, and to lengthen hours of work. It was in these terms that the resolution to introduce the literacy test was put to the 1897 AFL convention by the delegates of the Garment Workers' Union. And this easy-to-understand argument was advanced on numerous other occasions in labor journals and by labor spokesmen during the period.[5]

Implicit in these discussions was the fear and resentment felt by workers at the prospect of employers making gains whilst they themselves suffered losses. This apprehension about a shift in the balance of industrial power was made explicit in a measured article in the *American Federationist*, the journal of the AFL. Immigration was recognized as being "by far the most potent and effective of all the weapons which the enemies of labor organizations" had in their possession. For many years trade unions had struggled, with some success, to regulate the supply of labor in order to improve their members' working conditions. But employers had habitually relied on immigrants to weaken labor organizations. Immigration thus "militated against the upward striving of a people" and increased "the number of that class which by reason of its lack of intelligence, is slowest to appreciate the value of organization." Others more charitably attributed the immigrants' unresponsiveness to their European rural background. At stake was not only the more equitable division of the labor product between employers and workers but the very existence of trade unions. Furthermore, fairness and comparability demanded more effective restriction to provide the same protection of workers as employers received from the tariff.[6]

The maintenance of living standards was crucial if American families were to be protected from degradation and despair. A substantial majority of immigrants were single males or married men whose wives and families had remained in their homelands. The wages they received in the United States, though low by American standards, were considerably higher than their customary rates. However, American workers could not provide their families with an acceptable standard of living on the level of wages paid to foreign-born workers. The American workingman, it was said, had "duties and obligations and rights as a citizen, as a father, a member of a church," and the exercise of these "privileges" was expensive. Consequently, trade unions aimed to set a higher standard for the price of labor than its mere cost of production, and the criterion adopted was the standard of living. "Its maintenance in the United States at a higher level than elsewhere [was] more necessary because on it rested those institutions which made the United States a pride and a boast." Recent immigrants generally did not have to meet the expenses of long-established American citizens: the cost of sending children to school, the property tax, the poll tax, the church donations, the insurance premiums, and the contributions to benefit societies. It was recognized that in the course of time the immigrant himself acquired many of these obligations and learned to demand higher wages. But by then he, in turn, was finding his own bargaining position undermined by even more recent immigration. Unlimited entry of foreigners, therefore, offered the prospect of a steady decline in living standards and a withering of family obligations.[7]

Another criticism was the allegedly lower propensity of immigrants to spend their wages in the United States. Their aim was to maximize savings both to facilitate their return to their native countries with sufficient capital to establish economic security and, in the meantime, to send remittances to their families. This practice reduced consumer demand in the United States to the detriment of American industry. The situation was aggravated by the fact that mechanization had increased the productive power of unskilled immigrant workers, further widening the gap between their productivity and their level of consumption.[8]

Labor critics of immigration emphasized the tractable and passive character of the recent immigrants, which enabled employers to weaken the bargaining power of labor organizations. But restrictionists were prepared to use any argument, however contradictory, as long as it appeared to add weight to their case. It was sometimes asserted, for example, that immigrant workers, far from being subservient to their employers, were in reality the pliant tools of dangerous foreign-born agitators. Militant activity by immigrant workers usually exploded into violence, disorder, and bloodshed. The Poles, Hungarians, and Italians differed in their behavior from the native-born workers and the earlier immigrants from Northern Europe who had sought to redress their grievances "by the peaceable methods of mutual effort." The wrecking activities of the newcomers were damaging since they brought into disrepute all trade unions and labor organizations, identifying them in the public mind with disorder and violence.[9]

Some labor leaders hastened to assure their members that restrictionism had an altruistic side, reminding them that "the hundreds of thousands of workmen coming from Continental Europe [were] the prop which maintained aristocracies, autocracies and tyrants in their own country" and emphasizing that the demand for restriction was as "humanitarian for the people of other countries as it is wise, just and protective for the people of our own." If forced to remain at home in larger numbers, European workingmen would be compelled to "battle against injustice and work out their emancipation," which, John Mitchell predicted, would produce higher standards of living for the working class there. Even if such hopes were not fully borne out by events, restrictionists were confident that the populations of emigrant countries would benefit from the enforcement of a literacy test, since this would necessitate the provision of a better standard of education in those countries, assuming that their governments continued to seek the economic and social advantages associated with the emigration of their surplus population.[10]

These economic arguments were addressed to workingmen who actually felt the stress of wage and job competition. However, workers were also citizens with opinions on political and social issues. Recent immigration had implications for politics and posed questions about the future stability of the Republic. It also generated a multiplicity of languages, social customs, and forms of religious observance which cast grave doubts on the capacity of American society to assimilate the newcomers. As citizens, many workers shared these apprehensions, and the political and cultural arguments for restriction which they put forward derived from the common experience and understanding of all social classes. It is conceivable that workers adopted these arguments simply to ingratiate themselves with the general public and to win allies for their economic indictment of immigration. But this is to underestimate the genuine conviction of many members of the working class that unrestricted immigration undermined American culture and republican institutions.

For the members of the Wisconsin School of labor historians, the essentially economic character of labor's opposition to recent immigration was quite evident. Philip Taft asserted that it was "the adverse influence of the immigrant upon the labor market rather than opposition based on race or religion" which accounted for the attitude of organized labor. Similarly, the founder of the school, John R. Commons, wrote that what appeared often to be religious, political, or social animosities were "economic at bottom." Ethnic antagonism occurred between people at the same occupational or competitive level, but where different ethnic groups agreed on standards of wages, hours, and conditions, then antagonisms based on race or culture evaporated. So fundamental were divisions originating from differences in economic standards that they could break down even the strongest ethnic affinities; for example, Russian Jews in the United States were turning against the more recent Jewish immigrants because of their severe economic competition. Further evidence to support Commons's belief came from the Chicago stockyards, where trade unions in the early twentieth century recruited members from many different ethnic groups, resulting in declining interethnic hostility. "Association together and industrial necessity," the Irish and German union leaders said, "have shown us that, however it may go against the grain, we must admit that common interests and brotherhood must include the Polack and the Sheeny." But this association in unions evidently did not destroy, though it may have softened, mutual dislike and distaste among different ethnic groups.[11]

The pre-eminence of economic competition as a cause of ethnic hostility was a conviction which the Wisconsinites shared with men further to the left in the political spectrum. In his book *Immigration and Labor*, Isaac Hourwich asserted that "all doctrinaire theories of a civic character are accepted by organized labor in so far as they may be helpful in its campaign for restriction of immigration," but labor's "real attitude" was to protect jobs and wages. And, in similar vein, David Saposs proposed that "social and political differences gave an ethical veil to the economic motives." In both cases restrictionist arguments based on the defense of American culture or republican principles were seen as instrumental to the achievement of restrictive legislation desired on other grounds. The point was made quite explicitly by a labor editor in 1905, when he acknowledged that conversion of the public mind could not be made on economic grounds but "in the light of the highest benefit to the Republic" and of the mission of the United States in the world. Whilst trade unions were prepared to address their appeal in terms which would carry conviction to a wider audience, the "*argumentum ad stomachum*" remained for them the greatest and most powerful argument of all. For leaders like John Mitchell, the only ground for opposition was an inability on the immigrant's part to command a high wage, confirming Commons's point that ethnic hostility evaporated when there was agreement on wage levels.[12]

This "materialist" case implies that economic causes were "real" and other reasons for opposition advanced by labor organizations were elaborate rationalizations. Not all labor spokesmen would have accepted this interpretation. Even Saposs admitted that the reaction of English-speaking members of trade unions to the new immigrants' dress, mannerisms, language, and apparent unassimilability was one of "contempt, mingled with ridicule and often outright hostility." The antagonism based on race, religion, language, and tradition was genuine and deep; it could not be made to disappear by forthright assertions that the real basis of opposition was economic. Certainly Marx did not make the mistake of ignoring the existence of social groupings which cut across economic class divisions, for example the religious, social, and national allegiances which divided the English from the immigrant Irish workers in the middle of the nineteenth century. He was inclined to stress the role of employers in contributing to these antagonisms, but he did not deny their authenticity. Of course, Marx still believed that these noneconomic antagonisms would wither away under the scorching rays of socialist thought and action, although the history of the American labor movement in the early twentieth century does not bear out his expectation. So far from noneconomic groupings being "secondary, artificial or vestigial," they are, on the contrary, profound and fundamental and owe nothing to false consciousness. Human beings, as the anthropologist Claude Lévi-Strauss has argued, have an "instinctive antipathy, [a] repugnance for ways of life, thought or belief" to which they are unaccustomed. "The attitude of longest standing which no doubt has a firm psychological foundation, as it tends to reappear in each one of us when we are caught unaware, is to reject out of hand the cultural institutions—ethical, religious, social or aesthetic—which are furthest removed from those with which we identify ourselves." To assert that men should be bound together in economic groups irrespective of race or culture "is not very satisfactory to the intellect, for it overlooks the factual diversity which we cannot help but see." The power of race or ethnic differences to create division has been attested throughout history. "Gestures, sounds, the timbre of emotions in the voice, discipline or looseness in the body, spatial distances or the touching of flesh—all our routes of perception are heavily laden with affect. Man is primordially biological, and his body reacts to other bodies in spite of his mind or his beliefs."[13]

Whether these sorts of differences are derived from biology or culture is immaterial to this analysis. They exist and, as Grace Abbot pointed out, they may be overcome by intercourse and co-operative effort, as they were, partially, in the mineworkers' and meatpackers' unions. However, the continuing large volume of raw recruits to American industry from the rural areas of Europe meant that the task of breaking down barriers had to be completed again and again. It is not surprising that American labor preferred intensified restriction to the herculean task of forming unified economic organizations from such ethnically diverse peoples.[14]

Undoubtedly some labor representatives used political and cultural arguments as a screen for their economic objections or as a lever over public opinion. But others advanced economic arguments and cultural objections with at least equal energy and conviction. The Granite Cutters and the Iron Molders, whilst emphasizing the impact on wages, recognized that European immigration was a menace to all regardless of occupation. The Slavs, noted W. C. Pearce of the Mineworkers, had a lower standard of living and took a longer time to assimilate American ideas; they were "the principal menace to our wages *and* [author's italics] morals". But, the objection may be raised, both the granite cutters and the mineworkers were on the same economic level as the recent immigrants, and it might be expected that ethnic antagonisms would disappear if economic disagreements were ironed out. Such expectations were false. Consider the example of artisans' opposition to newly arrived immigrants in the 1770s when land was abundant, there was work for all, and frictions arose "out of cultural differences and mutual suspicions." Again, in the period we are now discussing, the subordination of cultural to economic factors did not apply in the case of the Locomotive Engineers or some of the other railroad brotherhoods, which took a deep interest in immigration from the early 1890s. Neither their jobs nor their incomes were threatened by the newcomers, yet they were among the first unions to clamor for more restriction on the grounds of cultural and political differences. As citizens they were concerned that the new immigrants were "too ignorant and too vicious" to appreciate the great values and benefits of American laws and institutions. They added, in a minor key, that the disturbance to the labor market caused by immigration was equally important.[15] The typographers were another group which suffered little from immigrant economic competition yet feared the impact of immigration on the family and on the future of the nation.

Here is solid evidence that noneconomic arguments for restriction were not invariably advanced in a self-serving, propagandizing, or rationalizing spirit, but that they often had an independent existence stemming from a deep and instinctive antipathy for the different and the strange, and that many working people were filled with apprehension and foreboding about the future of American values and ideals. "It is the *mental* aspect of culture," James Leyburn observed, "which gives us what security we have in life," and it is a threat to this which disturbs people most profoundly. It is true that economic motives figured most prominently in labor restrictionism; they certainly had the longest pedigree and held their ground throughout the period of restrictionist agitation, culminating in the restriction acts of the 1920s. Yet, to use Irwin Yellowitz's term, they "blended" with the prejudice that arose out of differences in religion, habits, attitudes, and appearance. Opposition on these grounds was slower to emerge; in a number of cases it may have acted as a rationalization or a smokescreen; it was only occasionally assigned priority; but the evidence is convincing that it represented a genuine and increasingly insistent commitment to the preservation of a way of life in the United States threatened by alien values and behavior.[16]

The threat was a twofold one, to American political culture, and to social customs and behavior. It is possible that the emergence of the literacy test as the most practical and widely canvassed form of restriction among the general public directed the attention of laboring men to the adverse social consequences of an increasing proportion of illiterates in the population. In any event, labor's indictment of the alien impact on political ideals and behavior was coherent, detailed, and vigorous, though too full of implicit self-congratulation. Labor's case was that good government depended on the virtue, intelligence, and independence of the citizenry. Illiterate immigrants were a menace to American citizenship because they had no knowledge or appreciation of American institutions or of impending political issues. "Ignorance," wrote an AFL spokesman, "makes possible oppression... A republic must conquer ignorance or be conquered by it." Recent immigrants compared unfavorably with earlier arrivals from Northern Europe who had experienced "an advanced state of civilization" in countries renowned for their "educational development, strict morality and sturdy independence of spirit." The more recent newcomers, by contrast, were unfitted to appreciate and enjoy the freedom and comfort offered by the United States to its citizens. The *Railroad Trainman* condemned them as "a vicious, ignorant [and] pestilential mob," but other observers understood the historical reasons for political backwardness on the immigrants' part, the generations of despotic rule in Eastern and Central Europe which debarred the subjects of Russian and Austrian monarchs from achieving the standards of citizenship which would have encouraged them to feel responsibility for public affairs. The most intelligent, energetic, and ambitious of these imperial subjects, it was said, were creamed off into the army and the church. It was therefore appropriate to insist that future immigrants should not be prevented by tradition or ignorance from appreciating the broader civilization and higher plane of life which prevailed in the United States. The most effective guarantee of a high standard of political behavior was the imposition of a literacy test, which would ensure an educated and intelligent alien community with good potential for citizenship.[17]

Recent immigrants were widely believed to be responsible for the deeply rooted corruption in political life, particularly at a local level. Their ignorance of the principles of free government and their previous reliance on face-to-face transactions with government officials in order to obtain personal favors or exemptions from particular laws made them the easy prey, or willing accomplices, of the city political machines. The corrupt naturalization process engineered by a number of the machines tightened the grip of political bosses over the political process and often enabled the foreign-born population to hold the balance of political power, though unfitted for such a role. The strength of the foreign-born in politics dissuaded many politicians from speaking out on sensitive issues through fear of electoral retaliation. Labor organizations had some direct cause for concern since it was not unprecedented for the foreign-born vote to be manipulated by the machine in the interests of the employers. There was, therefore, understandable apprehension that the American political system was being subjected to a once-for-all change and that since it was impossible fully to assimilate the newcomers, American republican ideals would be gradually eroded.[18]

Recent immigrants, then, were condemned by labor spokesmen for being the ignorant dupes of corrupt political bosses. However, their ignorance made them equally vulnerable to foreign-born agitators, anarchists, and nihilists. Compensating for their small numbers by their lawlessness and violent opposition to government, they found a natural recruiting ground among their fellow foreigners in American cities. Although they were highly educated themselves and able to skip through a literacy test, their potential supporters among the credulous and ignorant would be filtered out by the test. One labor editor warned of the danger from these anarchists who "hate our government, despise its institutions and are ready to incite their dupes to any deed of shame or blood." Examples of the power of foreign anarchy and crime were not far to seek. The 1891 lynching in New Orleans of Italians arrested for the murder of the local police chief but acquitted by the court was the occasion for the following outburst against the Italians, though it was equally, if unintentionally, applicable to the native-born lynchers. The "hordes of ignorance and crime," wrote this passionate critic, were "setting up their petty despotisms within our republic, substituting the decrees of their dark lantern tribunals for the decisions of our courts, frustrating the operation of our laws by their threats and bribes, and displacing the common rule of law and order by violence and anarchy."[19]

Machine politicians and anarchists, therefore, were twin threats to republican virtue, and both derived their power from recent immigrants from Southern and Eastern Europe. Restricting immigration would also remove the danger of the creation of a kind of fifth column within the United States, composed of recent immigrants with a dual loyalty to the European homeland and to their country of adoption. In the event of dispute or war between the United States and a European country, the American government could not be certain of the allegiance of its foreign-born population. The *Railroad Trainman*, ever alert to the immigrant threat, reported in 1895 that many Russians living in the United States had visited their country's consulate on the death of the tsar in order to take the oath of fidelity to the new sovereign. No one, the writer commented, could take the loyalty oath to Russia and be loyal "in all senses" to the United States. They signified by their oath where they would place themselves in any crisis.[20]

There were numerous dangers facing the American republic, and in almost every case, labor asserted, there was a close connection between them and the new immigration. But perhaps the greatest threat of all was to the American mission to maintain, sustain, and propagate republican forms of government throughout the world. The theme of mission and destiny had been invoked on several occasions in the past by labor leaders. Powderly, among others, had believed that the American experiment of human liberty and self-government had been under God's protecting and directing hand. They urged on Americans the duty of maintaining "the pristine purity and integrity" of their institutions and of transmitting them intact to posterity. This meant combatting the manifold dangers which confronted the country, "the greatest and most comprehensive" being immigration. Failure meant signing the death warrant of "the last effort of divine Providence in behalf of mankind," but success would result in a general revolution throughout the world. The restrictionists' invocation of Divine Mission proved to be useful in helping to combat the arguments of their opponents, who defended the open door for immigration partly in religious terms.[21]

These allegations about the political consequences of immigration were advanced in more apocalyptic terms than the discussion about the impact of immigration on social customs and institutions. Yet laboring men observed a real and growing threat to the social environment which would have to be confronted if Americans were to retain what was good in their inheritance. There was, they believed, a close connection between low wages and, a favorite term, "degraded" social conditions. Also, the increasing tendency for immigrants to congregate in the inner cities hindered assimilation and failed to neutralize harmful elements in the immigrants' culture. As in the debate over the effects of immigration on the political culture, labor representatives did not, in general, take up arguments about the connection between declining social conditions and voluntary immigration from Southern and Eastern Europe until the very end of the nineteenth century, and again the railroad brotherhoods were prominent in developing the indictment.[22]

Obviously immigrants were the products of different ethnic and national cultures. The question at issue was whether their cultures would adapt to American norms or whether they would, in part or completely, transform American social ideas and behavior and establish new or modified cultural patterns in the United States. There was no mistaking the distaste which many laboring men felt for alien cultures and social behavior. Newcomers were characterized as "diseased, poverty-stricken, ignorant and in many cases totally depraved," with "a fair proportion" in the criminal classes. They had "dispositions towards violence" and were contemptuous of law and order. They were "social outcasts from the least civilized parts of Europe," filling the hospitals, jails, and insane asylums and by their very presence degrading the American population. They existed in loathsome living conditions whose standards of sanitation bred disease and epidemics. A considerable proportion were illiterate. In short, whilst America was still an asylum, it now offered hospitality to very different guests, to criminals, paupers, the illiterate, and the ignorant. The issue was discussed in strikingly offensive trems. "That is not a wise host," remonstrated the editor of the *Locomotive Engineers' Journal*, "who opens the door of his clean, warm, healthy, virtuous, frugal and industrious home to the unclean, the vicious, the thriftless, the lazy and the lawless." Immigration had spread over American communities "the germs of European disease, sloth, vice and political error and crime" and exercised a contaminating influence over American homes. Of course, these alleged characteristics of new immigrants "owed more to prejudice and social distance than to reality," but that did not weaken the force of resentment which many workers felt.[23]

Resentment became apprehension when labor observers noted the apparently diminishing capacity of the American environment to transform immigrant cultures. They explained this by reference to the relative isolation of the newcomers in compact quarters of city centers where housing was cheap, unskilled laboring jobs were available, and coreligionists and fellow ethnics were present in large numbers to add a degree of familiarity to the strangeness of the new life in America. The herding of immigrants into colonies helped to preserve foreign customs, habits, and language, and in general to consolidate the newcomers' alien identity.

Labor organizations felt justified in insisting that the foreign-born should not be "debarred by tradition or ignorance from appreciating [a] broader civilization and higher plane of life," otherwise they would represent a real danger to American social customs and behavior. Unless conquered, the colonies would themselves expand and conquer the United States. Above all, the new immigration imperilled the welfare of the American family, and hence the future of the United States. Underpaid labor meant underfed families, uneducated children, insanitary homes, and low moral standards. "Verily the home is the heart of the nation, and our people must have good homes if our prestige among nations is to be retained and our progress is to be as great in the future as in the past." The literacy test, many thought, would provide the solution since it would help to lift the veil of ignorance, making immigrants more responsive to American stimuli and creating the opportunity for acculturation through the written word.[24]

In a revealing phrase, one advocate of the literacy test insisted that it was essential to "moral and social purity." There was no question for him of cultural syncretism; American culture was to be preserved undefiled, and the literacy test would facilitate that process. In their opposition to immigration on social and cultural grounds, labor adopted a revealing vocabulary, reiterating words like purity, contamination, cleanliness, poison, filth, darkness, health, degradation, preservation, depravity, and vice. An iron molder put the point in common sense terms: "We would not welcome to our home circle those whom we believed would exercise a contaminating influence. Why should we not apply the same discrimination when dealing with our greater family—the nation?"[25]

In all these attacks on aliens there was barely a trace of racism. American workers and their spokesmen did not claim that the political illiteracy and social degeneracy of immigrants were attributable to an inferior genetic inheritance. The views of William Howard of Washington, D.C., who wished to exclude all non-Aryans because of their "immutable and indestructible" racial characteristics, were quite exceptional. In almost every case where immigrants were criticized by labor, their behavior was attributed to the European cultures from which they sprang. For example, the virulent attack of David Black on the ignorance, debasement, immorality, and poverty of immigrants acknowledged these qualities to be the result of "centuries of tyranny and unrestrained despotism." This did not make the newcomers any more promising material for transforming into American citizens, but it did at least raise the possibility that they or their children would have the capacity to adapt and develop under the civilizing impact of the American environment. This was explicitly acknowledged by Edward McSweeney, ex–trade unionist and assistant commissioner of immigration, who connected the social degradation which accompanied the displacement of the native-born by the foreign-born in places of work with "the former state of servitude" and "the low degree of civilization" of the recent immigrants. Others were optimistic that the subjects of despots could, by joining labor organizations, learn the fundamental principles of free government and become citizens. The most liberal restrictionist position was that adopted by the editor of the journal of the Mineworkers' Union in the mid–1890s. Urging restriction, he condemned the influx into the mines of a class of workers who were undesirable because of their different standards and modes of behavior. Nevertheless, he confessed to no antipathy to these newcomers, claiming to recognize their manhood and common brotherhood with native-born Americans and earlier immigrants. Such attitudes were the very antithesis of racism.[26]

This attack on immigration by laboring men and their union representatives was weighty, deeply felt, and plausible, but, according to its critics, irrelevant to the major problems confronting the working class. Although restrictionists were ultimately able to secure a majority for the literacy test, they did not do so without a fight. Their opponents included those who, though restrictionists, remained opposed to the literacy test. However, the most coherent, vehement, and principled opponents of the test were those who opposed restriction altogether, except in the case of immigrants suffering from physical or mental illness. Their grounds for opposition were numerous and complex but may be summarized in the following way. The issue of immigration restriction was a distraction from the necessary process of social analysis which would reveal the fundamental reasons for working-class unemployment and impoverishment. Far from seriously damaging the American economy and the interests of its workforce, immigration even produced some clear economic advantages to the United States. Second, immigration restriction was a clear infringement of natural rights and notions of human brotherhood. Finally, limitation on the right of entry to foreigners was a blatant infringement of America's traditional role as asylum for the oppressed of other lands. Let us consider these arguments for the defense in turn.

In the earlier part of the period under discussion, from the mid- to the late 1890s, a number of workers' leaders emphasized that immigration restriction did not go to the root of America's economic and social problems. Their analysis reflected the considerable influence of Henry Georgeite, populist, and socialist ideas in the labor movement. In the early twentieth century, by contrast, these arguments were less widely discussed following the demise of the Knights of Labor and the relative decline of socialist influence in the trade unions. The essence of their case was that immigration was not a cause of low wages and unemployment, and therefore fighting immigration was not fighting the real disease. American workingmen were "accustomed to employ quack medicines and humbugs" for the cure of bodily ills and readily grasped a quack medicine as a panacea for economic evils. This was understandable, since immigrants presented a tangible target and their connection with unemployment seemed easier to grasp than a complex analysis of the characteristics of a capitalist economy.[27] Such critiques of capitalism had been available for a considerable time but only began to command widespread support in the 1880s and 1890s, when Henry George's single-tax proposal gained converts among agrarian and urban reformers alike. George's analysis had more influence among radicals than the Marxist critique, at least up to the mid–1890s, but subsequently, after the formation of the Socialist Party in 1901, the position was reversed. So, for those who were uncertain about attributing the major share of the blame for economic hardship to immigration, there were alternative and coherent explanations which allocated to immigration, at worst, a subsidiary role in causing distress.

In the early 1890s the journal of the Knights of Labor was to the fore in disseminating ideas about the crushing burden imposed on laboring people by the evil of land monopoly. Hundreds of thousands of acres were held off the market by land speculators, and men who would gladly have purchased small units of land at reasonable prices were prevented from doing so unless they consented to become tenants or to meet the exorbitant demands of land speculators. Yet everywhere "the world has more work that needs doing than there are hands to do [it, and] men who would gladly work are condemned to idleness and lands that need tilling must go unplanted." In the manufacturing towns men were idle or on short time, but the potential consumers of their products were kept off the land by speculators. Consequently, whilst the target of the urban unemployed was often the immigrants, a more appropriate object of criticism was the foreign land speculators who, like their American counterparts, restricted easy access to land ownership for aspiring small farmers. The solution to the problem was to restore railroad and other speculators' land to the people by means of the single tax, by government ownership of all monopolies, and an increase in the volume of money. Once this was done, immigration restriction would appear altogether unnecessary and unfraternal.[28]

The Knights' attack on the system of land monopoly broadened into a critique of property ownership in general which connected with subsequent socialist indictments. But there was an important intermediate stage in the development of the argument which focused attention on the impact of new technology as the major reason for economic distress. This criticism was partially shared by immigration restrictionists, but whereas the latter saw immigrants as permitting the introduction of new machines, and for that reason to be opposed, radical critics regarded immigration as a side issue, the principal target being the economic and social power wielded by capitalists through their ownership and control of modern machinery. Critics stressed that the surplus of labor was brought about by the "astounding" displacement of labor resulting from the development and extended application of machinery. The number of jobs would continue to decline if not a single immigrant were allowed in, since one machine in a factory or workshop could throw more people out of work than a whole shipload of immigrants.[29]

However, improved technology had many advantages to offer working people. Objections raised were not about machinery *per se* but about the uses to which it was put. The owners of the machines ultimately determined how and when they should be employed and to what purpose. Capitalism, by the use it made of machinery, was responsible for overstocking the labor market and for creaming off surplus value. That, ultimately, was the major cause of labor's low level of subsistence. "Don't blame the poor foreigners, it is the system," a painter and decorator declared on one occasion.

Even if immigration were cut off, the search for improved labor-saving technology would be stepped up; the recruitment of women would increase; there would be attempts to evade the immigration laws; and in foreign countries workers who had been denied entry into the United States would compete more intensively on the job market, leading to lowered wages and prices in their homelands. This would set on foot more intense competition in export markets, not excluding those of the United States. American manufacturers in turn would be forced to cut wage costs in the face of intensified competition from foreign goods. Given the ingenuity of the owners of capital in maintaining a labor surplus, the central issue of the time, according to one mineworker, was to change "the accursed wage system" by which labor, while producing everything, received no more in recompense than was sufficient to maintain its strength for work.[30] The campaign for new restrictive legislation therefore failed to touch the root of the problem and distracted working people from correctly analyzing the causes of their condition. Immigration had a part to play, it might be conceded, in sharpening the struggle for existence among wage earners, but it was not the cause of that struggle.[31]

Furthermore, by placing a higher value on profit than on production, capitalism negated the true purpose of an economic system, which was to maximize production to meet social needs. The immigration of the able-bodied, "the husky, brave, and ambitious foreign workmen," should be welcomed as adding productive resources to the American economy. There was no danger of overproduction "until every acre of ground is cultivated to the highest degree, until every mine is worked so as to supply the needs of the people, until all factories are run so as to produce enough food, clothing and other products to make all the people comfortable."[32] In the past the American economy had been developed by immigrants; in the future they had an equally important role to play, but only if the existing industrial system were overthrown by the forces of labor. If that were done, then the old welcoming refrain could once again be sung with conviction:

> Come along, come along, make no delay.
> Come from every nation, come from every way;
> Uncle Sam is big enough to shield you from all harm;
> He is also rich enough to give you all a farm.[33]

Of course every immigrant was a consumer as well as a producer and gave employment to others. Carpenters in New York State were said to oppose restriction because immigration stimulated the construction industry, and no doubt other groups of workers saw a direct connection between increased employment and immigration. Additionally, every immigrant brought in small sums of money which in aggregate represented a considerable gain to the American economy. This argument was not taken up by working people, possibly because they perceived that such an asset had to be offset against remittances to the home countries and the transfer of savings by migrants returning to Europe.[34]

When working-class opponents of restriction thought about immigration in the context of natural rights and human brotherhood, they revealed an intense idealism and a strong conviction that their arguments would have a powerful appeal. They firmly believed that the rights of emigration and immigration were natural rights, and a succession of labor spokesmen reiterated their commitment to this idea. "It was," wrote O'Neill McDarragh, "an infringement of the natural rights of man 'to proscribe his liberty to move to any part of the world which seems to him best'." It appeared to the president of the Colorado Federation of Labor that "every human being [had] a right to wander where he pleased upon the face of the earth." Nature meant the earth for all mankind, thought Thomas Kidd, and every right-thinking man believed in the words of Tom Paine, "The world is my country and to do good is my religion." George Clark, an immigrant coalminer from England and a member of the Western Federation of Miners, testified before the Industrial Commission that according to the "God-given right of humanity" no men had the power to prescribe where others should live. Even some restrictionists acknowledged the force of this idea. The editor of the *United Mineworkers' Journal*, for example, conceded that "to shut the gates of any land in the face of any man [was] essentially unnatural and wrong," though he declared, in reference to the tariffs, that if it was right to shut the gates against one commodity, it was equally right to shut them against another. These sentiments were summed up in a passage in the *Detroit Sentinel* in 1898: "There is a higher law than that of majorities:

the external moral law of the universe . . . If all men have an innate right to life, then it follows that all may live in whatever part of the earth's surface they desire." What, the author asked, was the legitimacy of political boundaries? Were they not merely "the arbitrary markings made by the bloody swords of historic bandits?"[35]

The argument based on natural rights should have carried particular conviction in the United States, as labor spokesmen were quick to point out. From the Declaration of Independence onwards, leading American figures had affirmed the right of men to migrate in pursuit of their natural rights to life, liberty, and happiness. In 1817 Daniel Webster avowed that the principle on which American institutions rested was "the right of a man in any country who is neither convicted nor accused of crime to change his domicile and allegiance with a view to the free exercise of his own faculties and the pursuit of happiness in his own lawful way." Consequently, an "American" ethical code which erected "American" right above human right was both "curious and cruel." In the words of Crèvecoeur more than a century earlier, "We know, properly speaking, no strangers. This is every person's country."[36]

In emphasizing natural rights, working-class leaders did not ignore ideas of human brotherhood and labor solidarity. At first they sought scriptural authority, but later the context became more secular and then socialistic. "Brotherhood," one writer affirmed, "allows no diminution in the measure of its love . . . Before all else it sets universality, solidarity." Or, as Walt Whitman put it, "We are aboard one ship, and what is port for one is port for all." The practical consequences for Americans included welcoming all immigrants with "that spirit born of the brotherhood of man and the fatherhood of God." But then the argument developed a stage further until it prefigured part of the socialist case against restriction in the decade before the First World War. Thomas G. Ryves expressed this view in 1895 when he wrote that labor was "the most cosmopolitan thing in the world," united by the demand for social justice and the equitable division of the product of industry. Capital recognized no political boundaries when trying to defeat labor organizations. Therefore, if the fight against capital was to be successful, national divisions and national prejudices had to be broken down in the interests of international working-class solidarity.[37]

If these arguments carried insufficient conviction to the audience at which they were aimed, there was a further shot in the antirestrictionists' locker designed to invoke antimonopoly sentiments among labor organizations. Restriction, simply, represented an attempt to monopolize a large section of the earth which had been made for all. It was inconsistent for trade unionists who complained of industrial and transportation monopolies to attempt to monopolize the United States for persons already living there. In any case, all Americans were foreigners or descendants of the foreign-born and had no right to set themselves up as dictators of who should and who should not be allowed in. Daniel De Leon's *People* went further in making the point that immigration restriction flew in the face of social and historical laws and was doomed to fail. People who owned more of the earth's resources than they needed would ultimately be unsuccessful in keeping away those who had less.[38]

Those who were unconvinced by the preceding antirestrictionist arguments could be appealed to on one additional ground, namely the right of the oppressed, wherever they lived, to seek asylum in the United States. Since the period of the American Revolution at least, the New World's role had been defined as offering, in Paine's words, "the *asylum* for the persecuted lovers of civil and religious liberty from every part of Europe," where "the outcast of every nation, where the child of every creed and of every clime" would breathe America's free air and participate in her free constitution.[39] This sense of obligation, duty, or mission towards the oppressed retained enough force in the 1890s for labor opponents of restriction to invoke it in defense of free access to the United States.

Eugene Debs, for example, asked what was the good of Columbus's discovery "if it did not afford an asylum to men who would escape from tyranny, and especially those who were workers." In describing for his own members the debate on restriction at the AFL convention of 1896, David Black of the Iron Molders' Union referred to the "storm of opposition" to restrictionism from those who believed that America should be preserved as an asylum and a refuge for the persecuted of the world. For some opponents of restriction, the definition of "the oppressed" broadened in the course of time to include all who had been expropriated or who had "fled to escape the clutches of starvation" or even those who simply desired to better their condition. But though the idea of asylum retained some of its vigor, the few references to it in labor journals indicate that its appeal was less potent than that of natural rights or the need to transform capitalism.[40]

The debate within the labor movement touched on almost all the arguments of restrictionists and antirestrictionists in this period, with the conspicuous exception of ideas derived from the pseudoscience of eugenics. This omission probably owed something to the somewhat attenuated but still extant internationalism of the working class and to the experience of migration in the families of most of them. But arguments alone did not change minds. The increasing power of the restrictionist critique in the first decade of this century owed much to changing economic and political circumstances. The aim of the next chapter is to identify these changes and to determine how they established a new direction in immigration policy for labor organizations.

NOTES

1. *Testimony Taken by the Select Committee of the House of Representatives to Inquire into the Alleged Violation of the Laws Prohibiting the Importation of Contract Laborers,*

Paupers, Convicts and Other Classes (50 Cong., 1 Sess., H. Misc. Doc. No. 572), Vol. 15, pp. 497–506.

2. *Official Journal of the Painters and Decorators*, August 1907; *United Mineworkers' Journal*, 23 August 1906; *Coopers' International Journal*, May 1908.

3. American Federation of Labor, *Report of the Proceedings of the Twenty-Second Annual Convention*, 1902, p. 21 (hereafter referred to as AFL, *Proceedings*); *Monthly Journal of the International Association of Machinists*, November 1893.

4. *Monthly Journal of the International Association of Machinists*, September 1904.

5. Ibid., November 1893; *The Weekly Bulletin of the Clothing Trades*, 23 June 1905; *Locomotive Engineers' Journal*, February 1897; *Detroit Advance and Labor Leaf*, 25 February 1888; *Memorial of the United Brotherhood of Carpenters and Joiners of America, Praying the Suspension of Immigration to the United States Indefinitely* (52 Cong., 2 Sess., S. Misc. Doc. No. 2); *American Federationist*, January 1911.

6. AFL, *Proceedings*, 1897, p. 56; 1903, p. 26; 1905, p. 75; *Coopers' International Journal*, May 1908; *The Railroad Trainman*, December 1892; *Granite Cutters' Journal*, July 1897, October 1897; *The Typographical Journal*, January 1903; *The Garment Worker*, December 1898; *Reports of the Industrial Commission* (56 Cong., 2 Sess., H. Doc. No. 495), Vol. 7, p. 392; *Granite Cutters' Journal*, November 1896. See also Edwin Fenton, "Immigrants and Unions, A Case Study: Italians and American Labor, 1870–1920" (Ph.D. diss., Harvard University, 1957), p. 412; *American Federationist*, December 1894, p. 216; *Locomotive Firemen's Magazine*, July 1891.

7. *Michigan Union Advocate*, 29 January 1904; Frank Julian Warne, *The Coal-Mine Workers; A Study in Labour Organization* (New York: Longmans, Green and Co., 1905), pp. 230, 236.

8. *The Railroad Trainman*, January 1893, August 1907; *Coopers' International Journal*, October 1905; *Granite Cutters' Journal*, March 1904; *The Typographical Journal*, May 1896.

9. *Locomotive Engineers' Journal*, May 1891, June 1899; *Reports of the Immigration Commission* (61 Cong., 3 Sess., S. Doc. No. 747), Vol. 1, p. 500; *United Mineworkers' Journal*, 17 June 1897.

10. AFL, *Proceedings*, 1905, p. 76; *The Weekly Bulletin of the Clothing Trades*, 29 April 1904; National Civic Federation, *Facts About Immigration* (New York, 1907), p. 70.

11. Philip Taft, *Organized Labor in American History* (London: Harper and Row, 1964), pp. 306–8; Philip Taft, "Labor History and the Labor Movement Today," *Labor History* 7 (1966): 75; John R. Commons, *Races and Immigrants in America* (1907; rpt. New York: Augustus M. Kelley, 1967), pp. 113–15; Carroll D. Wright, "Influence of Trade Unions on Immigrants," *Bulletin of the Bureau of Labor* No. 56 (1905): 4–5.

12. Isaac A. Hourwich, *Immigration and Labor; The Economic Aspects of European Immigration to the United States* (New York: Putnam, 1912), p. 45; David J. Saposs, *Left Wing Unionism* (New York: International Publishers, 1926), p. 112; *The Weekly Bulletin of the Clothing Trades*, 23 June 1905; *Amalgamated Journal*, 17 May 1906, p. 4.

13. Saposs, *Left Wing Unionism*, p 112; E. J. B. Rose, *Colour and Citizenship: A Report on British Race Relations* (London: Oxford University Press, 1969), p. 18; Norman J. Ware, *Labor in Modern Industrial Society* (New York: Heath and Co., 1935), p. 33; Claude Lévi-Strauss, "Race and History," in UNESCO, *Race and Science* (New York: Columbia University Press, 1961), pp. 224–26; *The Detroit*

Sentinel, 19 February 1898; Michael Novak, *The Rise of the Unmeltable Ethnics* (New York: Macmillan, 1972), pp. 81–82.

14. Grace Abbott, *The Immigrant and the Community* (New York: The Century Co., 1917), pp. 282–83.

15. *Granite Cutters' Journal*, December 1896; *Iron Molders' Journal*, May 1904; Charlotte Erickson, "Immigration and the American Economy: An Historical View," in Dennis Welland, ed., *The United States: A Companion to American Studies* (London: Methuen, 1974), p. 97; *Reports of the Industrial Commission*, Vol. 12, p. 100; *Locomotive Engineers' Journal*, July 1893, September 1893, February 1897, April 1897.

16. *The Typographical Journal*, April 1907; James G. Leyburn, "The Problem of Ethnic and National Impact from a Sociological Point of View," in David F. Bowers, ed., *Foreign Influences in American Life* (Princeton, New Jersey: Princeton University Press, 1944), p. 60; Irwin Yellowitz, *The Position of the Worker in American Society, 1865–1896* (Englewood Cliffs, N.J.: Prentice Hall, 1969), p. 11.

17. *The Railroad Trainman*, November 1894; *Advance Advocate*, August 1905, January 1907; *Monthly Journal of the International Association of Machinists*, May 1905; *Locomotive Engineers' Journal*, April 1897; *American Federationist*, June 1897, p. 69; Commons, *Races and Immigrants in America*, pp. 10, 112; AFL, *Proceedings*, 1902, p. 21; *Iron Molders' Journal*, July 1897; *Granite Cutters' Journal*, October 1897.

18. *Iron Molders' Journal*, May 1904, April 1906; *Amalgamated Journal*, 14 May 1903; *Granite Cutters' Journal*, March 1904.

19. *United Mineworkers' Journal*, 23 August 1906; AFL, *Proceedings*, 1905, p. 102; *Locomotive Engineers' Journal*, May and June, 1891; *The Railroad Trainman*, January 1896.

20. *The Railroad Trainman*, February 1895, January 1907.

21. *The Weekly Bulletin of the Clothing Trades*, 23 June 1905, p. 4; *Record of the Proceedings of the Eighth Regular Session of the General Assembly of the Knights of Labor*, 1884; *The Railroad Trainman*, November 1893; *Advance Advocate*, January 1907.

22. *Locomotive Engineers' Journal*, February 1892.

23. Leyburn, "The Problem of Ethnic and National Impact," p. 59; *The Railroad Trainman*, August 1904; AFL, *Proceedings*, 1907, p. 109; *Advance Advocate*, July 1905, August 1905; *Coopers' International Journal*, October 1905; *Iron Molders' Journal*, July 1897, June 1905; *Memorial of the United Brotherhood of Carpenters and Joiners of America, Praying the Suspension of Immigration to the United States Indefinitely*; *Granite Cutters' Journal*, December 1896; *Locomotive Engineers' Journal*, March 1891; Yellowitz, *Position of the Worker in American Society*, p. 12.

24. *The Railroad Trainman*, August 1905, February 1906; *Iron Molders' Journal*, July 1897, June 1905; *The Typographical Journal*, January 1903, April 1907; *Monthly Journal of the International Association of Machinists*, January 1905; *American Federationist*, December 1894, p. 216; *Reports of the Industrial Commission*, Vol. 7, p. 747 (testimony of D. F. Kennedy, AFL Organizer, Indiana); AFL, *Proceedings*, 1907, p. 207.

25. *Locomotive Engineers' Journal*, February 1898; *The Railroad Trainman*, August 1905, February 1906; December 1906; *United Mineworkers' Journal*, 17 June 1897; *Iron Molders' Journal*, July 1897, June 1905.

26. *The Journal of United Labor*, 4 May 1893; *Iron Molders' Journal*, May 1896; AFL, *Proceedings*, 1901, pp. 76–82; *Amalgamated Journal*, 14 May 1903; *United Mineworkers' Journal*, 12 September 1895.

27. *The People*, 26 December 1897; *The Journal of United Labor*, 16 April 1896; *Labor Compendium*, 12 December 1897.

28. *The Journal of United Labor*, 1 January 1891, 5 March 1896; *United Mineworkers' Journal*, 29 November 1894.

29. *The Journal of United Labor*, 9 June 1892, 30 April 1896; letter from Executive Board of Local 309, New York City, Brotherhood of Carpenters and Joiners, *The Carpenter*, 17 November 1897; *The People*, 22 March 1896, 9 May 1897, 26 December 1897; *Brauer-Zeitung*, 11 December 1897.

30. *The People*, 22 March 1896; letter from Thomas P. Abbott in *Official Journal of the Painters and Decorators*, November 1907; *The Carpenter*, 16 April 1896, 17 November 1897; *Brauer-Zeitung*, 11 December 1897, 29 December 1900; *United Mineworkers' Journal*, 10 January 1895; *International Woodworker*, December 1897.

31. *Official Journal of the Painters and Decorators*, November 1907; *The Journal of United Labor*, 16 April 1897 (letter from T. G. Anderson); *International Woodworker*, December 1897; *The People*, 12 April 1891; *Brauer-Zeitung*, 29 December 1900, 6 May 1905; *The Advance and Labor Leaf*, 3 September 1887; *The International Socialist Review*, July 1903; *United Mineworkers' Journal*, 10 January 1895.

32. *The Journal of United Labor*, 9 June 1892; *The Advance and Labor Leaf*, 2 March 1889; *Detroit Labor Leaf*, 27 January 1886.

33. *Monthly Journal of the International Association of Machinists*, November 1893; *The Advance and Labor Leaf*, 2 March 1889.

34. *Monthly Journal of the International Association of Machinists*, September 1897; *International Woodworker*, July 1896, December 1897; *Reports of the Industrial Commission*, Vol. 7, p. 302; *Testimony Taken by the Select Committee of the House of Representatives to Inquire into the Alleged Violation of the Laws Prohibiting the Importation of Contract Laborers*, Vol. 15, p. 658.

35. *United Mineworkers' Journal*, 29 November 1894, 10 January 1895, 12 September 1895; *Reports of the Industrial Commission*, Vol. 12, pp. 257, 335; *International Woodworker*, July 1896; *The Detroit Sentinel*, 19 February 1898; *The Typographical Journal*, March 1898.

36. *Committee on Immigration and Naturalization* (51 Cong., 2 Sess., H. Rept. No. 3472), Vo. 2, p. 19; *Liberty*, 11 February 1893; *Reports of the Industrial Commission*, Vol. 14, p. 265; *Brauer-Zeitung*, 4 December 1897.

37. *The Advance and Labor Leaf*, 2 March 1889; *Liberty*, 11 February 1893; *Monthly Journal of the International Association of Machinists*, September 1897; *The Carpenter*, July 1894.

38. *Monthly Journal of the International Association of Machinists* September 1897; *The People*, 22 March 1896.

39. Cecil D. Eby, "America as Asylum: A Dual Image," *American Quarterly* 14 (1962): 483; Peter Roberts, *The New Immigration* (New York: Macmillan, 1912), p. 248.

40. *Locomotive Firemen's Magazine*, May 1891; *Iron Molders' Journal*, January and July 1897; *The People*, 26 December 1897; *International Woodworker*, July 1896.

9

1900–1917: The Turning Point in Labor's Immigration Policy

It is widely recognized that in the first two decades of this century the American Federation of Labor was among the most important pressure groups seeking tougher U.S. immigration controls. In pursuit of this aim, it gave wholehearted and persistent backing to congressional attempts to enact the literacy test between 1906 and 1917.[1] However, there has been remarkably little discussion of the reasons behind labor's deep commitment. It has been assumed that the origins of AFL policy lay in the 1897 decision by its annual convention to support a literacy measure. Moreover, the key to an understanding of the AFL's approach, it is argued, is to be found in the circumstances surrounding that 1897 debate. Convinced by the arguments advanced at that time, delegates to future conventions simply reiterated them, though periodically presenting additional evidence in response to changing circumstances.[2]

The necessity for a reappraisal of this approach arises from doubts about the significance of 1897 as a turning point in labor opinion. Recent research has confirmed John Higham's judgment that organized labor "moved with the nativist tide in the nineties, but certainly not . . . with full assurance."[3] When the tide ebbed in 1898, so did labor's enthusiasm for the imposition of a literacy test. The AFL's apparent indifference to the problem of European immigration ended only in 1905 when once again it supported a resolution favoring restriction by means of the test. From then on all doubts seem to have disappeared; between 1906 and 1917, when the test became law, the AFL voted for resolutions in its support on no fewer than ten occasions.[4]

It is therefore more convincing to locate the turning point in labor's attitude to European immigration in the first decade of this century. Labor historians can no longer absolve themselves from the responsibility to understand the causes of this development by gestures in the direction of the 1897 AFL convention. Instead, an explanation of the AFL's conversion must be sought in the political, economic, and demographic conditions of the years 1904 to 1906. The consistency of its subsequent support for the test is explicable by reference to the events of the decade before 1917. Either the original causes of the AFL's conversion retained their strength in the prewar period, or new factors emerged to stiffen the federation's commitment to a restrictionist policy.

In his study of business attitudes to immigration, Morrell Heald argued that there was a positive relationship between these attitudes and economic fluctuations. He contended that it was possible "to chart the rise, the fall and the resurgence of prosperity in the years preceding 1914 through the discussions of immigration in the business press and at business meetings." The minidepression of 1904 excited great interest in the subject of immigration, and the same was true of the substantially more severe downturn in 1907–8. When economic recovery ensued, discussion of immigration flagged, only to pick up again after a further economic setback.[5]

Labor's attitudes parallel those of business, up to a point. The self-confidence and optimism associated with economic recovery after 1898 probably accounted for the lack of interest in immigration at AFL conventions before 1905. Samuel Gompers, the president of the AFL, certainly subscribed to this view, commenting that in a time of increasing industrial activity "the number of the unemployed was lower than it had been for some years before and fellow wage earners had a less keen sense of the effects of admitting immigrants without discrimination."[6] The upturn in unemployment resulting from the recession of 1904 was reflected in the anti-immigration resolution at the AFL's convention of the following year. However, the correlation is by no means perfect; the resolution was approved again in 1906 and in every subsequent year until 1917 despite the return of periods of prosperity. It seems clear, however, that the recession in 1904 triggered concern about the consequences of immigration for levels of employment and seemed to confirm the warnings of some trade union leaders about the fragility of prosperity. Douglas Wilson of the Machinists' Union had reflected in 1902 that "every thinking man in the ranks of organized labor is wondering how long the United States can supply work to the illiterate hordes of Eastern Europe if they continue to come in unchecked." Later, John Mitchell, president of the Mineworkers, contemplated the unemployment figures and urged immigration restriction since "the first duty of a community is to give its own members the opportunity of being employed at decent wages."[7]

Actual unemployment, or the fear of unemployment, succeeded in ter-

Table 6
Annual Totals of Immigrants: 1898–1907

Year	Number of Immigrants
1898	229,299
1899	311,715
1900	448,572
1901	487,918
1902	648,743
1903	857,046
1904	812,870
1905	1,026,499
1906	1,100,735
1907	1,285,349

SOURCE: Bulletin of the Bureau of Immigration, quoted in
American Federation of Labor, Report of the
Proceedings of the Twenty-Seventh Annual
Convention, 1907, p. 39.

minating labor's indifference to European immigration. The possible extent
of the threat to jobs was highlighted by the dramatic increases in the annual
totals of immigrants in the decade before 1906. Table 6 shows the dimensions of the problem.

It was not until 1903 that the labor press contained comments on the
significance of these immigration statistics, but subsequently the figures
were regularly reported in a number of labor journals. Gompers was among
the first to publish the figures and to comment on their implications for
working people, who had to bear the brunt of the fearful job competition
which resulted.[8] In 1905 the AFL reported that the number of immigrants
had broken the one million barrier; the resulting consternation was intensified by the fear that this figure would become the norm.

The figures were presented in a variety of ways in order to sharpen their
impact. Douglas Wilson calculated that of the five million immigrants to
reach the Atlantic coast since 1894, about 40 percent had arrived in the two
years preceding 1905. Others broke down the figures into monthly totals,
showing that the 150,000 immigrants in April 1906 were about two-thirds
of the number for the entire year of 1898 and represented the largest total
in any single month since the Bureau of Immigration was established.[9]
Indubitably the sheer size of the immigrant influx had enormous influence
in effecting a greater receptivity to restrictionist arguments. Even those like
John Mitchell, who claimed that wage earners had no sympathy with the
cry "America for the Americans" and who recognized the immigrant as a
fellow worker and brother, found it hard to believe that one million new-

comers a year could be absorbed and converted into Americans, or that profitable employment could be found for them. Immigration seemed "never-ending and overwhelming," a problem "shifting too quickly for adjustment, rising in new forms too swiftly to be met, inundating irresistibly and destroying from without."[10]

If immigration restriction was a way of limiting unemployment, it was no less valuable as a weapon against the employing class. Anticapitalist feelings were running high among members of trade unions as a result of new revelations about the steamship traffic. Furthermore, hostility was intensified by a vigorous campaign against trade unions waged by various employers' organizations. Labor was eager to seize any opportunity to weaken the power of the employers, and immigration restriction was recognized as an effective means of reducing their control over wages and conditions of work.

The publicity given in the labor press to the activities of the steamship companies engaged in the immigrant trade encouraged a more forceful criticism of immigration than might otherwise have materialized. The immediate stimulus to the campaign against the steamship companies was the so-called rate war on the North Atlantic. This allegedly boosted the immigrant traffic by reducing fares and created the belief that the shipping companies were a major influence on the levels of immigration. In their zeal for profits, it was said, they encouraged immigration even during depressions in the United States, so distorting the normal direct relationship between changing levels of economic activity and the volume of immigration.[11] From a later vantage point Gompers was able to portray immigration as having been the creation of an unscrupulous profiteering class working hand in hand with American employers to undermine working people's standards of life. It was to a very large extent induced, stimulated artificial immigration,

and hand in hand with it (as a part, indeed, of the machinations of the promoters, steerers, runners, sub-agents and usurers, more or less directly connected with steamship lines, the great beneficiaries of large immigration) run plans for the exploitation of the ignorant classes which often result in placing upon our shores large numbers of aliens who, if the fact were only known at the time, are worse than destitute, are burdened with obligations which they and all their relations are parties [sic], debts secured with mortgages on such small holdings as they and their relatives possess, and on which usurious interest must be paid.[12]

In short, the immigrant traffic had been so systematized by the shipping lines that it was almost as easy crossing the Atlantic as taking a ferry, and certainly as easy for the "shiftless and incapable" to travel to the United States as to stay in Europe.

This argument held a seductive appeal to the hesitant restrictionists in labor's ranks. It utilized the distinction between voluntary and induced immigrants, frequently drawn in the 1880s and 1890s, and conveyed the impression that virtually all immigrants from Southern and Eastern Europe were too poor to migrate without the artificially low fares and other inducements offered by the steamship companies. The publicity given to the shipping companies' activities enabled restrictionists to focus on a more comfortable target than the immigrants themselves, namely, the exploitative, profit-seeking capitalists who were undermining working-class living standards. By so doing, opponents of immigration could hope to win over doubters within labor's ranks with greater ease than if they had concentrated on the numbers and quality of the immigrants alone. This approach yielded positive results among even the most internationally minded sections of the labor movement.[13]

This hostility to employers was intensified as a result of the antiunion campaign, the so-called employers' counteroffensive. The merger movements in American industry, which reached a peak between 1898 and 1903, considerably augmented the power and resources of big business. Whilst this encouraged a firmer stand against trade unions, it also aroused anxiety among small businessmen at the threat to competition, leading them in turn to wage war against the unions in a bid to restore their freedom. The speed of union growth also caused alarm; membership rose from 447,000 in 1897 to almost two million in 1903.[14]

The employers' offensive against the trade unions took several forms. In some industries employers adopted a firm and unyielding position in strikes, which produced victories in the steel strike in 1901 and the packing house strike of 1904. A more general campaign against the closed shop was launched by employers' associations in particular localities. In 1903 the National Association of Manufacturers (NAM) became militantly antiunion and anti–open shop and formed a Citizens' Industrial Association to fight the "tyranny" of unions. A propaganda war was waged against trade unions, concentrating on the employer's right to carry on his business on "American" principles, without interference from the trade unions. By 1906 labor was under further attack from the widespread use of injunctions in industrial disputes and from the NAM's active intervention in elections to defeat allegedly prolabor candidates. Finally, one of labor's most effective tactics came under question in the courts. In the Danbury Hatters' case, initiated in 1902, and the Bucks' Stove and Range case five years later, the employers attempted to limit or prevent the use of the boycott in trade disputes. These two cases "made the danger to the labor movement of court interference exceedingly tangible ... it made the leaders as well as the rank and file feel that their unions were existing only at the sufferance of the law and the employers." The loss of members between 1904 and 1906 after the spectacular expansion between 1897 and 1904 intensified labor's sense of insecurity.[15]

In seeking a means of counterattack, trade unionists recognized that immigration had a bearing on the struggle with the employers. Both sides of industry were aware that a reduction in the volume of immigration would increase labor's bargaining power and assist it to enforce the closed shop. The employers had recognized that the upsurge in immigration after 1900 was a possible "counterpoise to the harm being done through the growth and domination of unionism which is adding so greatly to the cost of manufactured goods." It offered an opportunity to "restore the equilibrium" between employers and workers, stabilize wage costs, and assist in the destruction of unionism.[16] With sentiments like these emanating from business circles, it was inevitable that labor's attitude to immigration would harden. From labor's perspective, the employers' offensive and the inducements to cheap foreign labor were part of the same general strategy of cutting costs by weakening labor's power. Of course, increased trade union hostility to immigrants did not extend to those who "adjusted themselves" to American standards of living and who refused to be the pawns of employers by means of undercutting American wage levels. But there was little optimism that the mass of immigrants from Southern and Eastern Europe would be able to adjust in these ways: it was far more likely that they would afford the employers the means of overwhelming and destroying the labor movement.[17]

It was, indeed, the geographical and ethnic origins of the majority of immigrants which aroused deep anxiety among trade unionists. Native-born workers or immigrants of an earlier generation from Great Britain or Germany could not easily identify with the latest arrivals from the rural regions of Southern and Eastern Europe. The latent internationalism of the trade unions had played an important part in the debates on the literacy test in the 1890s, restraining the movement towards restriction. But at that time the share of Southern and Eastern Europeans in the overall immigration total had barely reached one-half. By 1906 the proportion of a much bigger overall total was almost 80 percent, and it seemed that the dominance of the new immigrants was of a permanent character. Few expressions of solidarity with these newcomers emanated from labor's ranks in that year. The ethnic, linguistic, and cultural divides were not easily bridged, and this resulted in frequent and critical assessments of the characteristics of the new immigrants in the labor press. There was widespread agreement that the Slavs, Italians, and Jews were not "of the right class and character" and that their moral, physical, and educational poverty would prevent them from adopting "American ways and understanding American ideals."[18] It was worrisome that the lions's share of the vastly augmented stream of immigrants should be composed of those Europeans least equipped to benefit from, and contribute to, American culture. In labor's eyes they were evidently inferior to earlier immigrants from Northern Europe who had "helped to make a great nation" of the United States. Numbers alone, no matter what the countries of origin, would have created a problem for trade unions. But the dominance of Southern and Eastern Europeans helped to ensure that labor opponents of immigration selected a discriminatory method of restriction aimed particularly at these latest arrivals.[19]

There were, however, other important influences which ensured that the revived enthusiasm for tougher immigration controls in the labor movement was channelled into support for the literacy test. The most significant was the impact on labor's thinking of the campaign to re-enact the Chinese Exclusion Law between 1900 and 1904. Gompers had warned that there was no question to be considered by the U.S. Congress "fraught with half as much import to the American people as is the question whether or not the Chinese shall be excluded from the United States." Once the law had been re-enacted in 1902, organized labor continued to fret over attempts by the employers to evade it and the possibility of Congress watering it down or not renewing the Chinese treaty.[20] Further alarm was aroused by the rising numbers of Japanese and Koreans arriving on the West coast.

It was difficult to prevent comparisons being drawn between Asiatic and European immigration, impossible to stop speculation that the restrictive methods applied in the one case might be appropriate in the other. Of course, these comparisons were only made possible by the transformation in the ethnic balance of European immigration. Nevertheless, the Asian example offered a precedent for a more rigorous exclusion policy which appeared increasingly appropriate in the light of comparisons between the Asian and the "new" European immigrants. Since this analogy is of crucial importance in explaining labor's choice of the literacy test, it requires more extended discussion.

The starting point is Alexander Saxton's contention that the Chinese case did indeed offer a precedent in the campaign against the new immigrants. He notes that the response of native-born workers to Chinese immigrants in California in the 1860s was to classify them with blacks and thus to exclude them from the producer class, which encompassed all white workers and employers actively engaged in the creation of wealth. Such a classification placed no inhibitions of solidarity in the way of a restrictive and discriminatory immigration policy. If the new immigrants from Europe could have been similarly classified, restrictionist elements would have gained a major advantage. But, as Saxton points out, Europeans were white and, for the most part, Christian, and Americans had a very long tradition of hospitality to such immigrants. "Guilt stirred by denial of such loyalties," he continues, "must somehow be set at rest before any reorientation on the matter of immigration would be possible. To this extent the Chinese experience had to be repeated." Saxton proposes that labor was, indeed, attempting such a reorientation by reference to the Chinese example.[21]

If his claim is true, the intensity of anti-Chinese emotions between 1901 and 1904 and the mounting concern over the Japanese would have strengthened the case against Southern and Eastern Europeans. In his support, Saxton quotes from a speech of Gompers in St. Paul in 1905, in which he warned that the "Caucasians" were not going to let their standard of living be destroyed by Negroes, Chinamen, Japanese, "or any others." Saxton presumes that the words "or any others" referred to the new immigrants. But, he asks, in which ways might they have been regarded as similar by the men whom Gompers represented? If they shared with the Chinese a number of "inferior" qualities, might that inferiority have been due simply to lack of educational and other opportunities rather than to membership of an inferior race? If such an opinion were widespread, it would have been unproductive to stress the genetic origins of Chinese inferiority, since this would have disqualified that Chinese case as a useful precedent. Accordingly, Gompers attempted to utilize the Chinese example by dwelling on their behavior, not their race. "There is no antipathy on the part of American workmen to Chinese because of their nationality," he asserted, "but a people which have allowed civilization to pass them by untouched and uninfluenced, a people who . . . menace the progress, the economic and social standing of the workers of other countries, cannot be fraternized with." The effect of this passage, in Saxton's opinion, "is to reinterpret the permissible hatred toward Chinese into language that can be applied directly to selected peoples of Europe."[22] Analogies based on common behavioral characteristics, therefore, were judged to be more persuasive than those which highlighted a common racial inferiority. Hence, when Gompers drew attention to the "slothfulness and submission to tyranny" in Europe of the new immigrants, he did not consider that he was betraying traditional American hospitality or working-class solidarity; the new arrivals from Europe were, like the Chinese, unfitted for entry by their cultural heritage.

Does evidence drawn from a wider range of labor sources than Saxton was able to call upon support his interpretation? There was one section of labor opinion which believed that there was nothing to choose between the Chinese and the new European immigrants. Both were on the same level, sharing a common inferiority; the only difference between them was that the Europeans could acquire the vote and thus apply pressure on politicians to oppose restrictive measures. Some felt that the Europeans were generally inferior "in honesty, morals and living," and that the Slavs and Italians in particular presented a greater danger to the Republic than the Asiatics in respect of illiteracy, criminality, and assimilative capacity.[23] Such opinions were not typical of the labor movement but do reveal the extent to which feelings of solidarity were being eroded.

More representative of labor opinion was the view that no proper comparison could be made between the Chinese and the new immigrants in respect of their capacity to assimilate and hence that a total exclusion law, whilst correct for the Chinese, was quite inappropriate for the Europeans. Somewhat paradoxically, one of the most forceful proponents of this view was the restrictionist, Samuel Gompers. In the following passage he makes a clear distinction between the kinds of restriction appropriate in each case:

However much we may oppose and with justice, unrestricted immigration from elsewhere, this Chinese question is not at all to be compared with or included in a general immigration law.... We can not afford to trifle with a race of people so utterly unassimilative, so ruinous to our general prosperity, and so blighting to our every prospect. Comparison with immigration of other peoples is only possible by contrast. While we object to an indiscriminate influx of other foreign laborers, we maintain that discrimination in the case of Chinese immigrants is impossible.[24]

In similar vein, James Duncan, one of Gompers' chief AFL lieutenants, conceded that there were grounds for complaint against indiscriminate immigration of Europeans but emphasized that such classes of immigrants could not be compared with the Chinese. Europeans were assimilable, and it was possible for them to become enthusiastic members of unions and to demand American wage rates. Gompers agreed, acknowledging "the noble possibilities in the poorest of the children of the earth who come to us from European lands." Their civilization was sufficiently near to the American, in his view, to permit their descendants to rise to the general level of the best American citizenship in one generation.[25]

How is this kind of sentiment compatible with support for an immigration restriction law which discriminated against "the poorest of the children of the earth"? Labor leaders agreed that the Chinese and the new Europeans were not identical and could not be treated in exactly the same way. Yet there were similarities between them. The significance of the agitation against the Chinese was that it presented an indictment of Chinese immigrant behavior which was directly usable by opponents of immigration from Southern and Eastern Europe. The repeated denunciations of the economic, social, and political behavior of the Poles, Italians, and Jews rivalled in tone and content the diatribes against the Chinese. It was not lost in labor opinion that similar behavior should meet a similar response. Of course, there were barriers against precisely equal treatment of the two streams since there were different reasons, genetic as against cultural, for similar patterns of behavior. Therefore, some action stopping short of total exclusion, but having the effect of reducing the flow of the "worst elements" from Southern and Eastern Europe, was highly desirable. Europeans from backward cultures emigrating *en masse* displayed mass behavioral characteristics which cast doubt on their assimilability, at least within a reasonable period. Individual immigrants from Europe could certainly be assimilated; one million a year could not be. Assimilation required time and opportunity; the constant pressure of more and more immigrants denied that opportunity.[26] Consequently, labor accepted that there should be tighter immigration controls for those ethnic and nationality groups which tended to weaken republican solidarity and cultural homogeneity. This appears to confirm Saxton's claim that Gompers's attempt in 1894 to change the focus of the discussion about the Chinese from their racial to their behavioral characteristics opened the way for comparisons between recent European immigrants and Asiatics. In sum, the resumption of the anti-Chinese crusade by the AFL in 1901, involving widespread publicity of Chinese coolie behavior and attitudes, increased support for the literacy test as the most appropriate method of dealing with the new immigration from Europe.

A final factor accounting for the choice of the literacy test was the recognition by labor's leaders that this measure commanded considerable support in the U.S. Congress. At the same time there was general agreement that it was futile to try to reform or more rigidly enforce the Contract Labor Law of 1885, which was still the main statutory means of controlling the flow of European immigration. The ineffectiveness of that law had long been clear, but further damning evidence in this respect was provided by the Industrial Commission in 1901, which concluded that "successive interpretations of the courts coupled with occasionally less strict administration" and a growing acquaintance with its loopholes by immigrants "rendered the law practically a nullity." It was widely recognized that the law could not be applied to the mass of European immigrants, whatever the original intentions of its authors.[27]

Awareness of the failure of the law was widespread at the very time, 1903–6, when worries were growing about the rising tide of immigration, the activities of the steamship companies, and the employers' offensive. This awareness strengthened support for the literacy test as a more effective method of reducing the number of immigrant workers. The literacy test was also the preferred method of restriction of those who were unwilling to draw too close a parallel between the recent European immigrants and the Chinese. Recognizing the differences between the groups implied the adoption of different solutions to the problems posed by each. Total exclusion was, therefore, a less satisfactory method of restriction than the literacy test, which would effectively exclude the "worst elements" of the European immigration and assist the process of assimilation.

By 1905–6, therefore, a rising tide of restrictionism engulfed the labor movement and bore it irresistibly towards adoption of the literacy test. Nevertheless, it is worth recalling that the restrictionist fervor of 1897 had vanished remarkably quickly with the onset of economic recovery. It is realistic to acknowledge that a similar improvement in labor's position after 1906, both in economic and political terms, might have stilled the clamor for restriction and produced the same indifference to the problem as characterized the years 1898–1904. However, on this occasion, there was no weakening of resolve on labor's part, and its support for the literacy test was reaffirmed on numerous occasions up to 1917. It is as important to understand the reasons for this as it was to establish the causes of labor's renewed commitment to the literacy measure in 1905.

Predictably, a number of factors combined to keep labor opinion firm in the decade after 1907. First, the effects of the economic depressions of 1907–9 and 1914 on employment and wages increased the doubts about the capacity of the economy to absorb vast numbers of new workers from abroad. Secondly, the recommendations of the Immigration Commission published in 1911 endorsed labor's support for the literacy test. Finally, the First World War and the possibility of American involvement generated powerful arguments in support of the test. Little emphasis was given to exclusionist arguments based on the new anthropological and genetic theories. Meanwhile the internationalist and open door approach to immigration, which was still quite influential in the labor movement in the 1890s, began a steady and uninterrupted decline after 1900 and became too weak to mount a challenge to the dominance of restriction in labor's ranks.

The recommendations of the Immigration Commission were profoundly significant in consolidating labor opinion behind the policy adopted by the AFL in 1905–6. Any organization whose policy on a matter of public importance has been endorsed by an independent and prestigious committee of enquiry has cause for satisfaction. It will campaign with renewed enthusiasm and confidently anticipate the ultimate success of its campaign. The commission's conclusions commanded widespread influence owing to the prestige of its members and the thoroughness of its research. "Everyone expected that it would uncover the facts about the immigration problem which would provide the basis for effective and unbiased legislation." In 1911 most Americans accepted its report as an objective and fair analysis. The apprehensions of antirestrictionists like Cyrus Sulzberger of the American Jewish Committee that the commission would be "disastrous" for the antirestrictionist cause if it produced a report hostile to immigration were amply confirmed.[28]

The commission did, in fact, adopt the main recommendations of the restrictionist lobby. Its declared aim was to exclude a sufficient number of immigrants to produce a marked effect on the supply of unskilled workers in the labor market. It proposed to deter those with no intention of staying and those who, "by reason of personal qualities," were least readily assimilated. After a résumé of the methods by which these objectives could be achieved, the majority of the commission plumped for the literacy test "as the most feasible single method of restricting undesirable immigration."[29]

On learning of these recommendations, Samuel Gompers was jubilant; they were a "splendid endorsement" of the policy he had recommended as early as 1896.[30] He took the opportunity presented by the commission's report to reflect on the evolution of opinion within organized labor. He recalled the strain which had existed, not only between restrictionists and

antirestrictionists, but in the minds of all trade unionists. Labor men had
been pulled in different directions by their allegiance to internationalism on
the one hand, and, on the other, their growing conviction that more stringent restriction was called for. Gompers clearly expected this tension to
diminish further following the commission's report. He boasted that there
finally existed authoritative, overwhelming, and convincing confirmation
of "the facts of the case as they have been accepted by the American Federation of Labor for decades."[31] Working men could now strengthen their
resolve, assuage their guilt, and sever their lingering adherence to the open
door. If further buttressing of judgment and confidence were required, the
report of the influential Industrial Relations Commission, published in 1915,
provided it.[32]

The realization that the weight of authoritative opinion was now firmly
on their side accounts for the greater confidence with which labor's representatives argued the restrictionist case between 1911 and the beginning
of the First World War. It may also partly explain why labor did not pay
more attention to the pseudoscientific racial theories then being peddled by
organizations like the Immigration Restriction League (IRL). Careful examination of the columns of many labor journals has produced few examples
of racist thinking applied to immigration. This was not the result of a failure
of nativist organizations to communicate with trade unions. Indeed, there
is evidence of a campaign by outside agencies like the IRL to persuade
organized labor to accept those racist ideas then current in certain intellectual
and genteel circles.[33] Concomitantly, a few scattered references appear in
the labor journals to some of the fashionable racial arguments. *The Railroad
Trainman*, always in the van of the restrictionist movement, quoted Prescott
Hall, the guru of the IRL, in support of limiting immigration. How much
of Hall's argument was absorbed by the readership is impossible to say,
but there is some evidence that the terminology of the racist thinkers was
beginning to spread among the labor audience and that the ideas, in a crude
form, were being discussed. Among the ideas mentioned in labor journals
were Francis A. Walker's hypothesis about race suicide, and also the notion
of hybridization. Apart from these references and a few scattered allusions
to "higher types" and "lower types," no space was given in the labor press
before 1917 to the ideas of immigration restriction based on concepts derived
from eugenics, genetics, and anthropology.[34]

One might expect that labor would have adopted at least some of these
ideas in support of its policy. That it did not was the result of several factors.
The first was a natural reluctance on the part of first and second generation
Americans to draw lines of race between themselves and more recent arrivals
whose region or nation of origin might have been contiguous to, or identical
with, their own. The new genetic and anthropological theories were highly
complex and not easily absorbed, but such difficulties would not have stood
in the way of their adoption in a vulgarized form had the motivation to

accept them existed. Labor was satisfied that a cultural explanation of ethnic differences adequately served its purposes and was more in harmony with its residual internationalism.

A second reason for labor's failure to utilize these theories was the confidence, largely generated by the Immigration Commission, that history was on its side. The case had been made and accepted; trade union policy had been endorsed; it now only remained to win over a few more votes in Congress to override presidential vetoes. However, after two failures to override the vetoes of Taft and Wilson in 1913 and 1915, new impetus for the restrictionist cause was needed. By that time it was provided, not by racial theory, but by the effects in the United States of the war in Europe.

Despite the exceptional prosperity of the majority of Americans from 1915 to 1917, labor officials were anxious about the effect of a future depression on wages and employment. Labor's concern over immigration was not diminished by the years of economic upswing. Like gamblers, they were hoping to consolidate during a good run to meet the inevitable spell of bad luck to follow. The socialist Scott Nearing pointed out that the immigration figures had fallen by more than two-thirds between 1914 and 1915 as a result of the war. At the same time there had been a great spurt in industrial output and a substantial increase in employment accompanied by higher wages for unskilled workers. Nearing implied that there was a connection between *de facto* immigration restriction and the improvement in wages and conditions, especially for the unskilled. Accordingly, he proposed a scheme to prohibit the admission of any immigrant who did not have a job at a "decent" wage. Labor organizations agreed with Nearing's analysis, believing that millions of war-stricken Europeans would escape to the United States after the war at a time when the American economy would be adjusting to peacetime conditions. In labor's view, these postwar economic difficulties must not be exacerbated by the immigration of millions of "illiterate and desperate men" from Europe. Trade union officials advocated an intensified campaign to persuade Congress to pass the literacy test, if necessary over a presidential veto, while there was still time.[35]

Considerations of national unity and preparedness also loomed large in labor's stepped-up restrictionist campaign. The main cause for apprehension was the disunity resulting from ethnic and religious heterogeneity; there was barely a reference in the labor press before 1917 to the danger from the immigration of radicals and syndicalists. The war in Europe had brought into sharp focus the dual loyalties and mixed identities of America's ethnic groups of European origin. Their campaigns to influence government policy towards the combatants had revealed to many observers, not least to those in trade unions, that some citizens of foreign birth and their descendants had shown more loyalty to their European countries of origin than to the land of their adoption. The lesson to be learned was how little assimilation had taken place and how such dual loyalty obstructed the path to preparedness. The awareness of disunity was, of course, a stimulus to the Americanization campaign, but it also gave momentum to the drive for immigration restriction, making it into "one of the imperative demands of the hour."[36] A policy of restriction, so it was thought, would enable the United States to face any future emergency with the patriotism resulting from the exclusion of heterogeneous foreign elements. It made no sense, after all, to spend millions of dollars on education in the United States whilst admitting millions of illiterate immigrants who had no knowledge of the aspirations and principles on which the American system of government was founded.[37]

There were, therefore, a number of factors between 1906 and 1917 which strengthened labor's support for the literacy test. One additional point has a direct bearing on this question. Political choice, it is well known, can as often arise from negative as from positive reasons. Besides the arguments in its favor, the literacy test had the negative advantage of appearing less objectionable than alternative methods of restriction. Various other possibilities had been reviewed by the Immigration Commission, but all had been discounted.[38] It was obvious that reform of the Contract Labor Law had little to offer, even though some unions still advocated it. Similarly, there were considerable difficulties in attempting to recruit foreign-born workers into trade unions as a means of protecting wages and conditions. Even the Ladies Garment Workers Union, with an impressive record of organization among the foreign-born, was aware of the perils of the policy as a means of neutralizing the effects of immigration. How much less appealing was such a policy for unions whose success in organization had been more limited and for whom the expenditure of time, effort, and money was daunting![39] Another possibility of controlling immigration involved American trade unions conducting a propaganda campaign in Europe to dissuade Europeans from emigrating. In 1913 the American Painters and Decorators Union agreed to send delegates to a Painters' International Congress in order to inform their European brothers of the true economic condition of the trade in the United States, in the hope that this would deter thoughtless and hasty emigration.[40] But the absence of support for this type of action in the rest of the labor press shows that labor did not see such a policy as a solution to the problem of immigration.

These countervailing forces to the growth of restrictionist opinion were weak, fragmented, and demoralized. However, the most powerful resistance to the adoption of the literacy test might have come from socialist trade unionists who had been the most dedicated internationalists in the 1890s. The strong opposition to the literacy test voiced at the AFL's 1896 and 1897 conventions bears witness, in part, to socialist influence. The dual unionism of Daniel De Leon, however, wilfully squandered the socialists' advantage in the AFL and alienated many sympathizers. This meant that at the beginning of this century, socialists were in a weaker position to influence policy making in the AFL. Attempts to restore their influence and to win votes for their party from trade unionists inevitably involved concili- ation and compromise. For many socialists the sacrifice of the out-and-out internationalism which had characterized their immigration policy in the 1890s was a small price to pay for labor support. Consequently, the brake on restrictionism in the AFL was eased, facilitating a deeper commitment to the literacy test. On the eve of the U.S. declaration of war in 1917, a majority of the socialist members of the AFL voted for the literacy test, illustrating the erosion of socialist solidarity over immigration.

However, a reading of socialist discussions on the immigration question soon disabuses one of the idea that the change of opinion was entirely motivated by tactical considerations. Many socialists were plainly troubled by the effects of unrestricted immigration on the Americn working class, and felt a clear tug of loyalty between their internationalism and their com- mitment to defend workers' living standards. It should be noted, however, that the Socialist party never compromised its internationalism to the extent of endorsing the literacy test; indeed, there is no record of socialists even debating that issue in their press or at their conventions. It appears that, sympathetic though they were to the condition of the American working class, socialists were more strongly influenced by internationalist ideals than the labor movement as a whole. In this connection we must bear in mind that recent immigrants were almost certainly more strongly represented in the Socialist party than in the AFL and that the dominance of skilled unions in the federation made it less sympathetic to unskilled workers, who con- stituted the majority of recent immigrants.

A comparison of opinion in the AFL and the Socialist party suggests that the crystallization of opinion which occurred in the trade unions over the literacy test in the first decade of this century had not taken place among socialists at that time. Rather, socialist debates reveal a similar degree of uncertainty about immigration to that present in the AFL in the 1890s. This is not to suggest that socialists would inevitably have adopted the literacy test. But they were on the lookout for some method of curtailing undesirable immigration which could be reconciled with their internationalist obliga- tions.[41] Hence, although the socialists were a substantial minority in the AFL in the pre–1914 decade, they spoke without conviction, compromised their internationalism, and fudged the issues in the interests of pragmatic politics. In this evaluation of the reasons for labor's commitment to the literacy test, the impotence of socialist internationalists in the labor move- ment cannot be ignored. But it surely pales into insignificance beside the other forces shaping labor's attitudes in the decades before the First World War.

The significance of the period 1905–17 in the history of labor attitudes to immigration is this: it finally resolved the tensions in the labor movement between sentiments of international solidarity on the one hand and the instinct for survival on the other. These conflicting tendencies had been in evidence in the three post–Civil War decades, but inroads on solidarity had been slight and could be rationalized by placing responsibility for undesirable immigration on the employers. By the mid–1890s many trade union leaders were convinced that the older traditions of labor solidarity and asylum would have to be modified to combat the challenge of economic depression, changing ethnic composition of the immigrants, and the evidence failure of the Alien Contract Labor Law of 1885 to control immigration. Although, under the leadership of Samuel Gompers, these officials were able to cobble together a majority in favor of the literacy test at the AFL convention in 1897, that discussion did not represent majority opinion among the rank and file, whose loyalty to international working-class solidarity remained strong. It required the experience of another decade to erode this traditional loyalty among union members and to ensure that the AFL's next vote in support of the literacy measure was truly representative of majority opinion in the trade union movement. From 1906 onwards internationalism in immigration policy was firmly subordinate to the impulse of protectionism; solidarity had been eclipsed by the instinct for survival.

NOTES

1. See, for example, John Higham, *Strangers in the Land: Patterns of American Nativism, 1860–1925* (1955: rpt. New York: Atheneum, 1963), p. 163, and George M. Stephenson, *A History of American Immigration, 1820–1924* (Boston: Ginn and Co., 1926), p. 161.

2. Philip Taft, *The A.F. of L. in the Time of Gompers* (New York: Harper, 1957), p. 306; Lewis L. Lorwin, *The American Federation of Labor: History, Policies, and Prospects* (Washington, D.C.: The Brookings Institution, 1933), p. 53; Henry Pelling, *American Labor* (Chicago: University of Chicago Press, 1960), p. 102.

3. Higham, p. 72; see Chapter Six.

4. American Federation of Labor, *Report of the Proceedings of the Thirty-Fifth Annual Convention*, 1915, p. 108; *Proceedings*, 1916, pp. 293, 335 (hereafter referred to as AFL, *Proceedings*).

5. Morrell Heald, "Business Attitudes toward European Immigration, 1861–1914" (Ph.D. diss., Yale University, 1951), pp. 331–44.

6. AFL, *Proceedings*, 1902, p. 21.

7. *Monthly Journal of the International Association of Machinists*, January 1902; *United Mineworkers' Journal*, 30 September 1909; see also *The Typographical Journal*, March 1909, and *The Garment Worker*, 5 March 1909.

8. AFL, *Proceedings*, 1900, p. 26; 1903, p. 26.

9. *Monthly Journal of the International Association of Machinists*, May 1905; see also *Michigan Union Advocate*, 3 August 1906; *The Carpenter*, 26 January 1906; *Advance Advocate*, July 1906.

10. *United Mineworkers' Journal*, 30 September 1909; *Michigan Union Advocate*, 15 January 1904.

11. *The Railroad Trainman*, August 1904; August 1914; *Advance Advocate*, March 1905, July 1905; *Monthly Journal of the International Association of Machinists*, September 1904.

12. *American Federationist*, July 1911.

13. See, e.g., *Brauer-Zeitung*, 21 September 1907.

14. John R. Commons et al., *History of Labor in the United States*, 4 vols. (1918; rpt. New York: Augustus M. Kelley, 1966), Vol. 4, p. 13.

15. Commons et al., *History of Labor*, Vol. 4, pp. 107, 122, 129, 155–56.

16. Heald, "Business Attitudes toward European Immigration," pp. 361–62, 372, quoting *The Commercial and Financial Chronicle*. At times the NAM blamed immigration for providing recruits to radical parties, thus connecting it with the growth of subversion and un-Americanism.

17. *Amalgamated Sheet Metal Workers' Journal*, 15 July 1904.

18. *The Carpenter*, July 1905, January 1906; *Iron Molders' Journal*, June 1905; *Advance Advocate*, January 1907.

19. The totals of so-called new immigrants rose from around 100,000 in 1897 to almost 1,000,000 in 1907. *Reports of the Immigration Commission* (61 Cong., 3 Sess., S. Doc. No. 747), Vol. 1, p. 13; *Iron Molders' Journal*, May 1904; with effect from 1899 immigrants were classified, not by countries or political divisions as formerly, but according to ethnicity. Consequently, the precise ethnic composition of the immigrant stream became unprecedentedly clear. The new classification was useful to restrictionists in that it highlighted the dominant position among immigrants of the "most backward" elements in the population of the East European empires. *Reports of the Industrial Commission*, (57 Cong., 1 Sess., H. Doc. No. 184), Vol. 15, Section 9, p. 132.

20. *Amalgamated Sheet Metal Workers' Journal*, 1901, p. 22; 1902, p. 89; *American Federationist*, June 1902, pp. 296–97.

21. Alexander Saxton, *The Indispensable Enemy: Labor and the Anti-Chinese Movement in California* (Berkeley: University of California Press, 1971), pp. 19–20, 274.

22. Ibid., pp. 273, 276–77.

23. *The Railroad Trainman*, August 1904; *Monthly Journal of the International Association of Machinists*, January 1906.

24. AFL, *Proceedings*, 1901, p. 22.

25. *Granite Cutters' Journal*, November 1905; *American Federationist*, May 1905, January 1911; *Michigan Union Advocate*, 13 May 1904.

26. *Report of the Committee on Immigration* (57 Cong., 2 Sess., S. Doc. No. 62), 1902, pp. 475–76 (statement of Frank Morrison, Secretary of the AFL).

27. *Reports of the Industrial Commission*, Vol. 15, Sections 58, 60, p. 26.

28. Harry Beardsell Leonard, "The Open Gates: The Protest Against the Movement to Restrict European Immigration, 1896–1924" (Ph.D. diss., Northwestern University, 1967) pp. 126 and 95–96.

29. *Reports of the Immigration Commission*, Vol. 1, pp. 45–48. Whereas public respect for the research and investigations of the commission was well merited, there was less justification for accepting its recommendations, since these did not emerge logically from the data it accumulated and published. This fact was understandably obscured from the general public at the time. The result was a shot in the arm for supporters of the literacy test, whose position had been endorsed by the commission.

30. AFL, *Proceedings*, 1911, p. 66.

31. *American Federationist*, January 1911; *Iron Molders' Journal*, January 1911.

32. *Report of the Commission on Industrial Relations* (64 Cong., 1 Sess., S. Doc. No. 415), Vol. 1, pp. 144–45.

33. United Brotherhood of Carpenters and Joiners of America, Local 161, Kenosha, Wisconsin, Minutes, 9 November 1905; *Brauer-Zeitung*, 23 September 1905; *Michigan Union Advocate*, 3 June 1904.

34. *The Railroad Trainman*, February 1905; *The Garment Worker*, 23 January 1905; *Monthly Journal of the International Association of Machinists*, September 1904; *Iron Molders' Journal*, February 1912.

35. *Miners' Magazine*, January and February 1917; *The Carpenter*, March 1916; *The Shoe Workers' Journal*, April 1916; *The Garment Worker*, 12 February 1915, 14 April 1916.

36. *The Shoe Workers' Journal*, December 1915, April 1916; *The Garment Worker*, 10 September 1915, 10 December 1915, 10 March 1916; Leonard, "Open Gates," pp. 219–20.

37. *The Garment Worker*, 7 April 1916, 14 April 1916; *The Shoe Workers' Journal*, February 1915; *Locomotive Engineers' Journal*, April 1916.

38. *Reports of the Immigration Commission*, Vol. 1, pp. 47–48.

39. *Coopers' International Journal*, October 1904; *Labor Compendium*, 15 December 1901. Trade unions which continued to advocate recruitment of foreign-born workers as an alternative to tough immigration restriction were the Coopers, the Painters and Decorators, the Brewery Workers, and the Ladies Garment Workers. See *Coopers' International Journal*, April 1911, May 1911; *Official Journal of the Painters and Decorators*, January 1906, January 1908; *Michigan Union Advocate*, 7 June 1907; *The Ladies Garment Worker*, November 1914.

40. *Official Journal of the Painters and Decorators*, October 1913.

41. For the Socialist party and immigration see, e.g., Howard H. Quint, *The Forging of American Socialism* (New York: Bobbs-Merrill, 1964); Morris Hillquit, *History of Socialism in the United States* (New York: Funk and Wagnalls Co., 1906); David A. Shannon, *The Socialist Party of America* (New York: Macmillan, 1955); Socialist Party of America Papers; *The International Socialist Review; Social Democratic Herald; Proceedings of the National Convention of the Socialist Party*, 1904, 1908, 1910, 1912.

10

The Eclipse of Solidarity, 1917–1924

The American Federation of Labor was entitled to some self-satisfaction after the passage of the 1917 Immigration Act. Its ardent support of the literacy test had been belatedly rewarded, and its Executve Council was confident that when peace and normality returned, the test would help to protect the nation from the dangers of excessive and undesirable immigration. Not that everyone shared this sense of the battle having been won. Frank Morrison, the federation's secretary, admitted to the House Committee on Immigration that only "time and experience [would] demonstrate what further legislation [would] be necessary in the interest and for the safety of the American people." Similarly, a spokesman for the Garment Workers thought it prudent to enact more stringent restrictive legislation before the war ended and the inevitable flood of foreign-born recommenced. In treating the 1917 act as the first step in a long process of tightening up immigration law, these labor representatives may be compared to the leaders of the Immigration Restriction League who, after a celebratory dinner, almost immediately began to plan additional legal barriers to the flow of immigration.[1]

Though fervent restrictionists were unlikely to be satisfied until complete exclusion existed, they were not typical of most trade unionists in early 1917. By the end of the war, however, labor opinion had moved much nearer to that of the restrictionist vanguard. In examining the reasons for this shift we should not draw a sharp distinction between labor opinion and the broader public opinion. General public attitudes towards immigration hardened owing to the war, which made a deep and lasting impact on an

entire generation of Americans, regardless of class distinctions. Consequently, an analysis of labor's attitudes to immigration after 1918 must first
explore the impact of the war on public opinion, within which labor opinion
was enfolded. The subsequent policies adopted by labor towards immigration in the period up to 1924 can best be understood in the broad context
of popular attitudes in those years.

America's entry into the war reinforced and intensified an already passionate national demand for total conformity and absolute loyalty from its
hyphenated population. The conflict could be won, most Americans were
convinced, only by complete identification with the nation's wartime goals.
The dual loyalty of so-called hyphenated-Americans was a shock to public
opinion, which had assumed that the process of assimilation had transformed the foreign-born into "American-thinking" people. Ethnic and political groups whose loyalty was suspect were urged to abandon their dual
identities, repudiate their un-American commitments, and subordinate
themselves to the national purpose. The German-Americans were the first
target of this so-called "one-hundred-per-cent Americanism," followed by
socialists, Wobblies, and pacifists, and all who in thought, word, and deed
opposed the war effort. The tenacity of the ethnic and national loyalties of
German-Americans clearly demonstrated the imperfect and partial nature
of acculturation. Accordingly, the war advanced the belief that further immigration restriction was vital to ensure the proper assimilation and Americanization on the nation's heterogeneous population. After all, once the
war was over, the pressures for conformity would probably ease and the
melting pot would function no more efficiently than before 1914. It seemed
imperative to restrictionists to limit postwar immigration still further to
ensure that the dual loyalty of wartime was not repeated in a future
emergency.[2]

Hopes for tougher immigration controls received some encouragement
immediately after the war. One hundred percenters and nativists, now
giving their full attention to radicals and socialists, wondered how the nation
could protect itself from these often alien Reds. The House Committee on
Immigration believed that immigration restriction was the only solution to
the Bolshevik menace and proposed a bill to this effect in early 1919. But
exclusionists made little progress in Congress, and other methods of dealing
with socialist subversives came to the fore. The Department of Justice led
a vigorous postwar campaign against them, and this diverted public attention from tighter immigration controls.[3]

The method chosen for dealing with alien radicals and socialists was
deportation, a more satisfactory weapon than restrictive immigration laws
in the eyes of the general public. The 1918 Alien Act, which provided for
the deportation of any alien who belonged to an organization which advocated revolt or sabotage, convinced Red-hunters that they were adequately armed for the roundup and exclusion of radicals. Nonetheless,

ardent restrictionists did not share this optimism and continued to warn the public about the dangers of immigration and the necessity for strengthening the law. In the end the nation came to share this view.[4]

In early 1920, as labor unrest declined and attempted Communist revolutions in Germany and Hungary failed, the drive began to go out of the anti-Red crusade. Nativism, however, did not die in 1920, it "simply separated from anti-radicalism." It became increasingly prominent, an intensification of the prewar hostility to Roman Catholics, Jews, and immigrants from Southern and Eastern Europe. But it was also, as John Higham suggests, a response to the fresh wave of immigration in 1920 and to the economic depression later in the year. Most importantly, it owed its scale and intensity to the wartime "supernationalism" and to the disillusionment of postwar society. The existing antiradical weapons were adequate, it seemed, but the challenge of new races required new measures. Consequently, public opinion became more responsive to demands for tougher immigration controls than it had been during the Red Scare.[5]

In May 1921 immigration began to pick up and provided the literacy test with its first real trial. As net immigration mounted to a monthly average of over 50,000 after midyear, it became obvious that the test was selective rather than restrictive and was unable to prevent anything near the prewar traffic. There was widespread alarm, deriving from newspaper and consular reports, that a great torrent of "war-torn Europeans" was about to inundate the United States. Soon a connection was made between this renewed stream of immigrants and rising unemployment, following the collapse of the postwar boom in late 1920. The slump continued for eighteen months, and its effects were seen in the decline of the gross national product, the fall in the wholesale price index, and the reduction in farm income. Meanwhile, the number of bankruptcies multiplied and unemployment rose to 4.7 million in the winter of 1920–21. Just as the short period of postwar prosperity and the low levels of immigration had reduced xenophobia, particularly when the wave of industrial unrest of 1919 had waned, so now the long-anticipated resumption of immigration and the economic depression found a new target for the still powerful and unassuaged wartime nationalism. The 100 percent Americanism of the war, which had promised to turn against immigration after 1918, but instead had focused on radicals, anarchists, and Communists, now found a new target in aliens from inferior races. Isolationism and nativism characterized Americans' persistent nationalism, which sought security by means of absolute unity and conformity.[6]

The most influential figure in the promotion of racial nativism was Madison Grant, whose *Passing of the Great Race* was reissued in 1921 and 1923 to meet public demand. Other noted popularizers of racism like Lothrop Stoddard and Kenneth Roberts took up some of Grant's ideas and reached a wide audience. Their message was that races differed enormously in capacity and achievements. Europe's population could be divided into three physical types arranged hierarchically, with the Nordics at the top, followed by the Alpines and then the Mediterraneans. Most Americans, they asserted, were descended from the Nordic races through the earlier immigration from Northern and Western Europe. The connection made by some writers between this anthropological classification and genetics enabled them to argue that cultural traits as well as physical characteristics were genetically transmitted. The Army IQ tests conducted during the war supported the new nativism, since they seemed to demonstrate that Nordic intellectual superiority, like the inferiority of the Mediterraneans, was not environmentally determined. Such speculations helped to explain the failure of the American environment to assimilate aliens from non–Anglo-Saxon ethnic groups.

Racists also offered another, though contradictory, proposition. They asserted that the admission of inferior non-Nordic races would inevitably result in interbreeding, which would produce a mongrel and hybrid type. Consequently, the new arrivals of different "racial proportions" threatened the existing types with annihilation. Since only superior people such as Nordics were capable of producing great civilizations, the preservation of their racial purity was a condition of social progress. At best, even if the new type resulting from ethnic intermixture did not turn out to be inferior, it would certainly be different and its precise qualities impossible to predict. Consequently, nativists advanced the idea that national greatness and the national mission depended on racial and cultural homogeneity, with obvious implications for immigration policy. In this atmosphere of "crisis bordering on hysteria," nativists presented a series of proposals to Congress designed to preserve the nation's racial foundations.[7]

The first result of this legislative activity was the 1921 Johnson Act, which set an upper limit on immigration from Europe of 350,000, each component nationality being restricted to a total equal to 3 percent of the number of foreign-born of that nationality resident in the United States at the time of the 1910 census. Its practical effect was that 55 percent of the total number of European immigrants would henceforth originate in Northern and Western Europe, and 45 percent in the South and East—a dramatic change in the prewar proportions, when more than 80 percent came from the latter regions. In Higham's view, the 1921 law represented the turning point in immigration policy, establishing the principle of an upper limit on immigration much lower than the prewar totals and, within that total, employing a quota system to effect a dramatic redistribution. Furthermore, it ensured that the foreign-born would cease to be a major factor in American history within a generation.[8]

Responding to pressure from restrictionists that the number of immigrants from Southern and Eastern Europe was still too high, Johnson and his advisers concentrated on reducing the quota. In the autumn of 1922 they proposed a new law under which the upper limit would be reduced by more than half and the quota for each nationality would be set at 2 percent of the number of that nationality in the 1890 census. Instead of a division of 55 percent for Northern and Western Europe and 45 percent for Southern and Eastern Europe, the relative proportions under the new legislation were to be 70 percent and 30 percent. However, it was not until 1924 that the new quotas became law. The legislation proposed a new formula for calculating the annual immigrant totals for each European nationality, based on so-called national origins, which would come into effect in 1927. The fundamental aim of this legislation was, in the words of the House Committee on Immigration, "to guarantee, as best we can . . . racial homogeneity in the United States," by keeping America for the Americans and by preserving the Nordic race from mongrelization and degradation.[9] Though there was some opposition to the 1924 legislation, the terms of the debates were set by the restrictionists, with opponents objecting to the merits of various quota plans rather than opposing the very principle of a quota.

Public attitudes and the legislation based on them have been discussed at some length in order to provide a general context for assessing the views of organized labor. As noted in Chapter Six, labor's official policy does not necessarily reflect the opinion of the rank and file. Members of trade unions play a number of other roles, as voters, consumers, parents, church attenders, club members, and party activists, which enable them to view issues of public importance from a variety of perspectives. In a period of heightened public emotion they are unlikely to be immune to the political passions of the time. Many members of trade unions, therefore, may have been so affected by the antiradical arguments in 1919, or the racist arguments prevalent after 1921, that their reasons for supporting immigration restriction diverged significantly from those officially adopted by their unions.

Although there was some opposition in the labor movement to more stringent anti-immigration laws, it is unquestionable that sentiment was overwhelmingly behind the new legislation. But why did labor support it? Did labor's reasons for backing restriction correspond to those being proposed in Congress and in the press? In other words, to what extent had labor opinion become racist over this issue, bearing in mind that arguments based on race had not been part of its case before 1917? Furthermore, were the grounds for labor's opposition to immigration, as expressed in the resolutions of trade unions and other bodies, shared by a significant section of restrictionist opinion in the labor movement? Can it be determined, that is to say, whether rank-and-file opinion was more or less racist than official opinion? More research will be required to provide an answer to the last question, possibly using a methodology similar to that employed in Chapter Six. However, an important first step is to try to clarify labor's policy, the reasons advanced in its support, and the nature and significance of the opposition to it which emerged between 1917 and 1924.

Our starting point is the impact of the war on conditions of employment. Mobilization into the army and the *de facto* termination of immigration created a labor shortage which was partly overcome by the recruitment of women and Southern black workers in manufacturing. Still, real wages had risen and working conditions had generally improved owing to the influence of the War Labor Board on employers. Unemployment had been virtually eliminated. The workforce had become accustomed to a degree of prosperity which it was determined to preserve when the war ended. Its expectations were strengthened by the publicly expressed views of prominent figures who embroidered the theme of "a land fit for heroes."

Unwilling to rely on these public expressions of goodwill, organized labor began to take practical measures to preserve its economic position. Accordingly, in December 1918, a special AFL committee on postwar problems decided to press for a two-year suspension of immigration. Frank Morrison, AFL secretary, testified in its favor before the House Committee on Immigration, and in the summer of 1919 the federation's annual convention ratified the proposal. Support for the principle of suspension was maintained by the AFL after the passage of the 3 percent bill in 1921, even though the latter was approved as a step in the right direction.[10]

The AFL's decision to back suspension requires explanation, particularly in view of the fact that only eighteen months earlier it had celebrated its major achievement, the enactment of the literacy test. Moreover, immigration had not even resumed by December 1918, when the original decision was taken, and the efficacy of the measure had not yet been tested. It would appear that labor was afraid that the literacy test would prove ineffective in stemming the flow of Europeans fleeing from a war-torn Europe. The test had hardly been designed with such an eventuality in mind. Moreover, labor was preoccupied with the transition from a wartime to a peacetime economy and worried about the loss of jobs this might entail. Over four million people had been employed, directly or indirectly, in war industries. Economists forecast that the ending of war contracts would inevitably lead to a run-down of economic activity and an increase in unemployment, at least until industry had time to adjust to peacetime conditions. These predictions were borne out in the first few months after the Armistice.

A rapid cancellation of war contracts occurred immediately after the war. By 1 January, 1919, Cleveland had some 60,000 unemployed, about 48,000 above normal for the time of year, composed of redundant war workers and demobilized soldiers. In Connecticut about 40,000 war workers had been discharged by mid-January 1919. All the major cities reported a high level of unemployment. This kind of economic readjustment was inevitable, though possibly the federal government could have prepared more adequately to cushion its impact. Equally inevitable was the demobilization of soldiers and sailors, which added to the labor force. The process began with 26,000 men returning from France in November 1918, and the peak rat~

was reached in June 1919 when 350,000 troops disembarked. Demobilization from units stationed at home occurred even more rapidly, so that over 1,600,000 officers and enlisted men had been discharged by March 1919. All told, some four million members of the armed forces were demobilized in 1919.[11]

This was precisely the outcome that labor had feared. Every trade union journal urged the need to protect employment prospects for demobilized servicemen and existing workers. Two of the AFL's most prominent figures, Matthew Woll and Frank Morrison, affirmed that labor's principal task was to control unemployment and to ensure that discharged soldiers and sailors obtained decent jobs. It would be wrong, they claimed, and productive of great bitterness, if soldiers returning to civilian life were denied employment owing to immigrant competition. They concluded that immigration should be prohibited until economic reconstruction had been completed.

As well as increasing unemployment, the resumption of immigration would serve to reduce wages and to worsen living standards. Employers' scare stories about a labor shortage owing to the remigration of many foreign-born workers were wide of the mark, since there was plenty of labor to meet demand. The wartime recruitment of women and blacks to work in Northern industrial plants had substantially increased the labor force. About half a million Southern blacks had migrated to the Northern cities during the war, and in Chicago alone about 50,000 blacks had arrived over an eighteen-month period in 1917–18. The riots and lynchings which occurred in some Northern cities in 1918 were partly due to social tensions and job competition, notably when blacks were hired as scabs during the 1919 steel strike. Small wonder, then, that the AFL believed the difficulties accompanying adjustment to a peacetime economy would be exacerbated by the resumption of immigration.[12]

But labor had other equally grave apprehensions. There were well-founded predictions that immigration would exceed even the prewar totals despite the existence of the literacy test. The German, Austrian, and Italian governments, it was claimed, were planning to rush over many of their laborers once the peace treaty had been signed in order to reduce their acute unemployment. But quite apart from governmental encouragement, there was sufficient incentive for the Europeans to flee the hardship and austerity of home and seek employment and opportunity in the United States. American industry, however, was not strong enough to absorb such a large influx of foreign workers in so short a period. Consequently, until the nation was back upon "a sound industrial basis," the suspension of immigration was absolutely vital. Matthew Woll in the *American Federationist* summed up labor's demands: "During this period of transition there rests on government the grave and important duty of creating a condition at home which shall present the opportunity to every able-bodied man to secure healthful and profitable employment under a wage [sic] of American standards of living and reasonable working hours." This duty involved complete suspension of immigration in the short term; thereafter, admission of immigrants should be regulated by levels of employment in the United States.[13]

These forecasts and apprehensions notwithstanding, unemployment did not become a major problem in the first eighteen months after the Armistice. After the initial period of layoffs, the economy began to prosper, and most of the demobilized soliders, as well as the workers employed in war plants, were able to secure jobs. This relative prosperity has been attributed to continued deficit spending by the federal government and to consumer expenditures deferred until peacetime. Military expenditures, too, remained high by prewar standards. The Federal Reserve Board pursued an easy credit policy, and a housebuilding boom got under way.[14] As a result, though industrial production declined by about 10 percent by mid–1919, it recovered to reach a new high in the second half of the year. Unemployment did not reach significant levels until 1920, after government spending began to decline. Yet, despite the reappearance of prosperity after the initial postwar economic downturn, labor's hostility to immigration remained intense. Its spokesmen claimed that the inevitable postwar depression had merely been deferred and that labor's pressure on the government for suspension of immigration had to be maintained in order to establish reasonable protection for working men in the hard times ahead. It is noteworthy, however, that labor's campaign against immigrants was not prompted solely by economic considerations: political and social anxieties reinforced apprehensions about economic prospects.

The war, for example, had increased labor's awareness that "many thousands" knew nothing about Americanism and cared less. In the camps, there were "numberless instances" in which military training began with the teaching of English. In civilian life, one union journal claimed, 80 percent of the disloyal were aliens, either self-styled internationalists or men and women still loyal to their former homelands. The melting pot, in effect, had demonstrably failed to secure a happy fusion of races and sentiments. In the future it would be necessary "to admit into the cauldron only such material as can reasonably be guaranteed as fusible." One criterion of "fusibility," an AFL committee proposed, was a willingness on the part of the foreign-born to become American citizens. It recommended that all eligible persons living permanently in the United States should be compelled to become citizens in order "to balance benefits with responsibilities." A union editor added that if "America is to be American, immigrants must not be allowed to come faster than we can assimilate them, not in the old-fashioned way of turning them loose to do the best they can, but in making American citizens out of them." This recommendation was embodied in a clause in the suspension proposal of 1919 which provided that, after the two-year suspension period, immigrants be admitted only on their written declaration to become citizens and be required to register annually until their citizenship was confirmed. This concern about citizenship and assimilation was a continuation of the prewar fears that American democracy would be irrevocably weakened by those who lacked knowledge of, or reverence for, America's laws and government. America's first duty was to perpetuate her role as the carrier and embodiment of democratic ideas.[15]

Developments in the immediate postwar world drew attention to another threat to democracy which labor had earlier neglected. Prewar labor leadership considered that the main danger to democracy originated with immigrants who were ignorant of American politics and uninterested in the democratic process. In the postwar years, however, some opponents of immigration stressed the danger from alien revolutionaries. Labor's change of emphasis reflected the widespread hostility to radicals during the war and the national hysteria triggered by the Red Scare. Labor spokesmen seemed even more sensitive to the threat from alien radicals, "the turbulent stream of bolshevist barbarians" as they were referred to on one occasion, when they contemplated the economic and political upheavals in Europe. The United States may have been intended as an asylum for the oppressed, but that did not include anarchists and "other elements" infected with the virus of bolshevism and intent on America's destruction. The formation of two Communist parties in 1919, composed primarily of Eastern Europeans who identified with the Bolshevik revolution and talked of the immediate overthrow of capitalism, was a salutary warning to Americans.[16]

Despite the growing importance attached to the alien menace, this aspect of labor's opposition to immigration still took second place to the economic threat. It is probable that labor's antiradicalism, real though it was, was inflated by the failure of the economy to remain depressed in 1919. Furthermore, labor's attitude toward alien radicals was ambivalent, unlike that of the wider public. Popular apprehension about a radical revolution in the United States in 1919 and 1920 fluctuated with the incidence of strikes, but it is worth recalling that a proportion of the strikes took place under the AFL's seal of approval, and many involved conservative craft unions attempting to maintain wartime gains. Consequently, labor's perspective on the strikes was rather different from that of the general public's. Conservative trade unionists could hardly become aroused by the spectacle of alien radicals engaging in militant strike action when they themselves were often involved. But labor could also draw distinctions between strikes and assess the implications of labor unrest. Strikes by native-born skilled workers were encouraged by union leadership, while industrial action by unskilled "new" immigrants, at times led by socialists or Communists, was highly suspect. The AFL's opposition to the Red menace was more informed and less hysterical than the public's in general, but it was equally firm. Only by a total suspension of immigration could the danger be averted and the threat to living standards lifted.

This policy was not without opposition among AFL affiliated unions, notably the Stereotypers, Ladies Garment Workers, and Tailors. One opponent made the cogent point that, since there had been a very heavy remigration to Europe in 1919, producing a net surplus of emigrants over immigrants, he failed to see the necessity for a suspension act. The International Ladies Garment Workers Union (ILGWU) membership originated mainly in Russia, Austria-Hungary, and Italy, and, not surprisingly, it had voted against the literacy test at the 1916 AFL convention. Its delegate to the 1919 convention rejected the allegation that "new" immigrants made bad unionists; on the contrary, foreign-born unionists were continuing the fight for a higher standard of living. Trade unionists should find alternative methods of dealing with economic difficulties, such as negotiating shorter working hours, as the ILGWU had done. The socialist president of the Tailors' Union invoked the familiar socialist argument: the maldistribution of wealth, not immigration, was the source of the workers' distress, a theme taken up by the Brewery Workers in their continuing battle against restriction. A Seattle delegate opposed suspension on the grounds that it would minimize contact with workers from other countries, and discourage the U.S. government from offering foreigners political asylum. But this was the sum total of AFL opposition to suspension, which may have aroused less forceful objections than either the preceding literacy test or the subsequent quota legislation because it seemed nondiscriminatory.[17]

John Higham has speculated on the reasons for labor's postwar support of total suspension. He discounted the factor of labor competition and its impact on employment and wages as an "old story." The key to the change in labor attitudes, he believed, lay in the impact of the war, which had demonstrated the nation's incapacity to Americanize the great prewar flood of immigrants. AFL leadership had argued along strictly economic lines until about 1916, when Gompers made an impassioned plea for developing "American character and national unity." "This explicit appeal to national homogeneity," he continued, "had not graced official A.F.L. declarations before the war period." It is not possible to accept Higham's interpretation without qualification. Earlier chapters have shown the importance labor attached to assimilating newcomers, and the literacy test was adopted as a major contribution to excluding the less assimilable immigrants. Labor repeatedly emphasized the importance of social homogeneity as a means of maintaining political and cultural standards. The war gave added impetus to the Americanization arguments in the labor movement, but can hardly be said to have originated them.

Furthermore, labor's support for suspension after the war was the product of a cluster of factors which Higham seemed to ignore. There was little in the way of available alternatives to the literacy test in 1918 and 1919 short of total suspension. The 1917 Immigration Act had only recently been passed, that there had been insufficient time to devise the next stage in a graduated response. Moreover, opposition to suspension in the trade unions was muted, perhaps on account of the measure's nondiscriminatory character. Discrimination in immigration law was probably less popular immediately after the war owing to the admirable prowar record of the majority of Southern and Eastern European immigrants. Labor also questioned whether discriminatory legislation would prevent the immigration of radicals.

Most important of all, labor was desperately anxious to maintain wartime economic gains. Unemployment might have been an "old story," as Higham remarked, but it lost nothing by age. The cutting off of immigration during the war made labor relatively scarce and highly priced, confirming what restrictionists had always asserted, but could never prove, namely, that immigration control was the key to workers' prosperity. Labor leaders were determined to preserve prosperity by any means, including immigration restriction. Labor's forceful reaction to the postwar resumption of immigration owed a good deal, as Higham argued, to the apparent failure of the melting pot in wartime, but there are other equally important factors to consider.

Despite labor's sturdy commitment to suspension in the immediate postwar period, other sections of the community failed to sustain their enthusiasm. Economic prosperity in the summer of 1919, a net surplus of emigrants, the policy of deportation, and, in early 1920, the decline in strike activity all helped to weaken support for this policy. It was not until midsummer 1920 that labor once again began to gain support for tougher immigration restriction. Thereafter, progress towards the goal of additional restrictive measures was virtually uninterrupted as public and labor opinion again converged.

Not surprisingly, labor opinion reflected the widespread economic anxieties existing immediately before the passage of the 1921 Johnson bill. Workingmen needed no reminder that labor bore the brunt of any economic depression. The increasing unemployment of late 1920 coupled with, and no doubt partially caused by, the rising immigration earlier in the year, fulfilled labor's predictions that existing legislation was inadequate. Throughout most of 1920 and into 1921 the labor press and trade union conventions deplored the increasing volume of immigration, and predicted that worse was yet to come. The prospect of an immigration of "record-breaking immensity," mostly originating in Russia, Poland, and Italy, was extremely disquieting. Once again, labor selected business as its principal target, claiming that employers were lobbying for a liberalization of immigration laws in their zeal to maintain profits and overcome labor shortages. Similarly opposed to further restriction, though hardly in alliance with employers, were internationalists, who, despising patriotism and state boundaries, aimed to accelerate social revolution by removing all controls on immigration. Labor identified a third component among antirestrictionists, the foreign-born, whose ambition to reunite their families and to welcome friends from Europe was likely to be thwarted by tighter immigration controls. This group was politically active, especially in the industrial areas of the Northeast, where congressmen were in no position to ignore the foreign-born vote.[18]

Immigration, in labor's opinion, had already created serious problems, and worse were in prospect. Unemployment overshadowed every other consideration. In July 1920, after immigration had begun to rise substantially, a union spokesman forecast that there would soon be a general labor surplus to add to the already existing surpluses in particular sectors. By November, it was claimed that the immigration rate would aggravate unemployment, and year-end observers noted that industries were shutting down, thousands were unemployed, and the standard of living was being depressed by wage cuts. Unemployment continued to rise until midsummer 1921, when it reportedly stood at five million. The distress and suffering associated with such figures could not be minimized, and there is little doubt that the effect on jobs and wages was the major evil of immigration, as far as labor was concerned.

But, as in the prewar period, attention was drawn to other adverse consequences. The influx of large numbers of aliens, many of them entirely ignorant of American democratic institutions, threatened republicanism and civic responsibility. This ignorance, rather than the radicalism of the immediate postwar period, was now recognized as the major political threat, as it had been before the conflict. Warnings about the danger of unassimilable aliens recalled similar prewar admonitions. One spokesman, in urging the exclusion of unassimilable races, equated the Slavs with the Japanese, which suggested that racism was being extended to European ethnic groups. In 1920, though, racism was still very much the attitude of the minority in the labor movement and would remain so in the future.[19]

Whatever arguments were advanced, the position was serious enough to demand immediate action. It was obvious to labor that the existing law was either inadequate or not being properly enforced, probably the former. Accordingly, the call went out for new legislation to prevent an influx of economic competitors. To the charge that this was a selfish policy, labor leaders replied defensively that self-preservation was the first law of nature. The two-year suspension was still the most favored measure. In practice, this meant supporting the bill proposed by the House Committee on Immigration. When it passed the House, labor doubted, and with good reason, whether the Senate would also affirm it. Delegates to the AFL's 1921 convention regretfully noted that the so-called 3 percent bill, not the suspension bill, had been passed by Congress. Despite its disappointment, however, the AFL welcomed the measure as an important step forward, though it reaffirmed its intention to try to obtain a complete, if temporary, suspension of immigration in the interests of reducing unemployment.[20]

Labor's determination to tighten up the law still further was heightened by administrative deficiencies in the 1921 Quota Act which soon became apparent. But even if procedures had been watertight, the law itself was inherently unacceptable to labor. The 3 percent quota was too liberal, permitting more aliens to enter than could safely be absorbed. It was satisfactory as a temporary measure in controlling the total number of immigrants, but it failed to improve their quality significantly. In an effort to improve the law, the 1922 convention of the AFL instructed its Executive Council to seek passage of a more stringent act at the expiration of the existing legislation. The AFL's favored solution was still the total suspension of European immigration. By 1924 it became clear that there was no practical political alternative to the Johnson-Reed Bill, based on the 2 percent quota. When the bill became law, it was welcomed by the AFL as being closest to its own demand for total suspension. From one union came forthright approval for the fundamental aim of the law, which was "to secure a larger proportion of immigrants from the North of Europe—from countries supposed to be more in accord with our culture and institutions."[21]

By 1924, therefore, the AFL had very nearly achieved its goal of total exclusion for European immigrants and had accepted the quota law of that year as the best deal it was likely to get. In view of the changed character of the national debate, where arguments based on racism became more prominent to the virtual exclusion of economic issues, it is noteworthy that organized labor's case against immigration hardly changed in this period. Admittedly, the question of immigrant radicalism was virtually ignored in the later period, in line with the public mood, but the major emphases on economic competition, failure of assimilation, and declining qualities of citizenship were retained. Virtually no inroads were made upon them by the widely fashionable argument of racial nationalism. True to itself and its traditions, the AFL adhered to the approach which it understood best and which had served it well. Yet in 1923 there had been a temptation to shift the focus from questions of wages and employment. After all, the economy was improving at that point, employment and wages were rising, and it was possible that there would be greater public sympathy for employers' lobbying against the quota.[22]

Despite the temptation to adopt popular racist arguments against immigration, labor remained loyal to its traditional cluster of arguments. In hearings before the House Immigration Committee on the Johnson 2 percent bill, the AFL stressed the need to protect American workers from unemployment and declining wages in order to achieve the "best possible standards in the workshop and in the homes for all American people." Samuel Gompers accused management of failing to come to terms with the problem of human waste in industry—of illness and accidents occurring at the workplace caused by employer negligence. Basing his argument on the presumably authoritative report of the Federation of American Engineering

Societies on the elimination of waste in industry, Gompers implied that an improvement in shopfloor conditions would not only be good for employees but would also increase labor supply without the need to lower immigration barriers. His emphasis on economic protection was followed by many union spokesmen, who stressed that unemployment was still a considerable problem, quoting the hundreds of job applicants at employment agencies in Northern cities. They drew attention to the augmenting of the labor supply by internal migrants, both white and black, moving from agricultural areas to urban centers. They concluded that there was no place for immigrants in industry because each additional foreign-born worker weakened working-class efforts to obtain reasonable living standards.[23]

Another traditional argument in labor's brief, one continually emphasized in this period, centered on the effect of increased immigration upon society's assimilative capacity. The wartime experience of dual loyalties, as we have seen, provided labor with a dramatic confirmation of its prewar claims. Enactment of the 1921 Johnson Bill did not calm labor's fears, partly because of inherent weaknesses in the act, partly because the employers' campaign to repeal it might succeed. During 1923 the AFL became concerned about one finding in the 1920 census, namely, that of the 15 million foreign-born in the United States, one and one-half million could not speak English and three million could not read or write it. Furthermore, over half the foreign-born had taken no steps to become citizens. The campaign for Americanization, the AFL concluded, needed to be intensified, and its success would be more certain if complete restriction were introduced. The most serious consequence of the failure to assimilate the foreign-born, in labor's view, lay in the field of citizenship. A large influx of foreign-born with different traditions, cultures, languages, religions, and styles of political behavior would weaken democratic institutions and divide the loyalties of many Americans in any future international conflict. Hence national survival was at stake. Experience had shown that attempts at forcible assimilation would not succeed, and that the only feasible alternative was to prohibit immigration altogether or to limit it to the smallest possible proportions.[24]

In making their point about assimilation, labor's representatives assumed that cultural differences rather than genetic ones made it difficult for newcomers to adopt American standards of citizenship. A small minority in labor's ranks supported the cause of racism, but the AFL rejected these ideas at its annual conventions. When, on occasion, racist sentiments crept into labor publications, they were quite likely to have been written by middle-class publicists. An exception was an article in the *Shoe Workers' Journal* in 1924 in which attention was drawn to the physically and mentally undesirable character of much of the alien inflow, as reflected in IQ results. The unrestricted entry of "degenerate stock," the article asserted, would determine the future of democracy and indeed of the "American race" itself.

The most notable example of this line of argument came from the pen of labor's most powerful and influential figure, Samuel Gompers, in the year that the second quota act became law. Writing for a labor audience, he seemed to espouse the racist argument which attributed genetically transmitted qualities to certain races which ensured their nonassimilability. He was determined, he wrote, "to maintain the general character given our institutions through the racial characteristics of those who have been the dominant force from the very beginning." Quoting Gino Speranza, he concluded that "the greater the homogeneity of its citizenship the better knit and spiritually united will be this or any other democracy." Gompers's comments, one scholar declared, meant that "for the first time in his long restrictionist fight openly, though with a certain reluctance, [he] embraced the idea that European immigration endangered America's racial foundations."[25] Gompers's autobiography, published around the same time, seems to confirm this judgment. It endorsed the principle that "maintenance of the nation depended upon the maintenance of racial purity and strength."

However, before accepting this judgment, we should inquire more closely what Gompers meant by racial characteristics. If he were influenced by Speranza, as the use of a quotation from him suggests, then he would have known that Speranza considered American institutions to be the product of the specific ethnic characteristics of the population. The United States was, Speranza believed, "in all the essentials of its life and character" grafted upon a historically definite and distinguishable North European or Anglo-Saxon stock. Upon that graft there developed a definite and distinguishable racial type—the historic American people. The words "racial type," he made clear, referred to North European origins. But, and this point deserves emphasis, the culture developed by that "racial type" was assimilable by other "racial types." Consequently, there was "room in the Republic for peoples whose views, beliefs and antecedents differ from those of historical American stock." However, Speranza conceded that too many newcomers of this type placed a strain on the culture and became a "denationalizing element within the republic and disrupting element within the democracy."[26] This, we will recognize, is essentially the same argument expressed by labor spokesmen in the past—that a vast multitude of newcomers from different cultures rendered the assimilation process virtually ineffective. It is probable that this is what Gompers meant, though he confused the issue by using the fashionable word "race."

This interpretation avoids the difficulty of explaining Gompers's apparent *volte-face* on this issue toward the end of his life, which seemed to put him out of step with labor opinion generally and with the views of the AFL in particular. The federation's attitude towards immigration was constrained by the need to recognize the susceptibilities of its foreign-born members, many of whom had their roots in Southern and Eastern Europe. The majority of unionist miners, for instance, were either first- or second-generation Americans who came from that region. In the large cities between 50 and 70 percent of the carpenters' union membership was foreign-born. The machinists' union had recently amended its constitution to admit semi-skilled and unskilled machine tenders, thus doubling its membership between 1917 and 1919, with most of the newcomers being foreign-born. There were also substantial numbers of immigrants among the electrical workers, the railroad carmen, the maintenance-of-way employees, and the meatcutters and butcher workmen, not to mention the ladies' garment and men's clothing workers.[27]

Since many trade unionists were of Slavic, Jewish, or Italian stock, it would have been insulting, as well as damaging to their own organizations, for union leaders to argue in favor of the exclusion of such newcomers on the grounds of their genetic inferiority and innate inability to assimilate. The trade unions had always affirmed that the problems of organizing newcomers had a cultural rather than a racial origin, and they maintained that position throughout the campaign for restriction. Their position, in short, was that the foreign-born were slow to assimilate American standards of living, working conditions, and wages. This was, of course, harmful to labor's interests, but the fact that many of the newcomers ultimately did join trade unions argued against the racially determinist point of view. The problem of slow assimilation could be solved by the quota legislation because, in Gompers's words, it would admit a carefully selected immigration of small numbers "most likely to become citizens, most likely to join intelligently and willingly in the effort to maintain standards of working conditions, standards of life and living and standards of citizenship built up through decades of hard effort."[28]

Although increasing recruitment by trade unions of Slavs, Italians, and Jews was probably a factor in restraining the adoption of out-and-out racist arguments for restriction, their membership in the unions had little effect in modifying labor's immigration policy. Most of the unions remained firm supporters of restriction. Unions in the needle trades, notably the ILGWU and the Amalgamated Clothing Workers (ACW), whose membership was predominantly Jewish and Italian, were exceptions to this rule. The ACW had endorsed free immigration since its foundation in 1914 and opposed the 1921 Quota Act on grounds of ethnic discrimination.[29] But compared with the ILGWU, the ACW kept a fairly low profile in the early 1920s, and the burden of opposing federation support for quota legislation fell almost completely on the former. It was almost certainly the ILGWU's opposition to which Gompers referred in 1924, when he criticized "racial groups" acting not as Americans but as aliens loyal to their fellow ethnics abroad. Noting their claim for the open door and their assertion that the American government acted unfairly in placing restrictions on the desire to migrate, he retorted that entry was a privilege, not a right, which the government had the power to confer or withhold.[30] But in selecting this argument for criticism, Gompers ignored other aspects of the ILGWU's position. Furthermore, he was silent about the negotiations which allegedly took place between the AFL and the ILGWU concerning a proposal to exempt Jews from the quota system. The ILGWU's stance on restriction had a private as well as a public aspect. Their inclination to depart from an absolutist antirestrictionist position by seeking preferential treatment under the quota system reflects the severity of restrictionist pressures in the early 1920s. In fact, the struggle between supporters and opponents of free immigration, long since won in the AFL by the restrictionists, was now being fought out among the Garment Workers. This conflict was not simply between union factions; it was also internalized by individual union members. One may nonetheless claim that the major opposition to legislation within the AFL emanated from the ILGWU.

Their public opposition to the Johnson Bill emphasized the traditional role of the United States as an asylum for refugees. ILGWU delegates at the 1921 AFL convention assailed the 3 percent quota proposal as "an inhuman attack on those who were compelled to flee from ravaged homes in the 'old country' in search of peace and better living." When, two years later, the terms of the 2 percent bill were reported, ILGWU convention delegates protested sharply that from its founding, the nation's policy had been one of offering asylum to all victims of racial, religious, and political persecution. The continuance of the policy was especially necessary in the early 1920s, owing to the "political, industrial and moral upheaval" of postwar Europe, which had produced renewed outbreaks of religious intolerance and political and racial oppression, driving thousands from their homelands. The Garment Workers' delegates clearly had Jews in mind. Their union's journal, in commenting on the drastically reduced rates for Russia and Poland under the proposed new quota, noted that the very countries whose populations were suffering most from oppression—that is, the Jewish inhabitants of these nations—would be permitted the least number of immigrants. The union's emphasis on America's role as an asylum may also be found in its response to Gompers's request for support for the Johnson-Reed Bill of April 1924. Agreeing that American workers should be protected against job competition, the ILGWU nonetheless stressed that priority should be given to considerations of humanity, and that the United States must not close its doors to those fleeing from religious, racial, or political persecution.[31]

This emphasis on the traditional ideal of asylum was significant. It was tactically sound to advance an argument which had proved to be persuasive among the general public and in Congress. Furthermore, it promised disproportionate advantages to the Jews of Eastern Europe, since they were the chief victims of persecution. It also permitted the Garment Workers to stand as opponents of the quota legislation even though their own anxiety about the economic impact of immigration was becoming acute. It enabled them to maintain an overt solidarity with ethnic or nationality groups from Southern and Eastern Europe whilst conceding the need for some restriction on economic grounds. Unless mass European immigration were checked, it believed, even the strongest American trade unions would be swept away and everything built up in the course of so many years would be destroyed. "Even our workers," its journal confessed, "are not so altruistic as to share their loaf of bread with the prospective arrivals." It recognized that the membership was torn between its sympathy for the sufferings of Europeans and the belief that unrestricted immigration might injure its interests and impair its own fight for a better life. There must be a certain amount of restriction, the journal conceded, but it should be made as humane and "devoid of brutality" as possible. For these reasons it opposed the Johnson Act.[32]

The ILGWU's singling out of "asylum" arguments in opposing the two Quota Acts was closely connected with the suggestion for some kind of special treatment for Jews. Further evidence of this was provided by Harry Lang in 1927. Lang, four years earlier, had recommended, in the *Jewish Daily Forward*, that Jews should be separated from other nationalities for purposes of immigration restriction. If this were done, it might be possible to induce the AFL to adopt a "hands-off" policy with reference to Jewish immigrants. It is significant that the ILGWU journal did not attack Lang's proposal on substantive grounds but solely because it exaggerated the AFL's influence upon the U.S. Congress. According to Lang, the plan he proposed was actually carried out. "Several committees of Jewish labor circles" conferred with the AFL in the hope that when the federation better understood the character of Jewish immigrants, it would then distinguish between them and other newcomers. Jewish immigration was special. First, it could not be criticized on economic grounds since it did not endanger work standards or compete in industries whose workers were mostly native-born. Second, Jewish immigrants generally arrived in family groups, which not only signified permanence but also offered a firmer guarantee of assimilation. Finally, the Jews had no homeland of their own, and so the argument that it was the responsibility of European governments to strengthen their own economies and to provide work for their own surplus workers did not apply to them. According to Lang, the Jewish labor delegation was able to convince the AFL, which agreed to lobby on its behalf. But, Lang sadly noted, nothing came of this agreement.[33]

Lang's evidence may not be trustworthy, but it is consistent with the ILGWU's own fear of the economic consequences of immigration and its acceptance of the need for "humane" restriction. Of all the antirestrictionist arguments, the defense of America as an asylum was the one most likely to attract support. Therefore, whilst the ILGWU was the strongest single opponent of the quota within the AFL, the evidence suggests that it was somewhat ambivalent on the subject of immigration and pursued a policy favoring Jewish immigrants at the expense of other ethnic groups from Southern and Eastern Europe.

When the literacy test was enacted as part of the 1917 Immigration Act, organized labor was pleased with the realization of a long-held goal, and only a few voices cast doubts on the probable effectiveness of the measure. Within little more than two years, however, the AFL became convinced that the test, its preferred method of restriction for at least a decade, would be incapable of offering adequate protection for its members. In calling for a total suspension of immigration for two years, the federation was probably hoping that this temporary ban would become permanent. By the end of the war most unions were convinced that the cessation of immigration was the key to their members' prosperity. Other threats to working-class living standards, like the transition from a wartime to a peacetime economy, seemed unavoidable; but the probable resumption of large-scale immigration, it was felt, could be prevented by an act of political will. Organized labor was also vitally concerned about the threat to democracy, either from a minority of foreign-born revolutionaries or from masses of ignorant Europeans incapable of speedy assimilation into the nation's political culture. Labor's anxiety was heightened by the obvious wartime failure of the melting pot and the very real limits to "fusibility" of the foreign-born. With these lessons in mind, labor proposed that if immigration were to resume after a period of suspension, aliens should not be admitted unless they declared their intention to become citizens. Unable to obtain total suspension, labor accepted the Quota Act of 1924 as being the most satisfactory available alternative.

Unlike the AFL's initial commitment to the literacy test, there were no deep divisions over the quota legislation. Support for it was overwhelming, and the few opponents of restriction recognized that of all the old arguments against it only one, the asylum idea, retained any wide appeal. Not that organized labor officially countenanced the racism which swept across the nation in the early 1920s. Awareness of the sensibilities of an important section of its membership reduced the temptation to engage in the politics of genetic determinism. But the pragmatic view that only very small numbers of European immigrants, and those mainly from the North, could be admitted with safety was all that remained of the internationalism and hospitality of labor's early years. The labor movement was now less generous, less humane, less altruistic, and less romantic, and a policy of self-preservation was the preferred alternative of all but a tiny minority of organized workers.

NOTES

1. American Federation of Labor, *Report of the Proceedings of the Thirty-Seventh Annual Convention*, 1917, pp. 118, 316 (hereafter referred to as AFL, *Proceedings*);

The Garment Worker, 14 April 1916, p. 5; 10 November 1916, p. 4; 9 February 1917, p. 4; John Higham, *Strangers in the Land: Patterns of American Nativism, 1860–1925* (1955: rpt. New York: Atheneum, 1963), p. 204; Robert De C. Ward, "Americanization and Immigration," *American Review of Reviews* 59 (May 1919): 513–16, quoted in Oscar Handlin, ed., *Immigration as a Factor in American History* (New York: Prentice-Hall, 1959), pp. 189–92.

2. See Chapter Nine; Handlin, *Immigration as a Factor,* p. 189.

3. Higham, *Strangers in the Land,* pp. 222–23, 225–26, 306; Burl Noggle, *Into the Twenties: The United States from Armistice to Normalcy* (Urbana: University of Illinois Press, 1974), pp. 91, 102–3; Stanley Coben, "A Study in Nativism: The American Red Scare of 1919–20," *Political Science Quarterly* 79 (March 1964), rpr. in S. Katz and S. Kutler, eds., *New Perspectives on the American Past,* 2 vols. (Boston: Little, Brown and Co., 1969), Vol. 2, pp. 209–21; David Brody, *Labor in Crisis: The Steel Strike of 1919* (Philadelphia: J. B. Lippincott Company, 1965), pp. 129–32. A brief depression after the war was followed by a period of prosperity, characterized by a rapid rate of inflation which put wage earners at a disadvantage.

4. Higham, *Strangers in the Land,* pp. 202, 221, 230; Noggle, *Into the Twenties,* pp. 88–89, 95–96.

5. Higham, *Strangers in the Land,* pp. 232, 265–70; Noggle, *Into the Twenties,* pp. 111–12, quoting William Preston.

6. Higham, *Strangers in the Land,* pp. 267, 308; Robert A. Divine, *American Immigration Policy, 1924–52* (New Haven: Yale University Press, 1957), pp. 6–8; Noggle, *Into the Twenties,* pp. 200–202; George M. Stephenson, *A History of American Immigration, 1820–1924* (Boston: Ginn and Co., 1926), p. 170.

7. Higham, *Strangers in the Land,* pp. 271–76; Divine, *American Immigration Policy,* pp. 11–14. Lothrop Stoddard's book *The Rising Tide of Color against White World Supremacy* was published in 1920. Kenneth Roberts's *Why Europe Leaves Home* came out in 1922, having previously appeared as articles in the *Saturday Evening Post.* Henry Pratt Fairchild, *The Melting-Pot Mistake* (Boston: Little, Brown and Co., 1926), pp. 123–24.

8. Divine, *American Immigration Policy,* p. 6; Higham, *Strangers in the Land,* p. 311.

9. Higham, *Strangers in the Land,* pp. 315, 322; Divine, *American Immigration Policy,* pp 14, 17.

10. David Burner, "1919: Prelude to Normalcy," in John Braeman, Robert H. Bremner, and David Brody, eds., *Change and Continuity in Twentieth-Century America: 1920s* (Columbus: Ohio State University Press, 1968), p. 4; Brody, *Labor in Crisis,* p. 48; *The Garment Worker,* 10 May 1918, p. 4; *United Mineworkers' Journal,* 18 April 1919; Noggle, *Into the Twenties,* p. 8; Higham, *Strangers in the Land,* p. 305; AFL, *Proceedings,* 1919, pp. 364–68; 1921, pp. 107–8, 307.

11. *The Garment Worker,* 31 January 1919, p. 4; Noggle, *Into the Twenties,* pp. 14–15, 68, 75–76.

12. AFL, *Proceedings,* 1919, pp. 364–68; *United Mineworkers' Journal,* 1 January 1919, 18 April 1919, 1 July 1919; *Cigar Makers' Official Journal,* December 1918; *The Garment Worker,* 5 September 1919; *The Railroad Trainman,* April 1918; *American Federationist,* August 1919, pp. 707–11; Noggle, *Into the Twenties,* pp. 155–58; Burner, "1919: Prelude to Normalcy," p. 21; Ward, "Americanization and Immigration," in Handlin, *Immigration,* p. 191.

13. *The Garment Worker*, 31 January 1919; *The Bricklayer and Mason*, September 1919; *American Federationist*, August 1919.

14. Stephenson, *History of American Immigration*, p. 170.

15. Noggle, *Into the Twenties*, pp. 75–76; Burner, "1919: Prelude to Normalcy," pp. 10–11; *The Bricklayer and Mason*, 22 February 1919, p. 18; January 1921, pp. 1–2; AFL, *Proceedings*, 1918; *The Garment Worker*, 5 September 1919; *The Shoe Workers' Journal*, April 1916 and April 1917; *Cigar Makers' Official Journal*, December 1918; *The Railroad Trainman*, April 1918.

16. AFL, *Proceedings*, 1919, pp. 364–68; *The Garment Worker*, 5 September 1919, p. 4; *Justice*, 28 June 1919, p. 4; *The Bricklayer and Mason*, September 1919, June 1921; *American Federationist*, August 1919; *The Railroad Trainman*, April 1918, pp. 289–92; see also Samuel Gompers to Matthew Woll, 11 February 1919, Samuel Gompers Letterbooks (microfilm, Library of the State Historical Society of Wisconsin, Madison); Noggle, *Into the Twenties*, pp. 90–91.

17. AFL, *Proceedings*, 1919, particularly pp. 364–68; Higham, *Strangers in the Land*, p. 267; Stephenson, *History of American Immigration*, p. 179; *Justice*, 28 June 1919, p. 4; *Brewery and Soft Drink Workers' Journal*, 3 May 1919, 17 January 1920. Suspension would inevitably have had more damaging consequences for the emigrant regions of Southern and Eastern Europe than for those in the North and West.

18. *The Railroad Trainman*, November 1920, pp. 677–79; June 1921, pp. 361–63; see also *The Garment Worker*, 2 July 1920, 30 July 1920, 26 November 1920, 7 January 1921; *The Shoe Workers' Journal*, November 1920; AFL, *Proceedings*, 1920, pp. 104–5.

19. *The Railroad Trainman*, June 1921; AFL, *Proceedings*, 1921, pp. 107–8; *The Garment Worker*, 2 July 1920; 26 November 1920, p. 4; 17 December 1920, p. 4; *The Bricklayer and Mason*, January 1921, June 1921; *The Shoe Workers' Journal*, November 1920, pp. 14–15.

20. *The Garment Worker*, 26 November 1920, p. 4; 17 December 1920, p. 4; *The Railroad Trainman*, January 1921, pp. 42–44; June 1921, pp. 361–63; AFL, *Proceedings*, 1921, pp. 107–8.

21. *The Railroad Trainman*, April 1922, pp. 253–54; November 1922, pp. 721–22; *The Shoe Workers' Journal*, May 1923, March 1924; AFL, *Proceedings*, 1922, pp. 181, 328–29; 1923, pp. 139–40, 350–51, 354–55; 1924, pp. 67–68; *American Federationist*, April 1924, pp. 313–17; *The Carpenter*, July 1924; *Locomotive Firemen's Magazine*, December 1923, p. 249.

22. *Advance Advocate*, June 1923, pp. 23–24; AFL, *Proceedings*, 1923, pp. 39–40; *American Federationist*, June 1923; *The Garment Worker*, 19 January 1923, p. 4; *The Bricklayer and Mason*, April 1924, p. 73; *The Shoe Workers' Journal*, May 1923, pp. 1–2; *Pattern Makers' Journal*, February 1924, p. 6.

23. *American Federationist*, February 1924, p. 144; June 1923, pp. 489–93; April 1924, pp. 313–17; *The Railroad Trainman*, October 1923, April 1924; *Advance Advocate*, June 1923, p. 24; *The Carpenter*, August 1930, pp. 25–26; *The Bricklayer and Mason*, April 1924, p. 73; *Locomotive Firemen's Magazine*, December 1923; *Pattern Makers' Journal*, February 1924, p. 6.

24. *The Railroad Trainman*, September 1921, pp. 555–57; February 1922, pp. 103–4; AFL, *Proceedings*, 1923, pp. 39–40; *The Shoe Workers' Journal*, May 1923, March 1924; *American Federationist*, June 1923, pp. 489–93; August 1923, pp. 657–59; *The Electrical Worker*, May 1924, pp. 390–91; *Pattern Makers' Journal*, February 1924, p. 6.

25. *American Federationist*, November 1922; *The Railroad Trainman*, January 1923, pp. 56–57; *The Shoe Workers' Journal*, March 1924, p. 25; Higham, *Strangers in the Land*, pp. 321–22.

26. Samuel Gompers, *Seventy Years of Life and Labor*, 2 vols. (London: Hurst and Blackett, 1925), Vol. 2, p. 160; Gino Speranza, *Race or Nation: A Conflict of Divided Loyalties* (Indianapolis: Bobbs-Merrill Co., 1925), pp. 14, 17.

27. David J. Saposs Papers, unprocessed MSS, folder entitled "Generalizations," typescript chapter "The Trade Union and the Immigrant," pp. 10–12 (State Historical Society of Wisconsin, Madison).

28. *American Federationist*, April 1924, pp. 313–17.

29. *The Advance*, 27 May 1921, 14 October 1921, 25 April 1924.

30. *American Federationist*, April 1924, p. 313.

31. *Justice*, 15 April 1921; 23 February 1923, p. 3; 7 March 1924; 4 April 1924, p. 2; 11 April 1924; AFL, *Proceedings*, 1923, p. 179.

32. *Justice*, 11 April 1924, pp. 6–7; see also 7 October 1927.

33. Ibid., 26 October 1923, p. 7; 7 October 1927, p. 5.

11

Conclusion

The enactment of the quota legislation in the 1920s, followed by the acute economic depression in the United States after 1929, removed the immigration question from the national agenda for a generation. From the earliest British settlements in North America, through the colonial and national periods, right into the twentieth century, immigration had been central to the American experience. Though conferring enormous economic and other benefits on the Republic, this inflow of peoples was, in the opinion of many Americans, a mixed blessing which had to be controlled by law if its undoubted advantages were not to be outweighed by the growing burden it placed on American society. Assessments of the benefits and costs of immigration varied widely, and a number of factors in the equation, like the question of natural rights, could scarcely be evaluated, still less precisely quantified. Consequently, the debate over immigration was as old as immigration itself, although the intensity of the discussion varied according to political and economic circumstances.

Nevertheless, despite fluctuations in opinion, there was a steady, and then accelerating, trend in the nineteenth and twentieth centuries towards enacting more rigorous immigration laws, with a view to excluding the less desirable types of newcomers and to controlling the total volume of entrants. The U.S. Congress, and by implication public opinion, was persuaded of the wisdom of the restrictionists' case. Labor organizations were among the most forceful advocates in the restrictionist *avant-garde*, and it is no exaggeration to say that the passage of the immigration laws of the early twentieth century owed as much, if not more, to labor as to any other single pressure group. Accordingly it becomes a matter of some historical importance to understand labor's conversion to restriction, how it occured, and why.

The process of conversion was markedly dialectical. For at least a century there was a contest in the labor movement (in the first half of the nineteenth century this took place among the urban artisans and mechanics, since a labor movement as such had not yet developed) between two impulses, which were refined and articulated into two contrasting political positions, even, one might say, two philosophies. On the one hand was the impulse to exclusiveness and survival, on the other the instinct for fraternity and solidarity. The former involved attempts to limit immigration by law or to restrict the political rights of the foreign-born, the latter meant challenging these proposals as contrary to American traditions. In time, restrictionists built on former legislative successes, as in the case of alien contract labor, to advocate more stringent limitations. A similar evolution occurred among their opponents, who tended to adopt the positions recently abandoned by restrictionists. By the early twentieth century the debate was largely between two sets of restrictionists, the radicals and the moderates, rather than between two diametrically opposed groups favoring exclusion on the one hand or complete absence of controls on the other. Supporters of the open door in immigration policy had not totally disappeared from the labor movement, but their influence was only marginal by that time.

This summary obscures the scale of the restrictionists' victory. The two sides did not start equal in the early nineteenth century, since, at that time, the ideal of fraternity towards European immigrants was the more deeply entrenched. It had to be uprooted, bit by bit, by those who believed that its practical results damaged the interests of urban workingmen. The early inroads on this ideal formed the foundation for further attempts to limit the application of solidarity in immigration policy. Gradually the balance of forces swung in favor of the restrictionists, and finally, by the 1920s, the instinct for fraternity was almost completely overcome by the demands of self-preservation.

The power of this open door tradition was evident during the nativist upheaval of the 1840s and 1850s, when the nativist groups and political associations advocated limitations on naturalization rather than restrictions on entry for the foreign-born. It was again apparent in the 1860s, when the National Labor Union, although disturbed by the effect of immigration on the labor market, confined itself to persuading European labor organizations to discourage their members from emigrating when unemployment was high in the United States. In the 1880s labor organizations like the Knights of Labor and the American Federation of Labor seized upon the Contract Labor Law as a means of reconciling the demands of solidarity with the needs of restriction. When it became apparent in the following decade that the law had failed, the literacy test was adopted by the labor movement to enforce exclusion of particular groups without being overtly discriminatory. Yet the 1890s was an important decade in the contest between solidarity and survival because, in choosing the literacy test, the AFL recognized that it would have to forfeit a part of its fraternal heritage. Allowing for the probability that the AFL did not reflect majority opinion among its members on this issue in the 1890s, we can still concede that within a decade the majority strongly backed the leaders' campaign for the literacy test. The incorporation of this test in law in 1917 whetted rather than satisfied labor's appetite for tough exclusion laws. The quota legislation which followed represented the eclipse of the impulse towards fraternity in the labor movement. Yet the very lengthy period required to accomplish this task is evidence of the tenacity of the ideal of solidarity.

What accounted for its attractive force? Its appeal lay in a combination of idealism, self-interest, and class politics. The ideals of asylum, natural rights, and mission, to take three examples from the eighteenth century, were invoked to justify a policy which was arguably in America's best economic interest and which appealed particularly to Americans who were themselves immigrants or the children of immigrants. In the nineteenth century solidarity received a further stimulus from the emergence of class-based political movements like the National Labor Union, the Knights of Labor, and the socialist parties. Admittedly, all these organizations made compromises over the immigration question, but the essential point is that in tracing the roots of working-class impoverishment to the financial manipulators and the capitalists, they averted the search for scapegoats for social problems and concentrated attention on the real rather than the symbolic causes of labor's dissatisfaction—for example, the diminution of opportunity, the loss of worker autonomy, and the impersonality of the work process. In their perspective, immigration was a peripheral matter or an irrelevance; what was necessary was fundamental social and economic reform, which could best be attained by a united movement of all workers, of whatever ethicity, religion, or culture.

However, these reform movements were never strong enough in themselves to reverse or seriously delay the almost inexorable progress towards immigration controls. More important in restraining restrictionists were their own hesitations and confusions. As legatees of the open door tradition, restrictionists could not support immigration controls without some embarrassment or guilt. This accounts for their irrational conviction that the Contract Labor Law of 1885 would exclude unskilled immigrant workers from Europe. They needed to believe in order to transfer their own guilt on to the shoulders of employers, whom they accused of importing these dependent, induced immigrants under contract. Their subsequent espousal of the literacy test represented a more realistic choice of means, as well as a willingness to bear the burden of guilt involved in modifying, if not quite rejecting, their fraternal inheritance.

All along, the question facing labor organizations was how to remain loyal to the open door when it was becoming increasingly evident that immigration resulted in so many economic, social, and political costs. Job competition, stagnant wages, displacement, worsened working conditions, and strikebreaking were compounded by political corruption, overcrowding, illiteracy, poverty, and cultural divergence to create a damaging indictment of the newcomers. Common sense indicated that a phenomenon apparently productive of so much social harm should be controlled. But common sense conflicted with inherited values; in this lies the drama of labor's anxious debate in the 1880s and 1890s. The matter might have been even more difficult to resolve if immigration had not become connected with industrial conflicts. When it was recognized that immigration permitted employers to establish an advantage in the labor market by means of strikebreaking, holding down wages, introducing new production methods, and weakening trade unions, the loyalty of many trade unionists to ideals of solidarity snapped or was stretched to breaking point.

Experience of the costs of immigration, then, gradually changed attitudes. But how many of these costs resulted from the size of the immigrant influx and its economic role, and how many from the changing ethnic, religious, and linguistic character of the immigrants themselves? Would the voices of protest have been as loud in the first decade of this century if the overwhelming majority of the European immigrants had been from Northern and Western Europe instead of from the South and East, as they had been 25 years earlier? Probably not, even though the numbers involved would inevitably have created friction and aroused disapproval. It was less the numbers than the character of the immigrants which was the source of tension. Or rather, the perceived character, since there was often a discrepancy between the actual social characteristics of the newcomers and labor's understanding of them, as was noted in Chapter Seven. Laboring men could see clearly enough that the latest immigrants were increasingly different in behavior and attitudes from the host society. The new arrivals failed to identify with their hosts in the ways previous generations had done (although the Famine Irish were often conveniently forgotten in such comparisons). Consequently, rather than conforming to conventional practices in industrial and social life, the more recent immigrants diverged from them in ways which undermined traditional standards. In other words, labor organizations from the 1880s onwards increasingly doubted the capacity and willingness of European immigrants to assimilate.

Doubts about assimilability are at the heart of labor anxiety about immigration. In the 1880s the pauperized, "degraded strikebreakers," recruited from Eastern Europe, were described as contract labor because Americans refused to believe that voluntary immigrants, who almost by definition identified with American ideas and values, would act in such unfraternal ways. Dependent upon, and servile towards, the employers, these contract laborers could not or would not adopt American standards. When it became clear that these workers were not under contract, as that was defined in the act, and consequently could not be excluded by the 1885 law, labor organizations adopted the literacy test as the best method of ensuring the assimilability of the new arrivals, since literacy was believed to hold the key of access to American culture.

The AFL's equation of "induced" with "unassimilable" was a gross but convenient oversimplification. It ignored the possibility that "voluntary" immigrants seeking economic opportunity and finding work through relatives and friends in the United States might be as unassimilable as their fellow ethnics imported by some labor agent. The AFL did not grasp this nettle until the First World War, when it called first for total suspension of European immigration and then supported the quota legislation. This new policy removed the distinction between voluntary and induced immigrants and implied that both types created problems of assimilation, with adverse consequences for labor. Yet, despite its increased scepticism about the possibility of assimilation, labor did not connect assimilability with genetic inheritance, at least as far as Europeans were concerned. It believed that culture was the product of environment, not race, and that in the fullness of time European immigrants, unlike the Chinese, could be assimilated in the United States. The problem was that there was insufficient time available and the sheer scale of the immigration tended to neutralize the assimilative potential of the American environment. If not absolutely impervious to American culture, then, immigrants were becoming sufficiently different in religion, language, and values to make the appeal for solidarity sound increasingly hollow. As labor leaders reiterated in the 1880s, solidarity was not a one-way process; it was effective only when all parties were responsive to its appeal.

Declining confidence in the assimilative capacity of the United States was not simply a function of the changing character of the newcomers; it also reflected internal developments in the Republic which produced uncertainty and anxiety among the population. As far as American labor was concerned, stagnant or only slowly growing real wages after 1890, recurrent economic depressions and their associated high levels of unemployment, and, above all, technical displacement created a climate of acute uncertainty. The transition from a traditional form of economic order, as in eighteenth-century America, to the commercial capitalism of the pre–Civil War period, and thence to the industrial and finance capitalism of the decades preceding the First World War involved vast and multifarious changes in economic structure, in methods of production and distribution, and in the scale of the production units. The pace of change so accelerated in the three or four decades before 1914 that numerous defensive organizations of workers emerged to try to impose stability and order on a seemingly chaotic process, and to safeguard craft skills and traditional work methods. In turn these defense organizations, the trade unions, recognized a threat to their own existence from the deskilling process and saw in it a means of decisively shifting the balance of power in industry to the employers, a process which would have further undermined the living standards of their members.

Labor organizations are neither inherently solidaristic nor inherently exclusivist; whether they are one or the other or a mixture of both will depend on circumstances. If it is possible, without excessive costs, to recruit all workers in an industry into a single trade union, this will strengthen the union and pay dividends in the collective bargaining process. Conversely, a union may be forced to exclude a proportion of the workforce if its appeals for solidarity are not met. Alternatively, it may choose not to recruit out of prejudice, misunderstanding, organizational difficulties, or the recognition that a part of the workforce has betrayed the ideal of solidarity by acting in the employers' interest against fellow workers. Some of these factors help to explain why American labor became increasingly exclusivist in the period between the Civil War and the 1920s. The identification of most European immigrants with the deskilling process involved in technical innovation, the precedent involved in the refusal to accept the Chinese immigrants as part of the American labor force, the trend away from nominally inclusive and solidaristic labor organizations like the Knights of Labor to exclusive craft unions, whose philosophy dominated the American Federation of Labor, particularly after the decline of socialist influence in its ranks, all served to divide the workforce and to produce demands for the restriction of immigration.

The trend away from solidarity to self-protection resulted essentially from the interaction of two sets of forces: the need to defend living standards and conventional work practices in the face of economic upheaval and technological change; and the perception that the unconscious agents of change were immigrants who seemed immune, through culture, tradition, and sheer numbers, to the appeal of solidarity. In short, unvoidable conflicts in the workforce were heightened by the changing ethnic character of immigration after 1880. Appeals to European newcomers to co-operate with the existing workforce in the interests of all fell on increasingly deaf ears. Organized labor inevitably concluded that its members' interests were better protected by abandoning solidarity than by trying to uphold it.

Bibliographical Essay

This bibliographical guide is not exhaustive, indeed it does not contain all the works cited in the notes. It is designed mainly as an aid to further reading, calling attention to some of the primary and secondary sources which the author found most helpful in the preparation of this study.

MANUSCRIPT SOURCES

The most interesting and intriguing source, and the most useful for this work, is the outgoing correspondence of Samuel Gompers, president of the American Federation of Labor (AFL) from 1886 to 1924 (with a break of one year in 1894–95). This correspondence is contained in his Letterbooks held in the AFL-CIO Building, Washington, D.C., and now available on microfilm. Although references to immigration are relatively infrequent, they are helpful in detailing Gompers' manipulative role at AFL conventions in obtaining endorsements for resolutions favoring immigration restriction. They also throw valuable light on the evolution of labor opinion in the two decades before, and in the period after, the First World War. Useful material for the last chapters of the book was found in the David J. Saposs Papers in the State Historical Society of Wisconsin at Madison. The society also holds a good collection of the minute books of local Wisconsin unions and trades assemblies, which were helpful in identifying grass-roots labor opinion about immigration. Among the society's other holdings, worth consulting are the Records of the International Workingmen's Association, 1871–76, the Socialist Labor Party Collection, 1866–1907, and the Papers of Daniel De Leon, Algie Simons, and Morris Hillquit, which cast light on the development of socialist attitudes to European immigration between the 1880s and 1914. In this respect the Socialist Party of America Papers, held in Duke University Library, Durham, North Carolina, and now available on microfilm, are exceptionally useful and repay close attention. Finally, the Joseph Labadie Collection at the University of Michigan, containing the papers of late nineteenth and early twentieth century anarchists, socialists, and political idealists, provides an interesting commentary on contemporary labor attitudes.

LABOR PUBLICATIONS, INCLUDING JOURNALS AND PROCEEDINGS

The most valuable descriptions of the discussions within labor organizations are to be found in the *Reports* of the convention proceedings of the AFL covering the period from 1886 to 1924, which is the chronological core of this work. Of much less wide-ranging significance, but still important sources for labor's debate on immigration in the 1880s, are the *Records* of the proceedings of the General Assemblies of the Knights of Labor and the *Reports* of the sessions of the AFL's immediate predecessor, the Federation of Organized Trades and Labor Unions (1881–86). More limited use was made of the reports of proceedings of individual assemblies, as in the case of the Knights, or of national unions affiliated with the AFL. Students of the debates in the Socialist party on the immigration question are referred to the very full accounts in the *Proceedings* of the national conventions of the party between 1906 and 1912.

The trade union and socialist journals consulted in the preparation of this work are too numerous to list here, although full references are given in the notes. The most widely used, because they contain frequent references to immigration and technological change either in editorials or correspondence, were the *American Federationist* (of the AFL), the *Iron Molders' Journal, The Journal of United Labor* (of the Knights of Labor), *Monthly Journal of the International Association of Machinists, The Carpenter, The Garment Worker, United Mineworkers' Journal, Locomotive Engineers' Journal, Railroad Trainman, Shoe Workers' Journal, Brauer-Zeitung* (of the Brewery Workers), and *Justice* (of the Ladies' Garment Workers). Among socialist journals, *The People*, of the Socialist Labor party, the *International Socialist Review*, and the *Social Democratic Herald* were informative on the evolution of socialist opinion. The *Appeal to Reason* and *Coming Nation* offered useful background.

GOVERNMENT PUBLICATIONS

The reports of three heavyweight commissions provide substantial evidence of the impact of immigration on American industry and industrial workers. In chronological order they are the *Reports of the Industrial Commission* (Washington, D.C., 1901), the *Reports of the Immigration Commission* (Washington, D.C., 1911), and the *Reports of the Commission on Industrial Relations* (Washington, D.C., 1915). They should be supplemented by the reports of congressional committees and the testimony taken by the committees on which their reports were partly based. The most useful sources of this kind derive from the Senate Committee on Education and Labor (1885), the so-called Ford Committee of the House of Representatives (1888), the Select Committee on Immigration and Naturalization (1891), and the House Reports on the Importation of Contract Labor (1890) and on Immigration and

Contract Labor (1892). The reports of the Senate's Committee on Immigration for 1896 and 1902, and the Conference Report of the House and Senate on the bill to regulate immigration, 1907, make one aware of the evolution of congressional opinion and point the way to emerging legislative proposals.

The various congressional reports are supplemented at the federal level by the annual and special reports of the Bureau of Labor. Among the most relevant of these are *Industrial Depressions* (Washington, D.C., 1886), *Railroad Labor* (Washington, D.C., 1889), *Strikes and Lockouts* (Washington, D.C., 1894), *The Italians in Chicago* (Washington, D.C., 1897), *Hand and Machine Labor* (Washington, D.C., 1898), *Strikes and Lockouts* (Washington, D.C., 1901), *Report on Conditions of Employment in the Iron and Steel Industry in the United States*, 4 Vols., (Washington, D.C., 1911–13), and *Report on the Strike of Textile Workers in Lawrence, Mass., in 1912* (Washington, D.C., 1912). The bulletins of the United States Department of Labor contain a number of valuable articles on labor conditions and the impact of immigration. Among the most helpful were "The Padrone System and Padrone Banks" and "The Italians in Chicago," both in the *Bulletin* for 1907, Frank Julian Warne, "The Union Movement among Coal Mine Workers" (1904), "Wages and Hours of Labor in Manufacturing Industries" (1905), Walter E. Weyl and A. M. Sakolski, "Conditions of Entrance to the Principal Trades" (1906), Emily Fogg Meade, "The Italian on the Land: A Study in Immigration" (1907), and Frank J. Sheridan, "Italian, Slavic and Hungarian Unskilled Immigrant Labor in the United States" (1907).

At a state level the annual reports of the Bureaus of Labor Statistics offer invaluable insights into conditions of employment and into labor's attitudes towards key contemporary issues. The most informative reports were those of Connecticut (1885 and 1887), Illinois (1885–86), Massachusetts (1871, 1872, 1888, 1894, 1904), New Jersey (1881, 1883, 1884, 1886), New York (1889, 1894, 1895, 1896, 1898), Ohio (1886 and 1889), and Wisconsin (1885–86 and 1887–88).

BOOKS, DISSERTATIONS, AND ARTICLES

Important and illuminating collections of published documents are Edith Abbott, ed., *Historical Aspects of the Immigration Problem: Select Documents* (1926; rpt. New York: Arno Press, 1969), and John R. Commons et al., eds., *A Documentary History of American Industrial Society*, 10 vols. (1910–11; rpt. New York: Russell and Russell, 1958). The most comprehensive and wide-ranging of the general histories of American labor are still John R. Commons et al., *History of Labor in the United States*, 4 vols. (1918; rpt. New York: Augustus M. Kelley, 1966), and Philip S. Foner, *History of the Labor Movement in the United States*, 4 vols. (1947; rpt. New York: International Publishers, 1962). They form an indispensable starting point for studies in labor history even though they are now widely regarded as somewhat dated in their different approaches. Falling into a similar category would be Philip Taft, *The A.F. of L. in the Time of Gompers* (New York: Harper, 1957). All historians of American labor in the late nineteenth and early twentieth centuries become aware of the towering importance of Samuel Gompers, whose autobiography, *Seventy Years of Life and Labour*, 2 vols. (London: Hurst and Blackett, 1925), commands attention even though its evident self-serving proclivities have to be discounted.

The outstanding and indispensable study of American responses to immigrants in the nineteenth and early twentieth centuries is John Higham's *Strangers in the Land: Patterns of American Nativism, 1860–1925* (1955: rpt. New York: Atheneum, 1963). Whilst business reactions to immigration have been charted in Morrell Heald, "Business Attitudes toward European Immigration, 1861–1914" (Ph.D. diss., Yale University, 1951), only recently has something equivalent been attempted for organized labor, in Robert D. Parmet's *Labor and Immigration in Industrial America* (Boston: Twayne Publishers, 1981), covering the period from the 1860s to the 1930s and devoting more space than the present work to the experiences and achievements of groups of immigrants in the labor market. Students of Chinese immigration, particularly those attempting to compare its impact with that from Europe, are indebted to Alexander Saxton's *The Indispensable Enemy: Labor and the Anti-Chinese Movement in California* (Berkeley: University of California Press, 1971). Similarly, Charlotte Erickson's *American Industry and the European Immigrant, 1860–1885* (Cambridge, Mass.: Harvard University Press, 1957), is an essential starting point for understanding so-called alien contract labor, which became so controversial after the Civil War. Methodological guidelines for the preparation of this work were derived from Lee Benson, "An Approach to the Scientific Study of Past Public Opinion," *Public Opinion Quarterly* 31 (1967): 522–66; and David Brody, "The Old Labor History and the New: In Search of an American Working Class," *Labor History* 20 no. 1 (Winter 1979).

Eighteenth-century American attitudes to immigration may be approached through Merle Curti, *The Roots of American Loyalty* (New York: Columbia University Press, 1946), Yehoshua Arieli, *Individualism and Nationalism in American Ideology* (Cambridge, Mass.: Harvard University Press, 1964), and James H. Kettner, "The Development of American Citizenship in the Revolutionary Era: The Idea of Volitional Allegiance," *The American Journal of Legal History* 18 (July 1974): 208–42. How artisans may have responded to the inflow of European newcomers to the labor market can be derived from Howard B. Rock, *Artisans of the New Republic: The Tradesmen of New York City in the Age of Jefferson* (New York: New York University Press, 1979), and Alfred Young, "The Mechanics and the Jeffersonians: New York, 1789–1801," *Labor History* 5 (1964): 247–76.

Early nineteenth-century nativist movements have received considerable scholarly attention: Thomas J. Curran, *Xenophobia and Immigration, 1820–1930* (Boston: Twayne Publishers, 1975), and Ira M. Leonard and Robert D. Parmet, *American Nativism, 1830–1860* (New York: Van Nostrand Reinhold Co., 1971), provide good introductions, which should be supplemented by Ray Allen Billington, *Protestant Crusade, 1800–1860* (New York: Macmillan, 1938), and Seymour Martin Lipset and Earl Raab, *The Politics of Unreason: Right-Wing Extremism in America, 1790–1970* (London: Heinemann Educational Books Ltd., 1971). There has been much recent research into working-class responses to ethnic competitors on the economic, social, and religious planes. Among the most valuable of the resultant studies have been David Montgomery, "The Shuttle and the Cross: Weavers and Artisans in the Kensington Riots of 1844," *Journal of Social History* 5 (Summer 1972): 411–39, Michael Feldberg, *The Philadelphia Riots of 1844: A Study of Ethnic Conflict* (Westport, Conn.: Greenwood Press, 1975), and Bruce Laurie, " 'Nothing on Compulsion': Life Styles of Philadelphia Artisans, 1820–1850," in Milton Cantor, ed., *American Workingclass Culture: Explorations in American Labor and Social History* (Westport, Conn.: Greenwood Press, 1979), pp. 91–120. An understanding of the tensions created by economic modernization for the urban artisans may be obtained from numerous studies of urban working-class communities, notably Susan E. Hirsch, *The Roots of the American Working Class: The Industrialization of Crafts in Newark, 1800–1860* (Philadelphia: University of Pennsylvania Press, 1978), Howard M. Gitelman, *Workingmen of Waltham: Mobility in American Urban Industrial Development 1850–1890* (Baltimore: The Johns Hopkins University Press, 1974), Alan Dawley, *Class and Community: The Industrial Revolution in Lynn* (Cambridge, Mass.: Harvard University Press, 1976), and Michael Frisch, *Town into City: Springfield, Mass., and the Meaning of Community, 1840–1880* (Cambridge, Mass.: Harvard University Press, 1972). The challenge from recent immigrants is discussed in Oscar Handlin, *Boston's Immigrants* (1941; rpt. New York: Atheneum, 1969), Robert Ernst, *Immigrant Life in New York City, 1825–1863* (New York: Columbia University Press, 1949), and William V. Shannon, *The American Irish* (New York: Collier, 1974).

In the Civil War and post–Civil War periods, indispensable guides through the complexities of labor politics are provided by David Montgomery, *Beyond Equality: Labor and the Radical Republicans, 1862–1872* (1967; rpt. New York: Vintage Books, 1972), and Gerald N. Grob, *Workers and Utopia: A Study of Ideological Conflict in the American Labor Movement, 1865–1900* (Evanston, Ill.: Northwestern University Press, 1961). Charlotte Erickson's *American Industry and the European Immigrant* (already noted) meticulously examines the methods by which American industry recruited or otherwise obtained labor from Europe in the period. One of labor's leading personalities at this time, William Sylvis, is the subject of Jonathan P. Grossman's *William Sylvis, Pioneer of American Labor* (New York: Columbia University Press, 1945), and speaks for himself in James C. Sylvis, ed., *The Life, Speeches, Labors, and Essays of William H. Sylvis* (Philadelphia: Claxton, Remsen and Hoffelfinger, 1872). American labor's internationalists ideals and its relations with the labor movements in other countries are analyzed in Samuel Bernstein, *The First International in America* (New York: Augustus M. Kelley, 1962), and Julius Braunthal, *History of the International, 1865–1914* (1961; rpt. London: Nelson, 1966), as well as in the relevant chapters in Charles R. Leinenweber, "Immigration and the Decline of Internationalism in the American Working Class Movement, 1864–1919" (Ph.D. diss., University of California, Berkeley, 1968).

Discussion of the Knights of Labor owes much to Grob, *Workers and Utopia*, and Erickson, *American Industry* (already noted), but other valuable sources are Norman J. Ware, *The Labor Movement in the United States, 1860–1895: A Study in Democracy* (New York: Appleton and Co., 1929), Nathan Fine, *Labor and Farmer Parties in the United States, 1828–1928* (New York: Rand School of Social Science, 1928), and Terence Vincent Powderly, *Thirty Years of Labor, 1859 to 1889* (Columbus, Ohio: Excelsior Publishing House, 1889).

There are numerous studies of the "philosophy" of the American Federation of Labor, notably Michael Rogin, "Voluntarism: The Political Functions of an Antipolitical Doctrine," *Industrial and Labor Relations Review* 15 (June 1962): 521–35, Louis S. Reed, *The Labor Philosophy of Samuel Gompers* (New York: Columbia University Press, 1930), and Philip Taft, "On the Origins of Business Unionism," *Industrial and Labor Relations Review* 17 (October 1963): 20–38. Good background on the growth of labor organizations is to be found in Robert F. Hoxie, *Trade Unionism in the United States* (New York: Appleton and Co., 1917), and in Lewis L. Lorwin, *The American Federation of Labor: History, Policies, and Prospects* (Washington, D.C.: The Brookings Institution, 1933). Valuable sources on the attitudes of individual unions include Jesse S. Robinson, *The Amalgamated Association of Iron, Steel, and Tin Workers* (Baltimore: Johns Hopkins Press, 1920), David Brody, *Steelworkers in America* (1960; rpt. New York: Harper Torchbooks, 1969), Herman Schlütter, *The Brewing Industry and the Brewery Workers' Movement in America* (Cincinnati, 1910), Augusta E. Galster, *The Labor Movement in the Shoe Industry* (New York, 1924), Charles B. Barnes, *The Longshoremen* (New York: Survey Associates, 1915), Herbert J. Lahne, *The Cotton Mill Worker in the Twentieth Century* (New York: Farrar and Rinehart, Inc., 1944), Frank Julian Warne, *The Coal–Mine Workers: A Study in Labor Organization* (New York: Longmans, Green and Co., 1905), Chris. Evans, *History of the United Mine Workers of America, 1860–1900*, 2 vols. (Indianapolis: United Mine Workers of America, 1918), and John H. M. Laslett, *Labor and the Left: A Study of Socialist and Radical Influences in the American Labor Movement, 1881–1924* (New York: Basic Books, 1970).

Labor's assertions about trends in the levels of wages and employment can be tested by reference to Clarence D. Long, *Wages and Earnings in the United States, 1860–1890* (Princeton, N.J.: Princeton University Press, 1960), Paul H. Douglas, *Real Wages in the United States, 1890–1926* (New York: Augustus M. Kelley rpt., 1966), and Albert Rees, *Real Wages in Manufacturing, 1890–1914* (Princeton, N.J.: Princeton University Press, 1961). The connection between economic trends and the volume of immigration is explored from different standpoints by J. W. Jenks and W. Jett Lauck, *The Immigration Problem*, 6th ed. (New York: Funk and Wagnalls, 1926), and Isaac A. Hourwich, *Immigration and Labor: The Economic Aspects of European Immigration to the United States* (New York: Putnam, 1912). A more statistical and objective analysis is provided by Simon Kuznets and Ernest Rubin, *Immigration and the Foreign-Born* (New York: National Bureau of Economic Research, 1954). Allegations about the higher degree of pauperism, criminality, and mental illness, and the decreasing levels of occupational skills among the "new" immigrants in comparison with their predecessors are challenged by Peter Roberts, *The New Immigration* (New York: Macmillan, 1912).

The crucial question of the relation between technological and organizational displacement on the one hand, and rising hostility to immigration on the other, may be pursued by reference to George E. Barnett, *Chapters on Machinery and Labor* (Cambridge, Mass.: Harvard University Press, 1926), Philip Taft, "Organized Labor and Technical Change: A Backward Look," in Gerald G. Somers, Edward L. Cushman, and Nat Weinberg, eds., *Adjusting to Technical Change* (New York: Harper and Row, 1963), pp. 27–42, and David Montgomery, *Workers' Control in America: Studies in the History of Work, Technology, and Labor Struggles* (Cambridge: Cambridge University Press, 1979). The allegedly demoralizing influence of modern capitalism is elaborated in Harry Braverman, *Labor and Monopoly Capital: The Degradation of Work in the Twentieth Century* (New York: Monthly Review Press, 1974). Covering similar ground, though with different emphases, are David F. Noble, *America by Design: Science, Technology, and the Rise of Corporate Capitalism* (New York: Oxford University Press, 1979), and Don Clawson, *Bureaucracy and the Labor Process: The Transformation of U.S. Industry, 1860–1920* (New York: Monthly Review Press, 1980). The impact of scientific management on work practices and labor morale is explored in Hugh G. J. Aitken, *Taylorism at Watertown Arsenal: Scientific Management in Action, 1908–1915* (Cambridge, Mass.: Harvard University Press, 1960), and

Milton J. Nadworny, *Scientific Management and the Unions, 1900–1932: A Historical Analysis* (Cambridge, Mass.: Harvard University Press, 1955). That economic modernization and the emergence of modern capitalism did not invariably spell hostility to those agents of change, the immigrants, is well brought out in John T. Cumbler, *Working-Class Community in Industrial America: Work, Leisure, and Struggle in Two Industrial Cities, 1880–1930* (Westport, Conn.: Greenwood Press, 1979), which shows how the complexity of local circumstances could modify, deflect, or postpone the impact of technical change and preserve community morale.

The debate between restrictionists and internationalists in the labor movement is best studied in the labor press, but useful insights and differing viewpoints are presented by Michael Parenti, "Immigration and Political Life," in F. C. Jaher, ed., *The Age of Industrialism in America: Essays in Social Structure and Cultural Values* (New York: Free Press, 1968), pp. 79–88, David F. Bowers, ed., *Foreign Influences in American Life* (Princeton, N.J.: Princeton University Press, 1944), UNESCO, *Race and Science* (New York: Columbia University Press, 1961), Isaac Hourwich, *Immigration and Labor* (already noted), and John R. Commons, *Races and Immigrants in America* (1907: rpt. New York: Augustus M. Kelley, 1967).

Labor's approach to immigration during and after the First World War is best studied in the labor press, but a valuable introduction can be found in Higham, *Strangers in the Land*, and in David Brody, *Labor in Crisis: The Steel Strike of 1919* (Philadelphia: J. B. Lippincott Company, 1965). General background may be obtained from Stanley Coben, "A Study in Nativism: The American Red Scare of 1919–20," *Political Science Quarterly* 79 (March 1964): 52–75, David Burner, "1919: Prelude to Normalcy," in John Braeman, Robert H. Bremner, and David Brody, eds., *Change and Continuity in Twentieth-Century America: 1920s* (Columbus: Ohio State University Press, 1968), and Burl Noggle, *Into the Twenties: The United States from Armistice to Normalcy* (Urbana: University of Illinois Press, 1974). Helpful guidance to American immigration policies in the postwar period is provided by Robert A. Divine, *American Immigration Policy, 1924–52* (New Haven: Yale University Press, 1957), and Marion T. Bennett, *American Immigration Policies: A History* (Washington, D.C.: Public Affairs Press, 1963), and the racial nationalism of the period may be approached through Madison Grant, *The Passing of the Great Race* (New York: Charles Scribner's Sons, 1916), Henry Pratt Fairchild, *The Melting-Pot Mistake* (Boston: Little, Brown and Co., 1926), and Gino Speranza, *Race or Nation: A Conflict of Divided Loyalties* (Indianapolis: Bobbs-Merrill Co., 1925). Samuel Gompers, *Seventy Years of Life and Labor* (already noted) is required reading.

Index

About the Author

A. T. LANE is Lecturer in History in the School of European Studies at the University of Bradford in England. In addition to his contribution of a chapter in *Hosts, Immigrants, and Minorities*, by Kenneth Lumm, his articles have appeared in *Journal of American Studies* and *Labor History*.